Writing on Drugs

Writing on Drugs

Sadie Plant

Farrar, Straus and Giroux

New York

Farrar, Straus and Giroux
19 Union Square West, New York 10003

Library of Congress Cataloging-in-Publication Data
Plant, Sadie, 1964–
    Writing on drugs / Sadie Plant.
      p.   cm.
    Originally published: London : Faber and Faber, 1999.
    Includes bibliographical references and index.
    ISBN 0-374-29334-1
    1. Drug abuse—Social aspects.   2. Drug abuse in literature.   I. Title.

HV5801.P595 2000
394.1′4—dc21   00-020822

Writing on Drugs is dedicated to
the man who wore a white shirt and a blue sarong

With thanks to Derek Johns and Jon Riley, and all
the friends who have contributed to the writing of this book.
Very special thanks to Hilda and Philip Plant.

Contents

Prelude

The man wore a white shirt and a blue sarong. He would have sold you anything: emeralds, Toyotas, Marlboros, teak. He smiled: "The best of everything. It all comes from Khun Sa." Across the street the border guards, smoking in the shade, feet up on their motorbikes, watched the deal being done. "Be cool," he said. "They're OK. The whole town trades. They won't say anything to you."

So you gave the man his dollars, went back to the house, and sat on the veranda through the late afternoon. Chasing the dragon as the sun went down, high above the outskirts of the border town.

You feel it now, a slow smooth rush as the day cooled off into the dusk. The whole world paused in that moment: the mists peeling off the mountains, wood smoke curling from the settlement below. Even the river's placid flow, the color of the earth, shallow, slow.

And then the pace picked up, you breathed again. The golden Buddha settled in the mountainside, and the temple bell began its strange uneven chime. You tuned in to the sounds of kids and laughter, cowbells in the hills, the clatter of Coca-Cola crates and two-stroke engines in the town.

The rhythm tightened when the darkness fell. Tree frogs and cicadas started singing as the mountain shadows crept across the valley and the sky. The house felt like a hide, bathed in candlelight, wrapped in the blanket of the blue-black world outside, a dark night broken only by the lights of vehicles on the road, strips of fluorescence, a smattering of stars. Everything was gentle, effortless, and calm.

Later still came music from the Burmese side. The disco mixes of another world. *"Sugar bah bah bah bah bah bah oh Honey Honey bah bah bah bah bah bah You are my candy girl and you got me wantin' you . . ."*

Chains of mountains, chains of thought, events . . . you ran with the dragon to the delta, out to sea, and into the arms of the whole wide world. You chased it to the makeshift factories, out to the poppy fields, the fertile soil, the harvest and its workers, the women and the kids, the seasons and the cycles of demand and supply. Brown sugar, black gold, warm white light: you watched the whole thing crystallize, running through its repertoire, its stories and songs, the art and design of its influence. You stalked it through a maze of waterways and ports, streetcar tracks and highways, hotel rooms and squalid squats, city squares and alleyways and off into a maze of deals and rackets and temptations, a long and tangled tale of prohibitions and desires. You saw the insights it had given and the lies it had told, the pain it had driven and the pleasures it had sold. It gave you its plots and its characters, the maps of its memories, its charts and diagrams, its tales of adventure in the far-off Western lands. It boasted of its wars and the battles it had won, the fortunes it had made, the damage it had done.

It kept running. Dragons never tire. It blazed its trails across your darkness, etching its tracks onto that black mountainside. It kept running through your mind, tempting, escaping, daring you to chase it just a little more. You kept running through the story, running its story through your mind. It danced ahead, it laughed at you, it knew you would fail. You heard it all, and still became the dragon's tail.

Writing on Drugs

Private Eyes

I begin to write, almost without realizing it, without thinking, busy transmitting these words I don't recognize, although they are highly significant: "Too much! Too much! You're giving me too much!"
Henri Michaux, *Darkness Moves*

A vast literature on drugs has assembled itself in the last two hundred years. It begins with the late eighteenth century's explorations of opium, wends its way through cannabis, coca, and cocaine, and later finds itself entangled with a wide variety of plant hallucinogens and synthetic drugs.

Like their writings and their writers, these substances could hardly be more diverse. Some of them are ancient, others very new. Some are synthesized in laboratories, and some grow wild. Some are widely used as medicines, a few are fatal in large doses, some have no toxicity at all. In the twentieth century, the vast majority of these substances find themselves controlled by some of the world's oldest international agreements and its most extensive national laws. But they do have their own common ground as well. Whether they are organic or synthetic, old or new, stimulating, narcotic, or hallucinogenic, all these drugs have some specific psychoactive effect: they all shift perceptions, affect moods, change behavior, and alter states of mind. And all of them have exerted an influence that extends far beyond their users. The laws and wars on drugs are symptomatic of the ways in which these substances provoke the same extreme reactions in cultures, economies—social, political, legal—and even military systems. Their effects on the human nervous system seem to repeat themselves wherever they occur. When drugs change their users, they change everything.

> Drugs snatch us out of everyday reality, blur our per-
> ception, alter our sensations, and, in a word, put the
> entire universe in a state of suspension.
>
> Octavio Paz, *Alternating Current*

Every drug has its own character, its unique claims to fame. The coca bush gets its name from the Aymara word *khoka*, meaning simply "tree"; the word *hashish* is derived from the Arabic word for herb, or grass, as if it were the herb par excellence; and the Mexican psilocybin mushroom is known as *teonanactl*, which translates as "flesh of the gods." But there is something about opium, with all its varied properties and histories, that allows this drug to set the scene. "Of all drugs," wrote Jean Cocteau, "opium is *the* drug."

Opium is extracted from the opium poppy, *Papaver somniferum*, which is cultivated and harvested today with the same techniques that have been recorded over thousands of years. Once the poppies have flowered, the seed heads are scored with a knife and left to bleed a sticky substance from their wounds. The seed heads are scored in the afternoons, with a three- or four-bladed knife, and the next day the latex is collected with a flat blade. The process is repeated several times until the seedpod's supply of opium has been exhausted.

The poppy head yields a number of potent psychoactive alkaloids that have allowed opium to play a very special role in the story of the human use of drugs. It is widely acknowledged to be one of the world's oldest, most powerful, and most effective medicines, and while the earliest uses of opium may have been purely medicinal, plenty of circumstantial evidence suggests that its use as an intoxicant is as old as the hills in which it grows. Evidence of its use has been found in several regions of the world: it can be traced to Neolithic settlements on the shorelines of Swiss lakes, the eastern Mediterranean, and the Black Sea coast. It was cultivated in Mesopotamia by the Sumerians, and later known in Egypt, where traces of it have been found in tombs dating back to the fifteenth century B.C. Opium was used in ancient Greece, where Plotinus was said to be a regular user of a drug to which Homer is thought to refer in the *Odyssey* when he describes "a medicine to banish grief." Opium was also known in Rome, where it acquired an association with Morpheus, the god of dreams, who later gave his name to morphine. Its Chinese use is lost in the mists of time.

Arab merchants were probably the first large-scale distributors of the drug, selling it for centuries across Asia and the Middle East, and by the sixteenth century, opium was widely traded and used in Turkey, Persia, and India. Western interest in the drug was growing fast as well. Paracelsus popularized its medical use in the sixteenth century and developed what would later become a popular preparation: laudanum. In the seventeenth century, Thomas Sydenham declared that medicine would be useless without opium. His statement remains true to this day.

By the eighteenth century, opium had been used, abused, and discussed by a great number of European scholars, doctors, and travelers, whose tales about its use in the East shrouded it in a seductive air of mystique. The vast bulk of the West's opium was imported from Turkey and other areas of the Middle East, where the quality was famously high. But opium poppies also grew wild in several areas of the British Isles, where the Society of Arts promoted the domestic cultivation of opium poppies, awarding medals for high yields and qualities. Even garden lettuce, closely related to the opium poppy, yielded *lactarium*, a mild opiate that eighteenth-century market gardeners processed and sold as a by-product.

Raw opium was the first drug to give up the secrets of its chemistry when, in 1804, morphine was extracted from it. Morphine was followed by codeine, and more than fifty alkaloids have been identified in opium itself. Morphine is its most powerful alkaloid, and, isolated from its organic base, it proved a malleable and efficient pharmaceutical. Although it was mainly taken orally in the early decades of its use, morphine's remarkable properties encouraged experiments with other means of ingestion. It was, for example, applied to patches of raw skin exposed by blistering or inserted under the skin on the tip of a lancet.

And then came the syringe, an instrument that shared its history with the drugs with which it has become so closely tied. Opium is thought to have been the first substance to be smoked in a pipe, and it also inspired the earliest attempt to get drugs straight into the bloodstream when Christopher Wren combined a quill and a bladder to produce the first syringe in 1656. This early experiment did at least prove that such injections were possible: he injected a dog with opium and the dog died. When the modern hypodermic syringe was developed in the 1850s, it was morphine that popularized its use.

Like morphine itself, the syringe was cleaner, safer, and more clinical than any earlier means of inserting drugs into the body. "The advantages of the hypodermic injection of morphia over its administration by the mouth are immense," wrote Francis Anstie, one of its leading protagonists. "Of *danger*, there is *absolutely none*." Both morphine and the syringe were promoted as sophisticated medical aids, and there was such enthusiasm for this double act that injections of morphine were even used to treat addiction to opium. Hypodermic morphine became so popular that, by 1870, there had developed increasing fears that morphine might itself become a problem. And then came the cure to end all cures. Diacetylmorphine, a synthesis of morphine and acetic anhydride, was first produced in 1874 by an English chemist, C. R. Wright. He thought its effects were too powerful and unpleasant to be pursued. But later chemists were intrigued, and by the end of the century, diacetylmorphine was being marketed as "Heroin." It was made by the German pharmaceutical company Bayer, which promoted it as a nonaddictive substitute for morphine, and its medical use was approved in several countries, including Britain and America. Contrary to Bayer's original claims, heroin is one of the most addictive substances in the world.

> The needle is not important. Whether you sniff it smoke it eat it or shove it up your ass the result is the same: addiction.
>
> William Burroughs, *Naked Lunch*

In both Britain and America, a wide range of opiated preparations were on sale for much of the eighteenth and nineteenth centuries. There were no restrictions on their use until the late 1860s, and even then they continued to be popular. One of the most common mixtures was tincture of opium, or laudanum, a drink made from opium mixed with alcohol and distilled water. Camphorated tincture of opium, or paregoric, was also widely used, and in Britain and America there were dozens of patent medicines—Chlorodyne, Godfrey's Cordial, Dover's Powder, and such tempting remedies as Battley's Sedative Solution and Mrs. Winslow's Soothing Syrup—many of which contained substantial quantities of morphine.

These were the first over-the-counter, self-administered drugs. Companies were not obliged to list ingredients until the early years of the twentieth century, and all the available statistics on imports and sales of opium suggest that the drugs were used by nearly everyone—as cures for illnesses such as dysentery and cholera, and also as painkillers and sedatives. In London, wrote Thomas De Quincey in *Confessions of an English Opium-Eater*, published in 1821, "the number of *amateur* opium-eaters (as I may term them) was, at this time, immense." In Manchester, he was "informed by several cotton-manufacturers, that their work-people were rapidly getting into the practice of opium-eating; so much so, that on a Saturday afternoon the counters of the druggists were strewn with one, two, or three grains, in preparation for the known demand of the evening." Opium was cheap, plentiful, and without prejudice: the perfect quick fix of its day. Mothers used it to keep babies quiet, and workers in the foundries, the factories, and the mills used it to sleep at night and survive the working day. As De Quincey observed, "Happiness might now be bought for a penny, and carried in the waistcoat pocket: portable ecstasies might be had corked up in a pint bottle: and peace of mind could be sent down in gallons by the mail coach." Although, as he quickly added, "nobody will laugh long who deals much with opium: its pleasures even are of a grave and solemn complexion."

It now seems remarkable that opium was ever such a simple fact of daily life. Even mild, medicinal doses can affect perceptions and states of mind; it is difficult to speculate about the impact of such widespread use on the social atmosphere, the culture's sensibility, the population's mood. Opium grew in popularity in the late eighteenth century, as the first steam engines sputtered into life and the first great factories were built. The populations of cities grew, and the old routines of rural life, with its sense of identity and continuity, were disrupted, sometimes wiped away. By the mid-nineteenth century, it was possible to look back and see that the whole landscape of the culture had been transformed. Railway lines were laid, canals were cut, bridges were suspended over wide rivers. Trade routes and colonies had multiplied, all the maps were different, all the goods were new. Minds had been changed by a wave of revolutions—in America and France, as well as in philosophy, science, and the arts. It seemed as if nothing was standing still.

"Already, in this year, 1845," wrote De Quincey in 'Suspiria de Profundis," the second of his essays on opium,

> what by the procession through fifty years of mighty revolutions amongst the kingdoms of the earth, what by the continual development of vast physical agencies—steam in all its applications, light getting under harness as a slave for man, powers from heaven descending upon ed-

ucation and accelerations of the press, powers from hell
(as it might seem, but these also celestial coming round
upon artillery and the forces of destruction)—the eye of
the calmest observer is troubled; the brain is haunted as if
by some jealousy of ghostly beings moving amongst us.

Already, in 1845? As if it was all happening too early, too
soon, too fast; as if something was already too late. Surrounded by new mediations and mechanisms challenging
man's "imperial nature" and interrupting his engagement
with the world, De Quincey felt himself losing track: "Even
thunder and lightning, it pains me to say, are not the thunder
and lightning which I seem to remember about the time of
Waterloo." De Quincey wanted to find his feet amid the great
new orchestrations of an industrial revolution that he felt had
"disconnected man's heart from the ministers of his locomo-
tion." He needed to be able to dream again in a world whose
dreams had become "too much liable to disturbance from the
gathering agitation of our present English life." And, as he
discovered, "some merely physical agencies can and do assist
the faculty of dreaming almost preternaturally. Amongst
these," he writes, "is intense exercise; to some extent, at least,
and for some persons, but beyond all others is opium."
De Quincey made his name as the opium eater par excellence when he published *Confessions*, but he was by no means
the first writer to turn to opium for some respite from the
"eternal hurry" and the "colossal pace of advance" that had
characterized English life since the late eighteenth century.
Nor was he the only one to have discovered opium's "specific
power" to enhance his dreams and memories. Scott, Shelley,
Wordsworth, Southey, Byron, Keats . . . reams of gothic fiction
and Romantic poetry had taken something of their character
from the drug. In many cases, opium exerted a subtle influence that is difficult to isolate from all the other themes explored by these writers. But sometimes the effects of the drug
are writ large in the stories and poems composed by writers

on opium. As De Quincey discovered in *Confessions*, the drug can be far more than an engaging theme, a literary device, an object of research: this is a substance that has powers and an agency of its own. "Opium, not the Opium-Eater, is the hero" of all these tales.

> In Xanadu did Kubla Khan
> A stately pleasure dome decree:
> Where Alph, the sacred river, ran
> Through caverns measureless to man
> Down to a sunless sea.

These are the opening lines of "Kubla Khan," a poem written in the late 1790s that has since become one of the modern world's most loved pieces of poetry. The poem had some vicious critics in its day, but Xanadu, the pleasure dome, and the sunless sea became well-known features of the modern imaginative landscape.

Nearly everyone who knows these lines knows the story of their writing too. Samuel Taylor Coleridge published the poem "as a psychological curiosity" and claimed it was a fragment of a much longer sequence that had been "given to him" in a dream induced by a dose of opium. While reading Purchas's *Pilgrimage*, which contains a passage very similar to his first lines, Coleridge fell into

> a profound sleep, at least of the external senses, during which time he has the most vivid confidence, that he could not have composed less than from two to three hundred lines; if that indeed can be called composition in which all the images rose up before him as *things*, with a parallel production of the correspondent expressions, without any sensation or consciousness of effort. On awakening he appeared to himself to have a distinct recollection of the whole, and taking his pen, ink, and paper,

instantly and eagerly wrote down the lines that are here preserved.

But then came a famous interruption, the all-too-prosaic arrival of "a person on business from Porlock." And when Coleridge returned to his work, he had lost the plot of his great dream. There were only "eight or ten scattered lines and images, all the rest had passed away like the images on the surface of a stream into which a stone has been cast, but, alas! without the after restoration of the latter!"

"Kubla Khan" was composed "from the still surviving recollections in his mind." The fragment dripped with tempting possibilities, even—especially—though so much was lost. Coleridge "frequently purposed to finish for himself what had been originally, as it were, given to him," but the moment was never recaptured: "The tomorrow," he wrote, "is yet to come."

Coleridge had posed a challenge that many of his readers found irresistible. Poets were enchanted by the possibility that such poetry could spring from the opiated edge of waking life, and philosophers found themselves intrigued by the status and the meaning of such intense dreams. Coleridge's preface to the poem marked the beginning of a long experiment that continues to this day.

> When I placed my head on my pillow, I did not sleep, nor could I be said to think. My imagination, unbidden, possessed and guided me, gifting the successive images that arose in my mind with a vividness far beyond the usual bounds of reverie.

Mary Shelley's *Frankenstein* is probably the most well known tale to have emerged from this fine line between waking life and sleep. And the scenes stayed with her: "On the morrow I announced that I had *thought of a story.*" And not just any story: *Frankenstein* became one of modernity's founding myths, "a modern Prometheus," as Mary Shelley called it. "I began that day with the words, 'It was on a dreary night of November,' " she wrote, "making only a transcript of the grim terrors of my waking dream." Like "Kubla Khan," her story was a transcript, but, unlike the transcriber of Xanadu, Shelley had remembered to remember the words. And she could have told both Coleridge and De Quincey what they had to discover for themselves: modernity's new means of creativity had a propensity to backfire.

It was opium's "exquisite pleasure" that had first enchanted De Quincey as a young man. In his late twenties, he began to use the drug more regularly, first to deal with what he described as a "most painful affection of the stomach" and later because he couldn't stop. In the course of this long opium career, De Quincey came to see the drug's ability to enhance and induce dreams as its "*specific* power." Time and solitude were in short supply, but opium was readily available, and it did indeed compensate for the new speeds and alien forces that overtook the gentle pace of preindustrial life. For the drugged De Quincey, everything slowed down. Now he did have time to think and dream again. The "fierce chemistry" of his new dreams allowed him to remember even the

minutest incidents of childhood, or forgotten scenes of later years . . . I could not be said to recollect them; for if I had been told of them when waking, I should not have been able to acknowledge them as parts of my past experience. But placed as they were before me, in dreams like intuitions, and clothed in all their evanescent circumstances and accompanying feelings, I *recognized* them instantaneously.

He described the theater that "seemed suddenly opened and lighted up within my brain" and related the activities of his "Dark Interpreter," a character "whom immediately the reader will learn to know as an intruder into my dreams."

This was the phantom figure of recollection who allowed De Quincey to keep track of times that were otherwise running ahead of themselves. It was under his influence that the past came flooding back—the events of a day, of a year, even of De Quincey's childhood, arranging themselves on new planes in his mind. The Dark Interpreter allowed De Quincey to remember everything in slow-motion replays, giving him an expanded bandwidth for memories that were now bathed in "cloudless serenity" and "the great light of the majestic intellect." Like the chorus of a Greek drama, the Interpreter functioned

> not to tell you any thing absolutely new, *that* was done by the actors in the drama, but to recall you to your own lurking thoughts—hidden for the moment or imperfectly developed, and to place before you . . . such commentaries, prophetic or looking back, pointing the moral or deciphering the mystery, justifying Providence, or mitigating the fierceness of anguish, as would or might have occurred to your own meditative heart—had only time been allowed for its motions.

De Quincey insisted that opium had nothing to do with the intoxicating effects of alcohol but had its own ability both to stimulate and to sedate: "Whereas wine disorders the mental faculties," he wrote, "opium, on the contrary (if taken in a proper manner), introduces amongst them the most exquisite order, legislation, and harmony. Wine robs a man of his self-possession: opium greatly invigorates it. Wine unsettles and clouds the judgement, and gives a preternatural brightness . . . opium, on the contrary, communicates serenity and equipoise to all the faculties."

Opium was a means for parting the veils "between our present consciousness and the secret inscriptions on the mind," and only the sick and the dying had known such secrets in the past. Feverish memories and the reports of the way in which life flashes before the eyes of the dying: all this, for De Quincey, was "repeated, and ten thousand times repeated by opium, for those who are its martyrs." He related the story of a woman who, as a child, had nearly drowned in a river and "saw in a moment her whole life, in its minutest incidents, arrayed before her simultaneously as in a mirror, and she had a faculty developed as suddenly for comprehending the whole and every part. This," added De Quincey, "from some opium experiences of mine, I can believe." Through death, fever, and now by way of "the searchings of opium," long-forgotten memories could "revive in strength. They are not dead," he wrote, "but sleeping."

At first, De Quincey was delighted by the drug's ability to restore his memories and enhance his dreams, not least when it appeared to allow him to live out the fantasies he chose: "A sympathy seemed to arise between the waking and the dreaming states of the brain," he wrote. "Whatsoever I happened to call up and to trace by a voluntary act upon the darkness was very apt to transfer itself to my dreams." But such compensations also tend to overshoot. De Quincey's deficit of dreams became a surplus with which he found it difficult to cope. He swung from the impoverishment of his imagination to its almost unbearable opiated wealth, and his quest to maintain equilibrium in the face of a fragmenting and accelerating world produced "nightly spectacles of more than earthly splendour," a "dream horror" that was "far more frightful" than the world he wanted to escape.

And opium restored far more than scenes from De Quincey's faded past. Opium, he discovered, has "a power not contented with reproduction, but which absolutely creates or transforms." There were new, strange scenes in his opiated dreams, and while the drug allowed De Quincey to collect his own thoughts and memories, it also gave him images of far-distant times and places. The dreams he was now dreaming were no longer his own. Scenes came unbidden, as if from elsewhere; his mind was invaded by flashback anticipations, sudden recollections, and unpredicted twists: "The caprices, the gay arabesques, and the lovely floral luxuriations of dreams, betray a shocking tendency to pass into finer maniacal splendours."

> I was stared at, hooted at, grinned at, chattered at, by monkeys, paroquets, cockatoos. I ran into pagodas: and was fixed, for centuries, at the summit, or in secret rooms; I was the idol; I was the priest; I was worshipped; I was sacrificed. I fled from the wrath of Brama through all the forests of Asia: Vishnu hated me: Seeva laid wait for me. I came suddenly upon Isis and Osiris: I had done a deed, they said, which the ibis and the crocodile trembled at. I was buried, for a thousand years, in stone coffins, with mummies and sphynxes, in narrow chambers at the heart of eternal pyramids. I was kissed, with cancerous kisses, by crocodiles; and laid, confounded with all unutterable slimy things, amongst reeds and Nilotic mud.
>
> I thus give the reader some slight abstraction of my oriental dreams . . .

These dreams enthralled his readers, but for De Quincey, they were terrible nightmares. He had a pathological hatred of all points east of London that seems to have preceded his Oriental dreams. He described South Asia as "the seat of awful images and associations," and China evoked fears and "feelings deeper than I can analyse." He feared the "mere antiquity of Asian things, of their institutions, histories, modes of faith," and felt overwhelmed by the vast populations of the Asian continent. De Quincey's Orient was not primitive: this he reserved for Africa, with its "wild, barbarous, and capricious superstitions," whereas Asia, epitomized by its "ancient, monumental, cruel, and elaborate religions," was a terrifying, teeming zone. "I have often thought," he wrote in *Confessions*, "that if I were compelled to forgo England, and to live in China, and among Chinese manners and modes of life and

scenery, I should go mad. The causes of my horror lie deep."
De Quincey's enmity for China was sealed when his twenty-
two-year-old son died there in 1842.

Opium turned the dreams back on, but it also took the off
switch away. As De Quincey lost the ability to distinguish between an increasingly hallucinatory waking life and the intensity of opiated dreams, the characters he met in the outside
world came to resemble dream figures. Of the druggist who
supplied him with his first opium, he wrote, "I believe him to
have evanesced, or evaporated, so unwillingly would I connect any mortal remembrances with that hour, and place, and
creature, that first brought me acquaintance with the celestial
drug." These encounters were the stuff of dreams, yet they
were as real as the world had always been: the druggist

> looked dull and stupid, just as any mortal druggist might
> be expected to look on a Sunday: and, when I asked for
> the tincture of opium, he gave it to me as any other man
> might do: and furthermore, out of my shilling, returned
> me what seemed to be real copper halfpence, taken out of
> a real wooden drawer. Nevertheless, in spite of such indi-
> cations of humanity, he has ever since existed in my mind
> as the beatific vision of an immortal druggist, sent down
> to earth on a special mission to myself.

And then there was his famous visitor, the Malay, who ate
enough opium "to kill three dragoons and their horses" and
"fastened afterwards upon my dreams." From where did
these characters come; where did they go? "What business a
Malay could have to transact amongst English mountains, I
cannot conjecture."

De Quincey felt increasingly possessed by opium, used and
abused by what had once been medicine, a puppet of the
characters it placed inside his head. In his sequence of Oxford
dreams, opium puts him under the influence of three Sublime
Goddesses, the Sorrows, whose mission is to "plague his heart

until [they] had unfolded the capacities of his spirit." Passing his life between them, the Sorrows condemn him "to see the things that ought not to be seen—sights that are abominable, and secrets that are unutterable." Their messages were scrambled, but opium allowed him to receive them

> not by sounds that perish, or words that go astray, but by signs in heaven—by changes on earth—by pulses in secret rivers—heraldries painted on darkness—and hieroglyphs written on the tablets of the brain. *They* wheeled in mazes; *I* spelled the steps. *They* telegraphed from afar; *I* read the signals. They conspired together and on the mirrors of darkness *my* eye traced the plots. *Theirs* were the symbols,—*mine* are the words.

Even the Dark Interpreter began to assume an air of autonomy. His interpretation "generally is but that which I have said in daylight, and in meditation deep enough to sculpture itself on my heart." But although he was the product of De Quincey's opiated mind and often his "faithful representative," there were also times when the Interpreter seemed "subject to the action of the god *Phantasus*, who rules in dreams." He was usually "anchored and stationary in my dreams," but at times "great storms and driving mists cause him to fluctuate uncertainly." The Interpreter "sometimes swerves out of orbit, and mixes a little with alien natures."

Opium had allowed De Quincey to stand "aloof from the uproar of life; as if the tumult, the fever, and the strife, were suspended," but it also made some of his worst dreams come true. It had allowed him to collect his thoughts and memories, but it also took him to zones teeming with ghostly beings and monstrous forces. He had run from the steam train's "annihilation of space and time," but his "sense of space, and in the end, the sense of time, were both powerfully affected" by the drug. Everything he most feared was now played out in the theater of his mind.

Even eloquent De Quincey, rarely stuck for words, found it difficult to convey the "revolting complexities of misery and incomprehensible darkness" and "the hieroglyphic meaning of human suffering" that his opiated nights contained. His dreams were often "accompanied by deep-seated anxiety and gloomy melancholy, such as are wholly incommunicable by words," and "horrors from the kingdoms of anarchy and darkness, which, by their very intensity, challenge the sanctity of concealment, and gloomily retire from exposition." Although his readers loved his luscious descriptions of Oriental travels and goddesses of the night, De Quincey always felt that they failed to understand the sheer intensity of his dreams, the terrifying worlds on to which his doors of perception could open. "I saw through vast avenues of gloom those towering gates of ingress," he wrote: they are "awful gates" that open on to "a shaft . . . into the worlds of death and darkness." Opium, he tried to insist, was notable "not merely for exalting the colours of dream-scenery, but for deepening its shadows; and, above all, for strengthening the sense of its fearful *realities*."

> And from junk sickness comes a heightened sensitivity to impressions and sensation on the level of dream, myth, symbol.
>
> William Burroughs, *Interzone*

Normal transmission was never quite resumed: "My dreams," wrote De Quincey after months of abstinence, "are not perfectly calm: the dread swell and agitation of the storm have not yet wholly subsided: the legions that encamped in them are drawing off, but not all departed." Things would never be the same. If De Quincey had wanted to compose himself, he now watched himself divide and multiply: "housed within himself—occupying, as it were, some separate chamber in his brain—holding, perhaps, from that station a secret and detestable commerce with his own heart," he feared that there was "some horrid alien nature." There was more, and worse, to come.

> What if it were his own nature repeated—still, if the duality were strictly perceptible, even *that*—even this mere numerical double of his own consciousness—might be a curse too mighty to be sustained. But how, if the alien nature contradicts his own, fights with it, perplexes, and confounds it? How, again, if not one alien nature, but two, but three, but four, but five, are introduced within what he once thought the inviolable sanctuary of himself?

De Quincey was haunted by this thought. He described his fear of "the horrid inoculation upon each other of incompatible natures. This horror has always been secretly felt by man," he wrote. "We read it in the fearful composition of the sphinx. The dragon, again, is the snake inoculated upon the scorpion." And now De Quincey could see it in himself. The drug had made itself indispensable, a crucial element in his life, a part of him, as necessary to his functioning as any other substance in his body and his brain. Life without opium had become impossible: the drug had "ceased to found its empire on spells of pleasure," and now "it was solely by the tortures connected with the attempt to abjure it, that it kept its hold." Opium had changed his body and his mind. It had put him back in touch with himself, but now he was a fabricated creature composed of man and drug, strung out between illusion and reality, suspended between life and death. "I saw that I must die if I continued the opium: I determined, therefore, if that should be required, to die in throwing it off."

> You see junk is death the oldest "visitor" in the industry.
>
> William Burroughs, *Naked Lunch*

De Quincey didn't die, or give up opium, for years. He continually returned to its themes, and his writings on the drug remain some of the most engaging accounts of opium's "sensual pleasure" and what he came to call its "accursed chain." But if he took the drug "to an *excess*, not yet *recorded* of any other man," even De Quincey had to admit that there was "one celebrated man of the present day, who, if all be true which is reported of him, has greatly exceeded me in quantity."

"Laudanum gave me repose, not sleep," wrote Coleridge to his brother George in a letter quoted by Elisabeth Schneider, "but you, I believe, know how divine that repose is, what a spot of enchantment, a green spot of fountain and flowers and trees in the very heart of a waste of sands!" Coleridge never quite recaptured his dream of Xanadu, but he kept repeating the experiment. Opium was the very stuff of his dreams and the reason why he had to coin a new word: *intensify*. "Though, I confess," he wrote in *Biographia Literaria*, "it sounds uncouth to my own ear." Opium excited Coleridge's fascination with the possibility that dreams might unlock some of the secrets of creativity and poetry, memory and imagination. He was convinced that the most intense dreams could not be explained in terms of the "present dogma, that the Forms and Feelings of Sleep are always the reflections & confused Echoes of our waking Thoughts, & Experiences." In his *Notebooks*, he carefully distinguished between different kinds of dream experience and argued that in addition to the dreams of ordinary sleep, to which the "present dogma" might well be adequate, there were also powerful reveries and dream states that could not be so easily ascribed to waking thoughts and experiences. They seemed to have their source in a very different world. Even more intense were nightmares, which Coleridge defined less in terms of their terrifying contents than by their emergence on the very brink of sleep. The horror of the nightmare is its tendency to leave its dreamers lucid while removing their control. It is "not a mere dream," he wrote in

Shakespearean Criticism, "but takes place when the waking state of the brain is re-commencing and most often during a rapid alternation, a *twinkling,* as it were, of sleeping and waking."

This "intermediate state," in which even "the strangest and most sudden transformations do not produce any sensation of surprise," fascinated Coleridge, and many later writers too. Robert Louis Stevenson was obsessed by the images "witnessed in that small theatre of the brain which we keep brightly lighted all night long, after the jets are down, and darkness and sleep reign undisturbed in the remainder of the body." Havelock Ellis later used the term *hypnagogic* to apply to this "ante-chamber of sleep, when the senses are in repose and waking consciousness is slipping away, or else when, as we leave the world of dreams, waking consciousness is flowing back again." Dreams experienced in these hypnagogic states are far more vivid and intense than those dreamed by night, or even ordinary daydreams. And they tend to present "a possible, though, it may be, highly improbable event. The half-waking or hypnagogic intelligence seems to be deceived by this element of life-like possibility."

For Coleridge, this was a privileged state in which the most bizarre discontinuities and chimeras could pass through a mind that would regard them all with calm ambivalence: "We pass no judgement either way," he wrote. Opium could take such dreams to extremes. And poets could turn them into poetry, taking the reader as far as they had been, leaving the audience suspended between the poles of illusion and reality, lost in the same worlds of life-like death and death-like life in which they had found their lines. It is this sense of suspended judgment that allows the most unlikely events to unfold on the stage or page. "We *choose* to be deceived" in the theater, he wrote, and "when we are enveloped in deep contemplation of any kind, or in reverie, as in reading a very interesting play or romance, we measure time very inaccurately; and hence, if a play greatly affects our passions, the absurdities of passing over many days or years, and of perpetual change of place, are not noticed by the audience." All writing should allow its audience to experience what Coleridge famously defined in *Biographia Literaria* as a "willing suspension of disbelief."

Like the landscapes and the story of "Kubla Khan," this phrase had an extraordinary impact on subsequent theories and critiques of poetry, theater, and later art forms, such as film, video, and multimedia—before it found a home in cyberspace. It became a kind of catchphrase, a repeated refrain, a part of the language that went on to be used without reference to the poet or the drug.

> We want to make theatre a believable reality inflicting this kind of tangible laceration, contained in all true feeling, on the heart and senses . . . the audience will believe in the illusion of theatre on condition they really take it for a dream, not for a servile imitation of reality.
>
> Antonin Artaud, *The Theatre and Its Double*

The willing suspension of disbelief introduced a profound sense of ambivalence that repeats itself in Coleridge's life and work and endlessly reiterates itself throughout the whole story of writing on drugs. With its juxtaposed images of "mingled measure" and a "sunny pleasure-dome with caves of ice," "Kubla Khan" itself is described by Elisabeth Schneider as "the soul of ambivalence." But if opium allowed Coleridge to explore life on the line between illusion and truth, it also made it difficult for him to reassert the difference between the two: he has always been accused of a remorseless willingness to fabricate, plagiarize, and lie, and "Kubla Khan" was a case in point: Was his preface a true story? Did he really dream the dream, and had his writing really been interrupted by a man from Porlock? Or had he simply made the story up in an attempt to excuse the poem's brevity? Was he inspired by Purchas, or had he simply stolen his opening lines from the pages of *Pilgrimage*? And if opium had given him the poem, could he really claim to be its author at all? Neither he nor his critics seemed able to decide whether he was a fine poet and philosopher, a shallow pretender unworthy of such praise, or, as seems far more pertinent, both of these and all of them at once: "One can say that Coleridge plagiarized," writes Richard Holmes, "but that no one plagiarized like Coleridge." The poet puts truth in abeyance and leaves it hanging there.

> There are degrees of lying collaboration and cowardice—That is to say degrees of intoxication.
> William Burroughs, *Nova Express*

The albatross around the hero's neck in "Rime of the Ancient Mariner" may not have been a reference to opium, but it made a perfect image for the opiated guilt that later came to weigh Coleridge down. The drug threw him into webs of deceit and depths of self-flagellation to which even De Quincey seemed immune: "Infirmity and misery do not, of necessity, imply guilt," he later wrote. But Coleridge could find no respite from the guilt that accompanied his use of opium. When he described the serpents, the tortures, the vicious circles in which he was trapped by his doses—fluid ounces first, then pints—of the drug, his remorse was palpable. In a passage quoted by Holmes as "the most frank and the most terrible" of Coleridge's letters on opium, he condemned himself for treating his friends with "silence, absence, or breach of trust" and launched into a devastating attack on his dependency on the drug. "What crime is there scarcely which has not been included in or followed from the one guilt of taking opium?" He fumed about his "ingratitude to my maker for the wasted Talents; ingratitude to so many friends who have loved me I know not why; of barbarous neglect of my family . . . I have in this one dirty business of Laudanum a hundred times deceived, tricked, nay, actually and consciously LIED."

In the words of total need: "Wouldn't you?" Yes you would. You would lie, cheat, inform on your friends, steal, do anything to satisfy total need. Because you would be in a state of total sickness, total posses-sion, and not in a position to act in any other way.

William Burroughs, *Naked Lunch*

In the early 1830s, so the story goes, Coleridge broke down in the kitchen of some London friends. He cried as he confessed how much he longed for opium, and, blissfully unaware of the implications of her advice, the young mistress of the house tried her best to console him. "Mr. Coleridge, do not cry," she said. "If the opium really does you any good, and you *must* have it, why do you not go and get it?" According to her son, who observed the scene, Coleridge immediately pulled himself together at these words: "The poet ceased to weep, recovered his composure and, turning to my father, said, with an air of much relief and deep conviction: 'Collins, your wife is an exceedingly sensible woman!'"

Harriet and William Collins were well known in the literary circles of the day: William was an artist, and Coleridge was one of many writers who commissioned him to paint his por-trait. Wilkie Collins was their first child, nine years old when he saw Coleridge weep for want of opium. "I was a boy at the time," he later wrote, "but the incident made a strong impres-sion on my mind and I could not forget it."

Coleridge seems to have impressed all the children he met: he used to read his poems to Mary Shelley's parents while she hid behind the sofa to listen after hours. As for Wilkie Collins, he grew up to be a prolific and hardworking writer, proud of the fact that his books were read as the pulp fiction of their day. He suffered from gout and several other complaints from a relatively early age and, like Coleridge before him, took opium to ease the pain for many years. At one time, he de-scribed the drug as "my only friend," and he became so inter-ested in the drug that he collected and studied reports of other writers' opium use. Several of his books—including *No Name, The Woman in White, The Moonstone,* and *Armadale*—give opium a prominent role, and the drug also seems to have supplied him with some of his most powerful and recurring motifs. Collins was fascinated by fraud, deceit, and mistaken identity, themes that figured in many of these books, and he had firsthand experience of his drug's tendency to induce a sense of duplicity: there was, he said, "another Wilkie Collins," who "sat at the table with him and tried to monopolize the writing pad."

Collins, like Coleridge, fine-tuned his scheming mind and honed his skills of deception on the drug. "I am in terrible trouble," he once said to his friend Fred Lehmann, with whom he traveled to Switzerland in 1868.

> I have only just discovered that my laudanum has come to an end. I know, however, that there are six chemists at Coire; and if you and I pretend, separately, to be physicians, and each chemist consents to give to each of us the maximum of opium he may by Swiss law, which is very strict, given to one person, I shall just have enough to get through the night. Afterwards we must go through the same thing at Basle.

The book Collins had just published turned such webs of deceit into the complexities of narrative. Opium finds its way into the very heart of *The Moonstone*. The stone of the title is a large diamond with a long, Oriental history. At the beginning of the story, the stone mysteriously disappears. At the end, it transpires that the diamond was taken by a character who is both culpable and innocent: Franklin Blake, the hero, stole the stone, but he did so in an opiated state that left him with no memory of his actions. Truth and lies, innocence and guilt: like De Quincey, *The Moonstone*'s thief cannot be held accountable for the crimes of opium. Only when the scene is recreated does he find himself remembering what he has done.

The mystery is solved by Sergeant Cuff. It is his careful examination of the facts, his calm and rational approach, that uncovers the influence of opium. But his evidence is circumstantial. Opium itself is his only chance of proving the hypothesis that the secret lies in opium. Only the drug can substantiate its role in the diamond's disappearance. And so the scene of the crime is re-created; Franklin Blake is given opium for what Cuff believes is a second time. "I gave him the dose, and shook up his pillows, and told him to lie down again and wait." Within an hour, the "sublime intoxication of opium gleamed in his eyes; the dew of a stealthy perspiration began to glisten on his face." Everything hinges on the outcome of this experiment. Cuff is almost overcome with excitement. He can't bear "the suspense of the moment" as it begins to look as if the experiment is working: "The prospect thus suddenly opened before me was too much for my shattered nerves. I was obliged to look away from him—or I should have lost my self-control." To Cuff's great relief, his suspicions are confirmed when Blake repeats his actions of the first night. Blake is exonerated, Cuff is vindicated, and opium provides the solution to its own mystery.

In his preface to *The Moonstone*, Collins wrote:

> Having first ascertained, not only from books, but from living authorities as well, what the results of that experiment would really have been, I have declined to avail myself of the novelist's privilege of supposing something which might have happened, and have so shaped the story as to make it grow out of what actually would have happened—which, I beg to inform my readers, is also what does actually happen in these pages.

As Collins's biographer William Clarke states, *The Moonstone* is "the first, the longest and the best of modern English detective novels." Its sheer length allowed Collins to explore the complexities of a plot that presents a multitude of characters and scenes, clues and leads, and possible solutions to the crime. Just like the novel's hero, Franklin Blake, Collins keeps his readers in suspense, gripped by the story, lost in a plot that allows its readers to revisit the opening scenes and see them in the light of the solution, opium. It is a story of shifting perceptions that shifts the perceptions of its readers too. Opium was there all along, a chemical solution to the mystery it makes, secreted in the first few pages of the book.

The Moonstone is often noted for its evocation of a sense of character. Collins wrote in his preface to the book that his earlier novels had traced "the influence of circumstances upon character. In the present story I have reversed the process. The attempt made here is to trace the influence of character on circumstances." *The Moonstone*'s Sergeant Cuff is one of the first characters really to *have* character, to be a personality in his own right. Collins portrays him in his working life but also makes him sensitive and multifaceted: he is, for example, an enthusiastic gardener as well as an intelligent detective. This animated figure was the first in a long line of larger-than-life characters to stalk the pages of detective fictions.

Wilkie Collins has often been chastised for swapping his literary skills for opium. Clarke points out: "that the drug prevented him from developing the plots on which his first novels depended is hardly in dispute." And after the publication of *The Moonstone*, Collins found himself subjected to a fashionable treatment for his love of laudanum. In 1869 he wrote:

> I am stabbed every night at ten with a sharp-pointed syringe which injects morphia under my skin and gets me a night's rest, without any of the drawbacks of taking opium internally. If I only persevere with this, I am told I shall be able, before long, gradually to diminish the quantity of morphine and the number of nightly stabbings— and so emancipate myself from opium altogether.

But if opium became an enslavement, compounded by the in-dignity of the syringe, Collins had been taking laudanum, sometimes in huge quantities, for some twenty years when he wrote *The Moonstone*. And if opium contributed to his subse-quent decline, there is no doubt that *The Moonstone* was its beneficiary, not its casualty. The drug that made the mystery, the solution, and the proof also had a hand in the writing of the book. Collins dictated *The Moonstone*, "the last part largely under the effects of opium," to a young girl. And just as Franklin Blake was unaware that he was the author of the crime, Collins found himself at one remove from his own opi-ated work. "When it was finished," he later wrote, "I was not only pleased and astonished at the finale, but did not recog-nize it as my own."

> It was the sort of spell that the story-teller cast over the tyrant in the Arabian Nights. And to the last he walked the world with the pride of a poet, and with the false yet unfathomable courage of a great liar. He could always produce more Arabian Nights if ever his neck was in danger.
> G. K. Chesterton, "The Dagger with Wings"

It was Edgar Allan Poe who had first used his writing to ex-periment with what he called "the anomaly of the most rigidly exact in science applied to the shadow and spirituality of the most intangible in speculation." The ineffable, insub-stantial worlds from which Coleridge had plucked "Kubla Khan" now became regions to be explored with the fine-tooth combs of what Poe defined as "the imaginative intellect."

"How very commonly we hear it remarked, that such and such thoughts are beyond the compass of words! I do not be-lieve that any thought, properly so called, is out of the reach of language." In "Between Wakefulness and Sleep," Poe de-clared that he had "never had a thought which I could not set down in words, with even more distinctness than that with which I conceived it." But even he, so full of confidence, found it difficult to convey a certain "class of fancies, of exquisite delicacy, which are *not* thoughts, and to which, *as yet*, I have found it absolutely impossible to adapt to language." He did not, he wrote, "altogether despair of embodying in words at least enough of the fancies in question to convey, to certain classes of intellect, a shadowy conception of their character." And if he did ever find a way, "even a partial record of the impressions would startle the universal intellect of mankind, by the *supremeness of the novelty* of the material employed."

Poe pursued Coleridge's attempt to delay "the lapse from this border-ground into the dominion of sleep," sustaining a moment in which he was often treated to what he described as "psychal impressions," or fancies. They were remarkably vivid and intense and had "nothing even approximate in character to impressions ordinarily received. It is," he wrote, "as if the five senses were supplanted by five myriad others alien to mortality." Fascinated by these "mere points of time where the confines of the waking world blend with those of the world of dreams," in which, for all their brevity, so much can occur, Poe was keen to sustain his suspension between sleep and waking life so that an "inappreciable *point* of time" could be stretched into a navigable space.

Poe filled his stories with voices from these twilight zones beyond the world of waking life. Many of his characters are trapped or traveling in these regions: there are journeys across oceans and trips through space, drug-induced adventures on the edge of consciousness. "Mesmeric Revelation" records his conversation with a mesmerized "sleep-waker," Mr. Vankirk. In "The Facts in the Case of M. Valdemar," the protagonist puts a dying man into a mesmeric trance for several months. "I had become a slave to opium," says the narrator of "Ligeia" as he moves from "passionate waking visions" of his dead lover to the point at which her corpse returns to life. "It had me in its clutches, and all my work and my plans had taken on the colour of my dreams." As Charles Baudelaire exclaimed in *Les Paradis artificiels*, "In how many marvelous passages does Edgar Poe, that incomparable poet and unrefuted philosopher, who should always be quoted on all the mysterious maladies of the soul, describe the somber and compelling splendors of opium?"

But such descriptions were not enough for Poe. He and his characters lived to tell their tales of half-life in the twilight zone, but he also wanted to express the inexpressible, to convey the singular intensity of his opiated dreams, to give his readers a chance to share his experience of abeyance between worlds. And if the borders between life and death were among the most engaging of Poe's themes, his quest to produce even a "partial record" of the impressions made by opium extended to the structure of his texts, the techniques and devices he employed in a tireless effort to make his horror stories horrify and keep his readers hanging in the states of suspension he described. It was this ability to evoke the effects he described that made Poe "the master of horror," for Baudelaire, "the prince of mystery."

Poe also inherited Coleridge's reputation as a plagiarist and a charlatan. Notorious for his sleights of hand, his literary hoaxes and deceptions, Poe was famous for his ability to fool his readers, in stories such as "The Unparalleled Adventure of One Hans Pfaall," with fictions pretending to be scientific fact. At a time when poetry seemed utterly incompatible with such scientific themes, his blends of fact and fiction, truth and fantasy, added to his reputation as a hoaxer and a fraud. Poe was delighted by the ease with which he could deceive his readers, especially intellectuals. In 1844, he wrote, "Twenty years ago credulity was the characteristic trait of the mob, incredulity the distinctive feature of the philosophic; now the case is exactly conversed." Although they brought him nothing but notoriety at the time, what were then dismissed as works of "pseudo-science" are now regarded as early examples of what has become a powerful and respected genre: science fiction.

It was in Poe's detective stories that his conviction that "the two divisions of mental power are never to be found in perfection apart" really came to fruition. "The *highest* order of the imaginative intellect is always pre-eminently mathematical; and the converse," he insisted as he wrote "The Murders in the Rue Morgue," the first of three stories to figure the detective C. Auguste Dupin. If *The Moonstone* was the first detective novel, "The Murders in the Rue Morgue" is widely regarded as the first piece of detective fiction. Poe's hero became famous for the mathematical precision of his thinking, his highly tuned skills of ratiocination and deliberation. Dupin is astute and perceptive, his powers of observation and intuition as highly developed as his analytic skills, his processes of reasoning far more significant to him and the story than the mysteries he solves. And Dupin's ability to run back through the steps that led to the mystery gives the narrative its own strange circularity as it wends its way back to the beginning, to and from the crime and its solution. Dupin's methods are unorthodox, resented by the police in the story but later adopted by real officers of the law.

Poe's attention to fine detail, his analytic prowess, and the nonlinearity of his narrative make the trilogy "almost a complete manual of detective theory and practice," as Dorothy L. Sayers famously declared; it seemed to initiate and complete a whole genre in one accomplished move. The summary by Philip van Doren Stern says it all:

> The transcendent and eccentric detective; the admiring and slightly stupid foil; the well-intentioned blundering and unimaginativeness of the official guardians of the law; the locked-room convention; the pointing finger of unjust suspicion; the solution by surprise; deduction by putting oneself in another's position (now called psychology); concealment by means of the ultra-obvious; the stage ruse to force the culprit's hand; even the expansive and condescending explanation when the chase is done;

all these sprang full-panoplied from the buzzing brain
and lofty brow of the Philadelphia editor.

Poe's Dupin duped everyone.

Artificial Paradises

> A deadening warmth pervaded my limbs, and de-
> mentia, like a wave which breaks foaming on to a
> rock, then withdraws to break again, invaded and
> left my brain, finally enveloping it altogether. That
> strange visitor, hallucination, had come to dwell
> within me.
>
> Fitz Hugh Ludlow, *The Hasheesh Eater*

De Quincey insisted that *Confessions* was not to be read as an
admission of guilt. This was a work of "self-accusation,"
which, he insisted, was a very different thing: "Infirmity and
misery do not, of necessity, imply guilt." Although his book
did reveal the depths of his despair, the weakness of his will,
and his loss of self-control, he also took some pride in his ability to resist the drug. Among De Quincey's declared purposes
in writing *Confessions* was the desire to correct what he considered the lamentable ignorance surrounding the drug. "I do
by no means deny that some truths have been delivered to the
world in regard to opium," he wrote.

> Thus it has been repeatedly affirmed by the learned, that
> opium is dusky brown in colour; and this, take notice, I
> grant: secondly, that it is rather dear; which also I grant,
> for in my time, East-India opium has been three guineas a
> pound, and Turkey eight: and, thirdly, that if you eat a
> good deal of it, most probably you must—do what is par-
> ticularly disagreeable to any man of regular habits, viz.
> die.

De Quincey also said that he wanted to dissuade other would-be eaters of opium from following in his footsteps. But he must have known how tempting even the worst excesses of his experience would be. And if De Quincey and so many of his compatriots had slipped into the opium habit by some kind of medicinal accident, many of the writers he inspired were far more deliberate in their attempts to emulate his adventures.

One of his keenest followers was an American editor, Fitz Hugh Ludlow, who worked for a succession of East Coast magazines, including *Vanity Fair*, and published *The Hasheesh Eater: Being Passages from the Life of a Pythagorean* in 1857. Ludlow was quick to acknowledge De Quincey's obvious influence on his work. *Confessions*, Ludlow wrote, had taken him

> beyond all the boundaries of the ordinary life into a world of intense lights and shadows—a realm in which all the range of average thought found its conditions surpassed, if not violated. My own career, however far its recital may fall short of the Opium Eater's, and notwithstanding it was not coincident and but seldom parallel with his, still ran through lands as glorious, as unfrequented, as weird as his own, and takes those who would follow it out of the trodden highways of mind.

Ludlow preempted accusations that his work was simply a poor imitation of De Quincey's masterpiece. Although he, too, tried opium, it was, he wrote, "impossible for any one known to have used the drug to make any intellectual effort whatever, speech, published article, or brilliant conversation, without being hailed satirically as Coleridge *le petit*, or De Quincey in the second edition." So Ludlow chose hashish instead.

Cannabis is one of the world's oldest cultivated crops, and in the eighteenth and nineteenth centuries, the rugged and less psychoactive varieties of hemp, or cannabis, were grown commercially across the Western world and used for making paper, banknotes, fiber, rope, and canvas (which takes its name from cannabis). Many other parts of the plant were commercially exploited: even the seeds were used in bird feed. One of the sweeter twists to the drug's tale is that writers on hashish have often written on paper made from the same plant. But cannabis indica, the variety then known to grow in India and across the Middle East, is the source of several powerful psychoactive alkaloids. Its pollinated female plants produce a sticky golden resin that can be gathered and used as hashish.

Cannabis is thought to have originated in central Asia or China. Its use in India is ancient too—there are references to the plant in the Atharva-Veda—and the plant is also widely distributed across the Middle East. Arab traders carried it to the east coast of Africa in the thirteenth century, and the use and cultivation of cannabis spread across the whole African continent. There are suggestions that cannabis was also native to the Americas, but the plants were certainly taken there by the first European settlers: the Spanish took them to South America, and the British took them to North America. In Canada, New England, and Virginia, cannabis was widely used in the production of textiles, and the crops were vital to the economic health of the American colonies.

Early uses of cannabis are thought to have been restricted to the commercial production of textiles and paper goods. It was not until the mid-nineteenth century that America gained an interest in the medical and psychoactive properties of cannabis, and Fitz Hugh Ludlow was one of the first people to experiment with the resin produced by the flowers of the female plant: hashish. Although grass is widely used today, the resin, hashish, is now relatively rare in the Americas and the Caribbean. Ludlow first encountered it on the shelves of a shop belonging to one of his friends, an apothecary. "In the very atmosphere of the establishment," he wrote, "loaded as it was with a composite smell of all things curative and preventive, there was an aromatic invitation to scientific musing."

And it was in this spirit that he took the drug. The musing led to the experiment: a brave one, given that so little was then known about the drug and its effects. He started with small doses of hashish, which was then eaten and measured in grains, increasing the quantity until the fateful night on which he found himself "in the power of the hasheesh influence. My first emotion was one of uncontrollable terror—a sense of getting something which I had not bargained for." Ludlow found himself in some amazing worlds, senses reconfigured, states of mind unknown. Afterward, he felt he'd seen enough mystery and wonder to last him a lifetime and was convinced he would not take the drug again. "For days I was even unusually strong; all the forces of life were in a state of pleasurable activity, but the memory of the wondrous glories which I had beheld wooed me continually like an irresistible sorceress." The experiment was bound to be repeated.

Ludlow was a careful student of hashish. He took great pleasure in identifying and analyzing many of the drug's effects. The drug's synesthetic effects also fascinated him: "The hasheesh-eater knows what it is to be burned by salt fire, to smell colours, to see sounds, and, much more frequently, to see feelings." He also reported the sense of sympathy hashish made him feel with other human beings:

a lively appreciation of the feelings and manners of all people, in whatever lands and ages—a catholic sympathy, a spiritual cosmopolitanism. Not only does this exhibit itself in affectionate yearnings toward friends that are about one, and an extraordinary insight into the excellencies of their characters, but, taking a wider sweep, it can understand and feel with the heroism of philanthropists and the enthusiasm of Crusaders.

There were also darker sides to his hashish use. As William Burroughs wrote, much later, in *Naked Lunch*, hashish brings the "disturbance of space-time perception, acute sensitivity to impressions, flights of ideas, laughing jags, silliness," and less pleasant results too: "It makes a bad situation worse. Depression becomes despair, anxiety panic." An early wave of paranoia inspired Ludlow to write, "I did not know then, as I learned afterward, that suspicion of all earthly things and persons was the characteristic of the hasheesh delirium." And when it came to leaving hashish in his past, Ludlow found himself unable, or at least unwilling, to forgo the drug. Even when it started to unnerve him with its strange images and vengeful gods, the splendors and horrors of his hashish-induced world compelled him to return time and again. Ludlow kept coming back for more.

It may seem surprising that hashish could have held him in such a powerful grip. Few of today's cannabis smokers would think that the drug could have such intense and addictive effects, although, as Alexander Trocchi has written, "It is a great pity to be without hashish at any time, indeed." But Ludlow and his contemporaries consumed large amounts of a drug that now tends to be smoked a little at a time and in much smaller quantities. There may have been an element of wish fulfillment, too: De Quincey's accounts of opium had colored expectations of all intoxicants, and there is little doubt that Ludlow was seduced by the drama of De Quincey's addiction. But Ludlow really does seem to have grieved for hashish when he tried to free himself from its influence. He wrote of the sense of "intense longing" he experienced on days of

clear sky and brilliant light. That beauty which filled the heart of every other living thing with gladness, only spoke of other suns more wondrous rolling through other heavens of a more matchless dye. I looked into the sky, and missed its former unutterable rose and sapphire; no longer did the whole dome of the firmament sound with grand unwritten music. It was a pain to look into that desert wilderness of blue which of old my sorcery had peopled for me with innumerable celestial riders, with

cities of pearl and symphony-haunted streams of silver. I
shut my eyes, and in a moment saw all that I had lost.

This acute sense of loss is a very real danger of any drug use.
The sober Ludlow found himself in an impoverished world
that was far more hollow and banal than it had ever been before he used hashish. He had seen a different world, and now
that he knew what he was missing, his drug-free life seemed
unbearably empty: "Henceforth forever, after abandoning
hasheesh, was all endurance with the external creation to be
denied me unless I could penetrate deeper than its mere outside." Hashish had shown Ludlow the depths of what otherwise appeared a bland and superficial world. Now he could
only do without hashish if he could find some alternative
means of accessing the depths it had revealed. But to one who
has known such exceptional intensity, some experience with
which nothing can compare, substitutes are difficult to find.
Only something better will really do the trick, and what could
be better than hashish? Ludlow did, however, find some kind
of cure in the shape of a doctor who took a "kind and lively
interest" in his case. It was thanks to him that Ludlow "began
once more to take an interest in the world, not through any renewed affection for its mere hollow forms, but for the sake of
that inner essence which they embodied." There was no way
back to life as he had known it before hashish, but he did begin "slowly to perceive the possibility of penetrating deeper
than the shard of things without the help, so dearly bought, of
hasheesh."

For at least one of Ludlow's contemporaries, the price was
far too high. The influence of hashish can be read in the work
of countless nineteenth-century French writers, but Charles
Baudelaire was the drug's most self-conscious and deliberate
explorer. He wrote several essays on hashish, which were
published in *Les Paradis artificiels: Opium et haschisch*, a book
he used as both a vehicle for his own reflections on hashish
and an opportunity to present a montage of translated ex-

tracts from De Quincey's work. This was not the first translation of De Quincey's *Confessions*—the first, by Alfred de Mus-
set, had appeared in 1828. In some ways, Baudelaire's work
was not a translation at all: he rewrote some sections of De
Quincey's book and added many comments of his own.

By the early nineteenth century, generations of French travelers had returned with news of hashish and its legendary
use, and, after Napoleon's Egyptian campaigns, troops
brought back the drug itself. Baudelaire's writings on hashish
were full of admiration for a drug whose very name, he
wrote, suggested that "in the one word *grass* the Arabs had
tried to define the source of every immaterial pleasure."
Hashish brought Baudelaire more subtle effects too, fine-
tuning his perceptions to the point at which "a new subtlety or
acuity manifests itself in all the senses. This development is
common to the senses of smell, sight, hearing, and touch. The
eyes behold the Infinite. The ear registers almost imperceptible sounds, even in the midst of the greatest din." Senses col-
lide into synesthesia: "Sounds clothe themselves in colors, and
colors contain music." Everything reveals its complexity and
depth: "Notes of music turn into numbers; and, if you are endowed with some aptitude for mathematics, the melody or
harmony you hear, whilst retaining its pleasurable and sen-
suous character, transforms itself into a huge arithmetical
process, in which numbers beget numbers, whilst you follow
the successive stages of reproduction with inexplicable ease
and an agility equal to that of the performer." Objects are distorted or transformed, assuming an unprecedented liveliness,
and space and time are caught up in "monstrous expansions,"
on which the hashish mind "gazes, with a certain melancholic
delight, down through the depths of the years, and boldly
plunges into infinite perspectives . . ." In *Les Paradis artificiels*,
Baudelaire described "an apparently interminable fancy" that
lasted for only a minute of real time. And then "a new stream
of ideas carries you away: it will hurl you along in its living
vortex for a further minute; and this minute, too, will be an

eternity, for the normal relation between time and the individual has been completely upset by the multitude and intensity of sensations and ideas."

These were effects writ large in all of Baudelaire's poetry and prose. But there were limits to his affection for the drug, and *Les Paradis artificiels* swings between love and hatred for hashish, which, he wrote, produced nothing like the "hieroglyphic" dreams experienced by De Quincey. "It is true that throughout its whole period the intoxication will be in the nature of a vast dream—by reason of the intensity of its colors and its rapid flow of mental images," he wrote, "but it will always retain the private tonality of the individual." Hashish could heighten perception and magnify the senses to extraordinary degrees, but it brought its users nothing really new, "nothing miraculous, absolutely nothing but an exaggeration of the natural." And this disappointed Baudelaire, whose Catholic beliefs seem to have given him a notion of real paradise with which hashish could not compete.

> Hashish, like all other solitary delights, makes the individual useless to mankind, and also makes society unnecessary to the individual.
> Charles Baudelaire, *Les Paradis artificiels*

Baudelaire's reservations blossomed into vehement and sometimes incoherent hostility toward both opium and hashish. His religious convictions underlined his insistence that there was something profoundly debilitating and debasing about the use of drugs. "It is the very infallibility of the method that constitutes its immorality," he wrote, even though he was convinced that the drug was far from infallible. Endorsing the position of the Church, which "regards only those riches as legitimate and genuine that are earned by assiduous seeking," Baudelaire condemned hashish as a means of circumventing the effort and the time it takes to reap such rewards, a shortcut to paradise, an attempt to "blot out the work of time," temptation incarnate, the flowers of evil: "in my opinion, not only one of the surest and most terrible means at the disposal of the Prince of Darkness for the recruitment and subjugation of deplorable humanity, but actually one of his most perfect embodiments." It was a shortcut to a paradise that was not a paradise at all.

Even at his most enthusiastic, Baudelaire remained committed to the tone set by the title of his book. The worlds revealed by both opium and hashish might be spectacular, but users were cheating, and cheated, by their experiences of artificial, ersatz heavens that did little more than trick visitors into thinking they had experienced some real paradise, an encounter with the Infinite: "The thoughts of the hashish taker, from which he counts on obtaining so much, are not really so beautiful as they appear under their momentary guise, clad in the tinsel of magic. They have much more of earth than of heaven in them." This was an artificial paradise.

Baudelaire was by no means the first to raise such doubts about hashish. Nor was his Catholicism the first context in which they were expressed. Islam has often been tolerant of hashish, and sometimes of opium as well: in the fourteenth century, as Farhad Daftary points out, "Hashish was discussed and utilized, even among the better classes of Cairo and Damascus, publicly and without inhibition." But the word *hashishiyya*, hashish eaters, was often used as a term of abuse in the medieval Levant, where many Muslim writers "stressed that the extended use of hashish would have extremely harmful effects on the user's morality and religion, relaxing his attitude towards those duties, such as praying and fasting, specified by the sacred law of Islam." Regular users of hashish were regarded as low-life delinquents, social outcasts threatening to Islam itself.

One of the earliest accounts of a drug-induced artificial paradise dates back to this period. The story of Hasan Sabbah, the Old Man of the Mountain, was popularized in the West by Marco Polo, but many other writers had already recounted the legend to the European world. The gist of the story is well known. In Marco Polo's version, Hasan Sabbah is said to have built "the largest garden and the most beautiful that ever was seen in this world" in the mountainous valley of Alamut. The garden was filled with "the most beautiful houses and the most beautiful palaces," fountains, and conduits, "through some of which it was seen ran wine and through some milk and through some honey and through some the clearest water." There were "ladies and damsels the most beautiful in the world," whose "duty was to furnish the young men who were put there with all delights and pleasures." There was music, fine food, silk, gold, love, and laughter. "And the Old Man made his men understand that in that garden was Paradise." The garden was said to have been modeled on the paradise described in the Quran. And it was with this simulated paradise that Hasan Sabbah was said to have convinced his warriors to fight. The young men he chose to be Assassins were given an intoxicating drink, sometimes defined as opium or as "a certain drink which put them to sleep," and then "taken in this deep sleep and put into that garden of his." When the young men wake, "they see all these things which I have told you, made just as the law of Mahomet says." They believe they really are in paradise. After several days of indulgence in the pleasures that surround them there, they are given another dose of opium and carried out of the gardens in their sleep. They are called before the Old Man, who "asks them whence they come." They tell him they have come from paradise.

The young men talk to everyone about their sojourn in this otherworld, convincing those who haven't seen it that the paradise is real and filling them with the desire to get there. The Old Man tells them all that paradise is indeed the reward for obedience. And when he sends his Assassins out to kill an enemy, they undertake the mission with no fear of death. Their desire to return to paradise is almost stronger than their desire to live.

Marco Polo's account of the Assassins was a synthesis of several other stories, most of which are now considered "no more than absurd myths." According to Daftary, it is inconceivable that such a well-disciplined and austere people could have been "the blind devotees of a deceitful leader who easily made them addicted to hedonistic pleasures and then demanded of them nothing less than self-sacrifice for his own diabolically selfish motives." The Assassin legends are "the products of ignorant, hostile 'imagination,'" much of it fostered by the Europeans but some of it the product of orthodox Islam. Sunni scholars regarded Hasan Sabbah's sect as dangerous and heretical, and it suited them to present the Old Man as a murderous and unscrupulous pretender to divinity. Marco Polo and the earlier European writers on which he drew may have been the innocent conduits of much older misinformation when they passed these stories on. One of the earliest Western accounts of the Assassins came from Arnold of Lübeck, a twelfth-century writer and traveler. In his version of the legend, the Old Man of the Mountain gains the loyalty of his followers "with such hopes and with promises of such pleasures with eternal enjoyment, that they prefer rather to die than to live." To those willing to kill on his behalf, and to face the revenge their actions might incur, the Old Man gives "knives which are, so to speak, consecrated to this affair, and then intoxicates them with such a potion that they are plunged into ecstasy and oblivion, displays to them by his magic certain fantastic dreams, full of pleasures and delights, or rather of trumpery, and promises them eternal possession of these things in return for such deeds." Whereas in Marco Polo's account the drug is used effectively to transport the young men in and out of the gardens, in Arnold of Lübeck's account the drug itself makes the gardens seem a paradise, to which the men, having glimpsed it, want only to return.

France's great nineteenth-century orientalist Sylvestre de Sacy drew on these and many other accounts of the Assassins in the memoir on the legend that he published in 1818. It was de Sacy who brought the story to the attention of a new generation of French intellectuals, and although he seems to have perpetuated many earlier misconceptions about Islam in general and the Assassins in particular, certain elements of the story he passed on are well-established matters of historical fact.

Hasan Sabbah's Assassins were Isma'ilis, a Shia sect whose beliefs set them apart from the Shia movement and Islam itself. The religion of the Druze, still alive in Israel, Syria, and Lebanon, is itself an offshoot of the Isma'ilis and remains one of the world's most secretive and self-sufficient cultures. Although, like all Shias, they believed in a lineage of imams in whom divine authority and intellect were invested, they considered Isma'il to be the seventh imam in the Shia lineage of twelve and so established an alternative line that more orthodox Shia regarded as a sham. They also argued that the Quran's instructions and prohibitions were matters of political convenience rather than divine teachings in themselves—a message with widespread appeal to disadvantaged Shia populations. By the eleventh century, Isma'ilism had become a powerful and popular movement whose influence extended from Atlantic Africa to the Indian subcontinent.

Hasan Sabbah, converted to Isma'ilism as a young man and rose to prominence as he tried to encourage an Isma'ili revolt against Turkish rule in Persia. In 1090, he seized the castle of Alamut, which remained the headquarters of his movement until the Mongols captured it in the mid-thirteenth century. Hasan Sabbah built gardens and cut canals in Alamut, making a fertile valley in what had once been an inhospitable region. And although he may have had no teams of trained assassins, his people were a formidable fighting force in the region for at least two hundred years.

De Sacy also discovered that the word *assassin* was derived from the movement's associations with hashish. The Assassins were known in their own time as *hashishiyya*, and *assassin* is simply the westernized equivalent of the term. Although de

43

Sacy concluded that hashish must have been the intoxicant used to transport Hasan Sabbah's followers to his incarnation of heaven on earth, the Assassins may have been called *hashishiyya* as a term of abuse. Either way, de Sacy sealed the connection between the Assassins and hashish and gave a generation of French writers a rich source of inspiring material.

And the Old Man continued to inspire his followers. His legendary artificial paradise gave Baudelaire the title of his book, and his movement gave its name to the loose collection of writers and artists with whom Baudelaire was associated in the 1840s: Club des Hachichins (they were unsure of the spelling). Meeting to converse and sometimes take hashish, the circle included Honoré de Balzac, the painter Eugène Delacroix, Théophile Gautier, and Gérard de Nerval. Their interest in the drug was encouraged by the presence of Jacques-Joseph Moreau, a doctor who published an influential study of hashish in 1845. Moreau's medical research led him to the study of several drugs, many of them stronger and stranger than hashish. More than a hundred years before psychiatrists began to experiment with the use of psychoactive substances in the treatment of mental disturbance, Moreau was developing such practices at the Parisian Hôpital de Bicêtre. One of his most effective remedies was datura, a plant closely related to henbane, belladonna, and a wide variety of other psychoactive—and highly toxic—plants. But it was hashish for which he reserved his greatest praise. "It is as if the sun were shining on every thought passing through our brain," he wrote. He, too, spread the rumors about Hasan Sabbah's paradise and is famous for the ominous promise with which he gave Gautier his first taste of hashish: "This will be deducted from your share in paradise."

"Hasheesh is indeed an accursed drug," wrote Ludlow, "and the soul at last pays a most bitter price for all its ecstasies; moreover, the use of it is not the proper means of gaining any insight." But he still thought it possible that hashish had given more than it took away: "Who shall say that at that season of exaltation I did not know things as they are more truly than ever in the ordinary state?"

Baudelaire would not have been convinced. Although he insisted that his objections to hashish had a serious ethical and religious basis, it was his inability to write on drugs that underscored his disapproval. In 1847, he ascribed his lack of literary success to both wine and laudanum. Three years later, the problem was hashish. The drug overwhelmed him with a listless apathy, the feeling that nothing was worth doing since nothing could compete with the drug. In a reversal of De Quincey's attacks on wine, Baudelaire insisted that "wine heightens the power of the will" whereas "hashish annihilates it. Wine increases bodily vigor, hashish is a suicide weapon. Wine encourages kindliness and good-fellowship, hashish isolates you. The one is industrious, so to speak, the other essentially indolent." Wine is the substance of Christian communion with God, and beer is the fluid stuff of social intercourse, the communion of human beings. Psychoactive drugs went against both the social and the religious grain.

"The point is," Arthur Rimbaud later answered him, with a mixture of opium, hashish, wine, and absinthe on his mind, "to arrive at the unknown by the disordering of *all the senses.* The sufferings are enormous, but one has to be strong, to be born a poet, and I have discovered I *am* a poet." The poet has to be *"in advance,"* he wrote, and this was bound to take him on a torturous path.

> A drug addict, apparently nothing but the wreck of a man, who seems to have learned nothing (since he's unable to say it), none the less sees others—be they scientists or important people—as shrunken beings.
>
> Henri Michaux, *Darkness Moves*

Even Baudelaire's contemporaries were critical of his condemnations of hashish. "It would have been better," Gustave

Flaubert once wrote to Baudelaire, "if you hadn't *blamed* hashish, opium, excesses. How do you know what will come of it all later?" Baudelaire's own writing was a case in point. His prose and poetry are full of the effects described in *Les Paradis artificiels*. In "La Chambre double," for example, the "furniture has lounging, prostrate, languorous forms. It seems to be dreaming, as if, like things in the vegetable and mineral worlds, it were endowed with a somnambulistic life. The cloth is speaking a silent language." There are experiences out of time: "There are no more minutes, no seconds, for time has been dethroned, Eternity holds sway instead." The world becomes enlivened, boundaries disappear, the line between poet and the world becomes unclear: "You are sitting smoking; you think you are sitting in your pipe and that your pipe is smoking you; you are exhaling yourself in the form of blue-tinged clouds."

Madame Bovary is the book most closely associated with Flaubert's drug-induced experiences, but his *Temptation of Saint Anthony*, which he wrote and rewrote over the course of nearly thirty years, was an even better answer to the question he posed to Baudelaire. St. Anthony was an early Christian mystic, living, it is said, in the Egyptian desert in the third century A.D. Flaubert's fictional saint spins off from this historical figure, giving him visions that take him back through time, and, "deep within this memory, which no longer belongs to him," he encounters a "resurgence of time" that "also produces a prophetic vision of the future. Within his recollections," wrote Michel Foucault, "Anthony encountered the ancient imagination of the Orient." And his journeys take him back into the heart of matter itself when, at the very end of the book, St. Anthony longs to

> have wings, a carapace, a rind, to breathe out smoke, wave my trunk, twist my body, divide myself up, to be inside everything, to drift away with odours, develop as plants do, flow like water, vibrate like sound, gleam like

light, to curl myself up into every shape, to penetrate each atom, to get down to the depth of matter—to be matter!

Flaubert's book is an extraordinary spectacle, a pageant of hallucinatory events and characters, stories folded inside stories, sequences chasing each other through a book that has its own "paradoxical shape" and "singular domain," a text that "gives rise to an extremely complicated space." In his "Fantasia of the Library," Foucault described it as "a book that develops according to the necessarily linear thread of its text" and "also opens a domain of depth." St. Anthony's visions are a long way from a world of vague imaginings and confused shadows. *The Temptation of Saint Anthony* is a piece of precision engineering, an intricate mesh of meticulous detail and elaborate analysis. St. Anthony's "domain of phantasms is no longer the night, the sleep of reason, or the uncertain void that stands before desire, but, on the contrary, wakefulness, untiring attention, zealous erudition, and constant vigilance."

"What strikes me as beautiful," wrote Flaubert, "what I would like to do, is a book about nothing, a book with no external tie, which would support itself by its internal force of style, a book which would have hardly any subject or at least where the subject would be almost invisible, if that can be so." Fitz Hugh Ludlow was convinced that hashish had already produced such a book. If the Old Man of the Mountain had colored French perceptions of hashish, the drug had traveled west surrounded by many other myths and legends from the East: the Turkish *Forty Viziers* contains many references to "the herb," and *The Arabian Nights*, or *The Thousand and One Nights*, includes several fond and funny accounts of hashish use. This collection of stories can be traced to the vibrant oral cultures of medieval Cairo and Baghdad, and further back again: Sinbad the Sailor is often read as a version of the same myth of Odysseus on which Homer based the *Odyssey*, and many of the tales are ascribed to older Arab and Indian storytellers.

The Thousand and One Nights was first translated into French by Antoine Galland in the early years of the eighteenth century, and then into English by an anonymous hack writer. By the time they were given their own idiosyncratic and literal translation by Richard Burton in the 1880s, the stories had inspired all of the nineteenth century's writers on drugs. The careful interlocking of the stories, all of them framed by a prologue that contains a fable of its own, gives the book a labyrinthine quality that seems alien to the straight lines of Western narrative. Many of the tales spin off from each other, and incidental characters from one story often become tellers of the next. Every chance for a new tale is taken, every link is made, every connection is followed through.

If De Quincey had been horrified by his Oriental dreams, his French followers were in love with the Eastern flavor of hashish and the stories with which it seemed to come equipped. And they were not alone: Ludlow also loved the fact that hashish seemed to bring these tales to life. His hashish put the "whole East, from Greece to farthest China," within easy reach of New York: "No outlay was necessary for the journey. For the humble sum of six cents I might purchase an excursion ticket over all the earth; ships and dromedaries, tents and hospices were all contained in a box of Tilden's extract." Or was this another deception? De Quincey had insisted that an opium eater who worked with oxen would dream of them, and, as Daftary reports, it was often said that hashish users "see the objects they like best: those who enjoy the sight of orchards see orchards; lovers see their mistresses; warriors see battles." There seems little doubt that its nineteenth-century dreamers were fulfilling their own fantasies as well. But Ludlow was convinced that the drug did bring something more than an exaggeration of his existing sensibilities and desires: not the paradise for which Baudelaire had hoped, but some kind of affinity with the cultures in which hashish was widely used. The Oriental character of the images and sequences in his dreams could not, he argued, be explained upon the hypothesis that the experimenter remembers it as an indulgence in use among the people of the East, for at the acme of the delirium there is no consciousness remaining in the mind of its being an unnatural state. The very idea of the drug is utterly forgotten, and present reality shuts out all inquiry into grounds for belief.

Hashish convinced Ludlow that he gained a privileged connection, a sympathetic link to all the cultures in which the drug had ever been used. He was being treated to dreams with a quality that had been dreamed time and again by the world's hashish users. He wasn't seeing the East in his dreams, but he was sharing its experience of the drug. And this was precisely the experience, he argued, that must have always enjoyed a pervasive influence on the cultures in which hashish is widely used. Ludlow was convinced that the drug was "the antecedent instead of the result of the peculiar characteristics of Oriental mind and manners." Ways of thinking, writing, building, and designing: all of these aspects of the cultures that used hashish were, for Ludlow, shaped by the drug that had enabled him to tap into the states of mind, perceptions, and imaginative events that influenced and formed generations of its users in the East. Those who take the drug also share the states of mind: "It is hasheesh which makes both the Syrian and the Saxon Oriental," he wrote. "Wherever this drug comes into contact with a sensitive organization, the same fruit of supernatural beauty or horror will characterize the visions produced."

Could hashish really induce the "same fruit" in different cultures, different times, and different individuals? Did the drug really have the same effects on every "sensitive organization" with which it came into contact, regardless of set and setting, the cultural contexts in which it was used? Ludlow's interest in hashish and the cultures from which it came had been roused by his childhood fascination with *The Thousand*

49

and One Nights. Surely he had been influenced by such factors as much as, if not more than, by the drug itself? Ludlow was more than happy to admit that *The Thousand and One Nights* had made an impact on his thinking, long before he took hashish. But this only fueled his argument that hashish induced a sensibility of its own. Ludlow claimed that it was quite impossible for thoughtful readers of *The Thousand and One Nights* to "close the mystic pages that have enchanted them without an inquiry as to the influences which have turned the human mind into such rare channels of thought." And this provoked the opening question of his book. What was the source of the "singular energy and scope of imagination which characterize all Oriental tales, and especially that great typical representative of the species, the *Arabian Nights*?" What had allowed the East to tell such tales, so rich in detail and complexity? Was there some ingredient to which the Western imagination had not been exposed?

Ludlow found his answer in hashish. "I unlocked the secret," he declared, "not by a hypothesis, not by processes of reasoning, but by journeying through those self-same fields of weird experience which are dinted by the sandals of the glorious old dreamers of the East." Ludlow's experiences with the drug had satisfied him that it could induce the same sensibility that had inspired the authors of *The Thousand and One Nights*:

> Standing on the same mounts of vision where they stood, listening to the same gurgling melody that broke from their enchanted fountains, yes, plunging into their rayless caverns of sorcery, and imprisoned with their genie in the unutterable silence of the fathomless sea, have I dearly bought the right to come to men with the chart of my wanderings in my hands, and unfold to them the foundations of the fabric of Oriental story. The secret lies in the use of hasheesh.

The tales told during the thousand and one nights are prefaced by the story of Shahriyar and Shahzaman, two brothers, both kings, each of whom has discovered the infidelity of his respective wife. During a journey they undertake in an effort to find out if they are alone in their humiliation, the kings meet a woman who, although held in captivity by a genie (or jinni), manages to add them to her ninety-eight previous lovers behind her sleeping captor's back. Reassured that even a jinni could be so deceived, the kings go home, and Shahriyar, the elder of the two, resolves to take a new wife every night, a virgin who will then be killed at dawn to guarantee that he will never be betrayed again. Not surprisingly, the supply of available virgins eventually runs dry, and the king's vizier, charged with finding the wives, begins to despair. The vizier himself has two daughters, Shahrazad and Dunyazad, and Shahrazad suggests that her father give her in marriage to the king one night. The vizier protests and tries to persuade his daughter not to sacrifice herself. But Shahrazad insists. She has a plan. She is well versed in poetry and stories, and just before she marries, she asks Dunyazad to request a story from her as soon as the marriage is consummated. The king is so enchanted and intrigued by Shahrazad's tale that he cannot bear to have her killed. She tells her stories for a thousand and one nights, bears the king three sons, and is finally spared.

If the Old Man of the Mountain took the fear of death away, *The Thousand and One Nights* kept death at bay—until, that is, Edgar Allan Poe decided to make Shahrazad push her luck with an unlikely trip through modernity. The story "The Thousand-and-Second Tale of Scheherazade" ends with her death: "She derived, however, great consolation (during the tightening of the bow-string) from the reflection that much of the history remained still untold, and that the petulance of her brute of a husband had reaped for him a most righteous reward, in depriving him of many inconceivable adventures."

> *Life/Death*: the paradigm is reduced to a simple click, the one separating the initial pose from the final print.
>
> Roland Barthes, *Camera Lucida*

Drugs were not the only chemical responses to the speeding changes of the nineteenth century. Photography gave Baudelaire another reason to despair: Susan Sontag quoted him complaining about it as "a new industry which contributes not a little to confirming stupidity in its faith and to ruining what might have remained of the divine in the French genius." Just as De Quincey found his memories bottled in laudanum, the camera made its own attempts to record change and preserve memory, capturing the past in enduring images, making memories that would not fade.

Photography was another chemical solution, an attempt to fix and preserve the past, another way of dealing with speeds and changes that seemed too fast. And, in a sense, another failure: the image captured life but arrested it as well. "All those young photographers who are at work in the world," wrote Roland Barthes, "determined upon the capture of actuality, do not know that they are agents of Death." And, like opium, photography did far more than reproduce the existing world. The street scenes photographed by William Henry Fox Talbot were full of details that had escaped the photographer, but not his new artificial eye. "Sometimes inscriptions and dates are found upon buildings, or printed placards most irrelevant are discovered upon their walls: sometimes a distant sundial is seen, and upon it—unconsciously recorded—the hour of the day at which the view was taken." And if the camera picked up on such details, it was also capable of capturing far more than the familiar world. "Now, for an absurdly small sum, we may become familiar not only with every famous locality in the world, but also with almost every man of note of Europe." This was a journalist, writing in London in 1861. "All of us have seen the Alps and know Chamonix and the Mer de

Glace by heart, though we have never braved the horrors of the Channel . . . We have crossed the Andes, ascended Tenerife, entered Japan, 'done' Niagara and the Thousand Isles, drunk delight of battle with our peers . . ."

One of the first travel books illustrated with photographs was John Thomson's *Illustrations of China and Its People*, published in 1873. And if photography allowed everyone to see images of such distant worlds, it also revealed a completely different take on reality. The camera had a perspective of its own. "A different nature opens itself to the camera than opens to the naked eye," wrote Walter Benjamin, "if only because an unconsciously penetrated space is substituted for a space consciously explored by man."

Both opium and photography introduced new perspectives, new perceptions of a world that had once been seen only with the naked eye. But while drugs were substances for private eyes, the camera's artificial sights could be shared by everyone. Writers such as Coleridge and Poe had struggled to communicate the peculiar qualities of their opiated dreams, but the camera put its visions of the world on a plate.

When De Quincey wrote *Confessions of an English Opium-Eater*, he had no photographic images, still less the cinematic vocabulary of moving pictures with which to describe the "nightly spectacles of more than an earthly splendour" that opium presented in the "theatres opened and lighted within my brain." Opium nevertheless ensured that the nineteenth century was photographic long before the camera arrived. And when the theaters that had opened in De Quincey's brain were transferred to the silver screen, filmmakers found themselves struggling to deal with many of the same themes that had obsessed the opiated writers of the nineteenth century. As Gilles Deleuze has pointed out, early European cinema found itself dealing with a fascinating "group of phenomena: amnesia, hypnosis, hallucination, madness, the vision of the dying, and especially nightmare and dream." By the end of the Second World War, film had become what it is today: "a mass industry," writes Paul Virilio in *War and Cinema*, "basing itself on psychotropic derangement and chronological disturbance." The century would continue to reel from such effects: television, video, multimedia, virtual reality, the Net, cyberspace.

Unconscious

As the nineteenth century progressed, a proliferation of new techniques allowed the living to approach death without tipping over the fatal line. Opiates had opened up the possibilities, and photography had captured them, but anesthetics took the suspended states explored by Coleridge and Poe to a new, and far more literal, extreme. Now bodies really could be suspended on the edge of life and death.

A statue of Joseph Priestley, chemist, philosopher, and revolutionary, stands outside the library in Birmingham, England. Priestley is one of the city's most famous sons. His radical political convictions took him to revolutionary America, where his religious convictions led him to develop the Unitarian Church, and his scientific work was more impressive still: he discovered oxygen and, in the course of this research, isolated many other gases too.

There's a guy who often sat on the library steps, looking at the monumental image of the man whose work had inadvertently changed his life. "Thrilling intimations of transcendent reconciliation and synthesis swept through me," he later wrote. "All manner of my mundane preconceptions were suddenly glimpsed entirely recontextualized within vast cosmological perspectives." Having worked in a hospital theater for more than ten years, this anonymous explorer one day decided to inhale some nitrous oxide, or laughing gas. The experience was profound. "I underwent a classic unbidden bliss experience in which an incredibly brilliant gold-white light suddenly flooded down on me, and I felt—or rather I knew with absolute certainty—that I was being touched by a higher presence." He spent much of the next ten years attempting to unravel this experience. He tried other drugs, drank a lot of alcohol, and wrote *Anaesthetic Inspiration*, an impressive account of his encounter with laughing gas.

Not everyone has such intense experiences with nitrous oxide, but its use is common enough. Mark Twain wrote "Happy Memories of the Dental Chair," and nitrous oxide is still administered by some dentists, in an effort less to remove the pain than to remove the patient's awareness of the experience.

Joseph Priestley isolated nitrous oxide in the 1770s. Although he found no medical use for his discovery at the time, the gas was one of several to be studied at the Pneumatic Institution near Bristol, a medical establishment founded by Thomas Beddoes in 1798. Beddoes was a highly respected doctor, fascinated by the possibility of treating diseases such as asthma with inhaled vapors. He was also one of the doctors consulted by Coleridge, who wanted "to open to him the whole of my case" but missed his chance when the doctor died before Coleridge had gained the courage to confess the extent of his problem with opium.

Beddoes's principal assistant was Humphry Davy, a young man who laughed all the way to the history books after he discovered the remarkable properties of Priestley's gas, nitrous oxide, in 1799. In a detailed account of his experiments, *Researches, Chemical and Philosophical; Chiefly Concerning Nitrous Oxide, or Dephlogisticated Nitrous Air, and Its Respiration*, published in 1800, he observed that the gas not only could be safely inhaled but had anesthetic properties as well. It also left him "absolutely intoxicated" and, he wrote, "made me dance about the laboratory as a madman, and has kept my spirits in a glow ever since." Davy's work was followed by Michael Faraday's 1818 observations about the anesthetic properties of ether, or sweet oil of vitriol, which had first been synthesized by Frobenius in the sixteenth century.

The possibility of using these and other substances for the purposes of painless surgery was not seriously discussed until *A Letter on Suspended Animation* was published by Henry Hill Hickman in 1824. Hickman was so "confident that animation in the human subject could be safely suspended" that he volunteered to be put in such a state himself. But there was widespread skepticism about the notion that a living, feeling organism could be numbed to the point of unconsciousness and then revived and resensitized. In both England and France, where he also tried to get the medical profession interested in his work, Hickman was utterly neglected in his own short lifetime. True, he was recommending the use of carbon dioxide as a narcotic agent, and his first experiment—on a dog that painlessly lost an ear to his knife—involved simple asphyxiation. But he was convinced that "the hitherto most agonizing, dangerous and delicate surgical operations, may now be performed, with perfect safety, and exemption from pain, on brute animals in a state of suspended animation" and "that the same salutary effects may be produced on the human frame, when rendered insensible by means of the introduction of certain gases into the lungs."

Even in 1839, it was still being said that anesthetized surgery was simply a contradiction in terms: "The abolishment of pain in surgery is a chimera. It is absurd to go on seeking it today. 'Knife' and 'pain' are two words in surgery that must forever be associated in the consciousness of the patient. To this compulsory combination we shall have to adjust ourselves." But within a few years of this statement, a number of operations using nitrous oxide and ether had been performed, and in 1846 the first public demonstration of anesthetized surgery was performed in Massachusetts. The headlines read: HAIL HAPPY HOUR! WE HAVE CONQUERED PAIN!

William Thomas Green Morton was the first to administer anesthesia in a witnessed operation conducted in 1846. This was a milestone in the history of medicine, and its practical and ethical implications were extensive. Patients who had once screamed and writhed through delicate operations were now rendered passive and insensible, and critics wondered about the morality of removing pain, not least for women in childbirth. There were fears that anesthetized bodies would be traumatized by pains they were unable to recognize and concerns about the powerlessness of anesthetized patients. The daughter of Crawford Williamson Long, the doctor credited with the first operation using ether, described her father's anesthetic as "a strange medicine by which he could put people to sleep and carve them to pieces without their knowledge."

It is difficult to imagine the scale of these developments. The possibility of deliberately manipulating the body in and out of unconsciousness was completely new, and a nineteenth century already fascinated by dreams and suspended animation was amazed by the possibility of inducing a controlled state of unconsciousness, a sleep so profound that the body could be cut open and remain undisturbed. This was a temporary and voluntary sojourn in a twilight zone previously known only in cases of disease or injury. Opium afforded pain relief, but these techniques were capable of deadening all the sensations that had once been identified with life itself.

There were other novel aspects of this condition. John Collins Warren, the surgeon who performed the first anesthetized operation, wrote, "Who could have imagined that drawing a knife over the delicate skin of the face might produce a sensation of unmixed delight? That the turning and twisting of instruments in the most sensitive bladder might be accompanied by a delightful dream? That the contorting of anchylosed joints should coexist with a celestial vision?" Such talk of visions and delights encouraged other uses of the anesthetic gases. "Ether frolics" and nitrous-oxide highs were enjoyed by chemists, dentists, and surgeons with ready access to these compounds. After inhaling six quarts of laughing gas, Davy wrote of a pleasure that "diffused itself over the whole body, and in the middle of the experiment was so intense and pure as to absorb existence. At this moment, and not before, I lost consciousness; it was, however, quickly restored, and I endeavoured to make a bystander acquainted with the pleasure I experienced by laughing and stamping."

In America, where the regulation and professionalization of medicine was less advanced than in England, it was said that "the boys and girls of many small towns were familiar with laughing gas as an excitant. There was scarcely a gathering of young people which did not wind up with one of these frolics." Crawford Williamson Long had introduced several young men to the pleasures of ether by the time he used it to surgical ends. "They were so much pleased with the exhilarating effects of ether," he wrote, "that they afterwards inhaled it frequently and induced others to do so, and its inhalation soon became quite fashionable in this county, and in fact extended from this place through several counties in this part of Georgia."

If anesthetics had both medicinal and recreational uses, they were also valued as experimental tools. Several nineteenth-century writers were impressed by the new zones between life and death that anesthetics seemed to open up. Humphry Davy gave nitrous oxide to Peter Mark Roget, author of *Thesaurus of English Words and Phrases*, and to Coleridge and Robert Southey, who was so impressed that he thought the "atmosphere of the highest of all possible heavens must be composed of this Gas." In *Les Paradis artificiels*, Baudelaire paid tribute to "the admirable services rendered by ether and chloroform from the point of view of a spiritualist philosophy." A later generation of thinkers was similarly impressed. William James discussed "the anaesthetic revelation" of chloroform in *The Varieties of Religious Experience*:

> I thought that I was near death, when, suddenly, my soul became aware of God, who was manifestly dealing with me, handling me, so to speak, in an intense personal present reality. I felt him streaming in like light upon me . . .

I cannot describe the ecstasy I felt. Nitrous oxide and ether, especially nitrous oxide, when sufficiently diluted with air, stimulate the mystical consciousness in an extraordinary degree. Depth beyond depth of truth seems revealed to the inhaler.

The gas made him think; it changed his mind:

One conclusion was forced upon my mind at that time, and my impression of its truth has ever since remained unshaken. It is that our normal waking consciousness, rational consciousness as we call it, is but one special type of consciousness, whilst all about it, parted from it by the filmiest of screens, there lie potential forms of consciousness entirely different.

Drugs arouse the powers of analogy, set objects in motion, make the world a vast poem shaped by rhymes and rhythms.

Octavio Paz, *Alternating Current*

With the publication of *The Interpretation of Dreams* in 1900, Sigmund Freud gathered all the nineteenth century's experiences of unconscious states and potential forms of consciousness together under one new term: *the unconscious*. It was a move that effectively drew a line under these long years of drug-induced experiment. His theories of the unconscious exorcised many of the ghosts encountered by the opiated dreamers who had first explored what he now defined as the unconscious mind. Fantasies were not to be explored but turned into memories and fulfilled "in a hallucinatory manner by dreams," which were no longer to be intensified but understood, domesticated, privatized. All dreams, Freud insisted in this phase of his work, are means by which unconscious wishes are fulfilled without disturbing the organism as a whole, and even the most self-destructive tendencies could be integrated "if they emerged as memories or dreams instead of taking the form of fresh experiences." Drug-induced encounters with alien forces, Oriental visitors, and demonic powers were now explained as matters of projection. The opiated scenes played out on De Quincey's screens—or in the theater of his mind—were emanating not from some external source but from the recesses of his own mind.

For De Quincey, opium had been a means for parting the veils "between our present consciousness and the secret inscriptions on the mind." The sheer intensity of De Quincey's opiated dreams encouraged his interests in questions of perception, memory, and what he called "the machinery of dreaming," and he was frustrated that these more abstract concerns had been overlooked by readers absorbed in what he regarded as the superficial contents of his dreams: the figurative scenes and images, the landscapes and characters of his visions. In "Suspiria de Profundis," he explained that while *Confessions* was "written with some slight secondary purpose of exposing this specific power of opium upon the faculty of dreaming," his real concerns were "much more with the purpose of displaying the faculty itself."

Freud's interest also lay with the contents of dreams, rather than with De Quincey's machinery. What De Quincey had described as the "magnificent apparatus" of the dreaming mind no longer forced "the infinite into the chambers of a human brain" but instead performed a complex set of condensing and censoring operations on dreams that now belonged to the individual. There were no more "dark reflections from eternities below all life" but instead scrambled recollections of the dreamer's private past. De Quincey's "great tube" became a "royal road" to a zone that now resembled the large entrance hall of a bourgeois Viennese house. In his *Introductory Lectures on Psychoanalysis*, Freud describes a narrower drawing room, the conscious mind, leading off this hall, and "on the threshold between these two rooms a watchman performs his function: he examines the different mental impulses, acts as a censor, and will not admit them to the drawing room if they displease him." The Dark Interpreter became a border guard.

White Lines

Also, he told an astonishing tale about coca, a vegetable product of miraculous powers; asserting that it was so nourishing and so strength-giving that the native of the mountains of the Madeira region would tramp up-hill and down all day on a pinch of powdered coca and require no other sustenance.
Mark Twain, "The Turning Point of My Life"

Cocaine is derived from the leaf of the coca bush, *Erythroxylon coca*, a plant native to the uplands of South America. It has white flowers, red fruit, and green leaves rich in the cocaine alkaloid. Coca has been cultivated and used for centuries in many regions of the Andes, particularly Bolivia and Peru, where it has long been revered as a source of physical energy and divine nourishment. Its leaves are chewed and held in the mouth, sometimes mixed with lime to make an alkaline paste. Their juices trickle out like liquid sun, fueling a body that can then endure long treks at the same high altitudes favored by the plant.

Coca had both practical and mystical importance in its native cultures. It was used as a measure of both exchange and time: the Incas preferred to be paid in coca rather than silver or gold, and Indians from the Peruvian sierra measured journeys in *cocadas*—the time between doses of coca. The distended cheeks of the coca user feature on many of the oldest Incan ceramics, and the plant figures in many Incan myths and rituals. It is sometimes said that Manco Capac, divine son of the sun, brought coca to the people as a gift when he brought his father's light to earth at Lake Titicaca. Another

61

myth tells the story of Mama Coca, who in some accounts is Manco Capac's wife, a beautiful woman who was killed because of her adultery and lies buried at the roots of the first coca bush.

> Actually, by Mama Coca, I knew he was referring to the small amounts of cocaine fixed in the leaf, but it would have been rude for me to suggest that Mama Coca was nothing more than a cheap alkaloid you could pick up on any city street.
>
> Ronald Siegel, *Intoxication*

Coca's effects seemed mild and benign to the first Europeans who encountered the plant. One proponent described coca as the means by which "any person might be enabled, like the Peruvian Indian, to live and labor in health and spirits for a month now and then without eating." Its users were not transformed but merely strengthened and improved. There were concerns about the myths and rites with which coca was associated, and at one point the Spanish issued a royal decree that condemned it as a demonic influence. But the use of coca was integral to those cultures now under Spanish rule. And although the Church did its best to rid the plant of its mystical and magical associations, Mama Coca seduced the Jesuits even as they excommunicated her devotees. The imperatives of trade overrode every moral, political, and theological concern: both the Spanish Crown and the Catholic Church thrived—and sometimes depended—on revenues they earned from their coca plantations.

It was not until the mid-nineteenth century that coca found its way back to the Old World. One of the earliest serious European studies of the plant and its effects was "On the Hygienic and Medicinal Virtues of Coca," published by an Italian neurologist, Paolo Mantegazza, in 1859. "As soon as one chews one or two drachms of coca and swallows its juice," he wrote, one starts to experience a feeling of warmth—I should say filibriform—spreading all over the body. Sometimes one experiences a very soft buzzing in the ears. At other times one needs space and would like to run forward as if searching for a wider horizon. Little by little, one starts to feel that the nervous powers are increasing; life is becoming more active and intense; and one feels stronger, more agile, and readier for any kind of work.

Eighteen drachms, or drams, of coca—a dram is a sixteenth of an ounce—induced a delirious state that gave him "pleasure by far superior to all other physical sensations previously known to me."

With his pulse racing at 134 beats per minute, Mantegazza began to hallucinate.

I was at that time fully aware of myself, but I felt isolated from the external world and saw images that were more bizarre and splendid, in terms of color, than could ever be imagined. Neither the brush of the most brilliant painter nor the pen of the fastest stenographer could have transmitted for a single moment those marvelous apparitions, which were tied to each other not by relationships or associations, but through the whims of unleashed fantasy and a rich kaleidoscope.

He listed a few of these visions—glass threads of lightning piercing Parmesan cheese, a golden tortoise in a cave of lace, and Chinese flowers with burning silver stamens. And these are just a few of the images he caught: "For each one I managed to transfer to paper I missed ten on account of their rapid succession."

Coca made him feel supreme: "I sneered at the poor mortals condemned to live in this valley of tears while I, carried on the wings of two leaves of coca, went flying through the spaces of 77,438 worlds, each more splendid than the one before." He tries to describe what is happening to him, but all his words are inadequate to the task. "An hour later I was sufficiently calm to write these words in a steady hand: 'God is unjust because he made man incapable of *sustaining the effect of coca* all life long. I would rather have a life span of ten years with coca than one of 1000000 . . . (and here I had inserted a line of zeros) centuries without coca.' "

Coca leaves do not travel very well, and few Europeans were aware of their powers until cocaine, their principal alkaloid, was isolated in the nineteenth century. The extraction of cocaine is sometimes attributed to Friedrich Gaedecke's 1855 discovery of a compound he called erythroxyline and was certainly achieved by Albert Niemann, who published descriptions of its extraction in 1860. Even then, interest in coca and cocaine was minimal in both Europe and the United States until the 1880s, when their popularity coincided with a new era of economic and technological change.

If opiates had provided De Quincey's generation with a means of escaping the ravages of the mechanical age, coca and cocaine woke everyone up to an era humming with new distributions of power and new forms of mass communication. Electricity and telephones wired the world, and both energy and information were now running in fast-moving currents with which everyone felt compelled to keep up.

An increasingly enthusiastic medical establishment recommended coca for a variety of conditions and complaints thrown up by these stressful times of rapid change. Patent medicines containing cocaine were readily available, and coca found its way into endless syrups, pastilles, wines, and elixirs. Mama Coca's legendary fine looks and long tresses were woven into the art nouveau swirls of advertisements for an endless stream of products. From Chicago came Peruvian Wine of Coca, "For Nourishing and Giving Strength to the Body"; in Paris, Popular French Tonic Wine "Fortifies and Refreshes Body and Brain" and "Restores Health and Vitality." Angelo Mariani, who gave his name to one of the most famous brand names, solicited and received endorsements of his drink from a string of celebrities, including popes, princes, and presidents. Jules Verne, rushing around the world in only eighty days, declared that "the wonderful tonic wine" was capable of "prolonging life," and Louis Blériot made the first flight across the English Channel with a bottle of Mariani in his pocket. Bartholdi, the architect responsible for the Statue of Liberty, said, "Vin Mariani seems to brighten and increase all our faculties; it is very probable that had I taken it twenty years ago, the Statue of Liberty would have attained the height of several hundred meters." Everyone loved coca then.

Mariani's coca wine was joined by an extraordinary variety of coca preparations. Many used a combination of coca and extracts from the kola nut, rich in caffeine. Kos-Kola, Kola-Ade, Café-Coca Compound, Dr. Don's Kola, Rococola, Wise-ola: there were endless variations on the theme in America and Europe. In Paris, Vélo-Coca was specially prepared for cyclists. Coca-Bola was made to be chewed—like coca leaves themselves—and there were other preparations to be smoked, inhaled, injected, used as ointments and powders.

Interest in the properties of coca encouraged pharmaceutical companies to produce and market cocaine with the same cheerful enthusiasm that accompanied coca itself. Merck, the first European manufacturer of cocaine, described the drug as "a stimulant which is peculiarly adapted to elevate the working ability of the body, without any dangerous effect." An 1885 report from Merck's American rivals, Parke-Davis Pharmaceuticals, presented it as a substance that could "supply the place of food, make the coward brave, and the silent eloquent." And these glowing reports about cocaine were by no means confined to the advertisements. Generations of users would enthuse about its ability to enhance physical, emotional, and intellectual performance. For William Burroughs, in *Naked Lunch*, it was to be the ultimate hit: "the most exhilarating drug I have ever used."

The cocaine craze had plenty of detractors, too. As early as

1885, cocaine was being defined as "a new danger. Before long," one commentator predicted, "a remedy will be demanded for the cocaine habit." Cocaine, said another user, "relieves the sense of exhaustion, dispels mental depression, and produces a delicious sense of exhilaration and well-being. The after-effects are at first slight, almost imperceptible, but continual indulgence finally creates a craving which must be satisfied."

> I had long since prepared my tincture; I purchased at once, from a firm of wholesale chemists, a large quantity of a particular salt, which I knew, from my experiments, to be the last ingredient required; and, late one accursed night, I compounded the elements, watched them boil and smoke together in the glass, and when the ebullition had subsided, with a strong glow of courage, drank off the potion.
>
> Robert Louis Stevenson,
> *The Strange Case of Dr. Jekyll and Mr. Hyde*

Opium was the hero of a thousand nineteenth-century tales, the perfect drug on which to write. But coca and cocaine have their own stories to tell. Mark Twain found himself "fired with longing to ascend the Amazon" after he read about the river and the bush that grew toward its source. "Also with a longing to open up a trade in coca with all the world. During months I dreamed that dream, and tried to contrive ways to get to Para and spring that splendid enterprise upon an unsuspecting planet." Twain did set off, with a fifty-dollar bill he found in the street. And although he went no farther than New Orleans, it was here that he became a Mississippi river pilot and made his name: which name? Mark Twain was a pseudonym which, among its many connotations, encapsulated his obsession with difference, division, split identity, and twins: he was convinced that he was one of a pair and had lost his other half at birth, and "mark twain" was a way of re-marking on them both.

If Twain had traveled farther south and found his "veg-etable product of miraculous powers," he might have found something of his lost twin.

The Strange Case of Dr. Jekyll and Mr. Hyde is the story of a man who takes a drug to give life to what has previously been one side of his character, a personality secreted within his own. Anxious to defer to the sober demands of social re-spectability, Jekyll has often felt as if there were two of him, one an upright moral citizen, the other a more wayward ad-venturer, indulging in pleasures the story leaves unnamed. When this double life becomes unsustainable, Jekyll makes no attempt to reconcile his dissociated elements.

> If each, I told myself, could but be housed in separate identities, life would be relieved of all that was unbear-able; the unjust might go his way, delivered from the as-pirations and remorse of his more upright twin; and the just could walk steadfastly and securely on his upward path, doing the good things in which he found his plea-sure, and no longer exposed to disgrace and penitence by the hands of this extraneous evil. It was the curse of mankind that these incongruous faggots were thus bound together—that in the agonized womb of con-sciousness, these polar twins should be continuously struggling. How, then, were they dissociated?

The drug is the answer to this question. "I hesitated long be-fore I put this theory to the test of practice. I knew well that I risked death; for any drug that so potently controlled and shook the very fortress of identity might, by the least scruple of an overdose or at the least inopportunity in the moment of exhibition, utterly blot out that immaterial tabernacle which I looked to it to change." But after some initially traumatic effects, his first experiment assuages his fears. As Edward Hyde he "felt younger, lighter, happier in body," and "within I was conscious of a heady recklessness, a current of disordered sensual images running like a mill race in my fancy, a solution of the bonds of obligation, an unknown, but not an innocent freedom of the soul." This was not just a transformation of the personality: as Hyde, his body is different, too, smaller than Jekyll's, his hands and face quite changed, his posture ugly and ungainly.

Anxious to resist arrest for his crimes and relishing the freedoms peculiar to his temporary periods of existence, Hyde is never tempted to stay around for long. "Think of it," he says. "I did not even exist! Let me but escape into my laboratory door, give me but a second or two to mix and swallow the draught that I had always standing ready; and, whatever he had done, Edward Hyde would pass away like the stain of breath upon a mirror." But Hyde becomes increasingly hungry for life, and when one night the switch from Jekyll to Hyde is made without the drug, Jekyll "began to spy the danger that, if this were much prolonged, the balance of my nature might be permanently overthrown, the power of voluntary change fortified, and the character of Edward Hyde become irrevocably mine."

If Jekyll succeeds in telling his two sides apart, he and Hyde do not become simple representatives of two extremes. Hyde may be evil incarnate, a unified figure whose simplicity is part of his attraction, but Jekyll remains the ingenuous fusion of goodness and malevolence. The contradiction is not overcome but instead displaced: three-quarters of his two halves are now on the wrong side of the moral tracks. Eventually Jekyll determines to "bid a resolute farewell to the liberty, the comparative youth, the light step, leaping pulses and secret pleasures, that I had enjoyed in the disguise of Hyde." But the temptation proves too much. Jekyll is "tortured by throes and longings, as of Hyde struggling for freedom; and at last, in an hour of moral weakness, I once again compounded and swallowed the transforming draught." Having been denied existence for so long, the Hyde that emerges this time is even more horrific than before.

The callous nature of Hyde's personality has already been revealed, not least when he launches a meaningless assault on a child. But when he emerges from Jekyll this time, he goes to new extremes and murders a public figure in a frenzied and violent attack. Appalled by this crime, Jekyll then stays in control for some time—until he wakes up as Hyde without the assistance of the drug. After this, the drug will allow him only brief periods as Jekyll. Worse still, the supply of what turns out to have been an impure and therefore unique batch of the drug is fast running out. He has known all along that he is risking his life, but it has not occurred to him that there might be a finite supply of the drug. And when his very last dose wears off, Jekyll's experiment proves fatal to them both. He is finally condemned to Hyde, and Hyde, condemned for murder, commits suicide.

Robert Louis Stevenson wrote *The Strange Case of Dr. Jekyll and Mr. Hyde* during six days and nights of a cocaine high. In spite—or perhaps because—of his poor state of health, he shut himself away and reappeared with the story complete. "That an invalid in my husband's condition of health should have been able to perform the manual labour alone of putting sixty thousand words on paper in six days, seems almost incredible," wrote his wife, Fanny. Cocaine was the substance of this new legend, and, not surprisingly, the potion used by Jekyll is a telling caricature of Stevenson's drug. The "throes and longing" that torture Jekyll, the desperation with which he has "London ransacked" in his search for a new supply of the drug, the doubled personality and the sense of some new character inside the normal mind, the sweet sense of lost responsibility that each time welcomes the advent of Hyde, even the sadistic, uncaring violence: these effects take the drug to the same extremes that can now be experienced on crack cocaine.

Stevenson's Dr. Jekyll says he has long been convinced "that man is not truly one, but truly two. I say two," he continues, "because the state of my own knowledge does not pass beyond that point. Others will follow, others will outstrip me on the same lines; and I hazard the guess that man will be ultimately known for a mere polity of multifarious, incongruous and independent denizens."

This sense of multiplicity had always obsessed Stevenson. It was integral to the shape of *The Strange Case of Dr. Jekyll and Mr. Hyde*, which uses three narrators, each of whom gives a different and partial account of the events. In an 1888 essay called "A Chapter on Dreams," in which Stevenson described a life strung out between waking reality and vivid, sequential dreams, he explored his relationship with the entities he called the Little People, or Brownies, the characters who, he said, wrote his plots and dreamed his scenes for him. They "have more talent" than the author. "They can tell him a story piece by piece, like a serial, and keep him all the while ignorant of where they aim. Who are they, then? and who is the dreamer?"

Stevenson can answer for the dreamer. "He is no less a person than myself." As for the talented Little People: "What shall I say they are but just my Brownies, God bless them! who do one-half my work for me while I am fast asleep, and in all human likelihood, do the rest for me as well, when I am wide awake and fondly suppose I do it for myself." The crucial elements of *The Strange Case of Dr. Jekyll and Mr. Hyde* had, he explains, been given to him by these little creatures as he slept. They gave him "the matter of three scenes, and the central idea of a voluntary change becoming involuntary" that was so crucial to the novel. While Stevenson claims authority over the meaning of the tale—"I do most of the morality, worse luck!"—these were the characters who performed the more imaginative work. And, since they "have not a rudiment of what we call a conscience," it was also the Little People who contributed the drugs to the story: "The business of the powders, which so many have censured, is, I am relieved to say, not mine at all but the Brownies'."

With Jekyll and Hyde, it seemed as if the nineteenth century's experiment with drug-induced characters had reached some kind of fatal conclusion. De Quincey's Dark Interpreter always hovers on the brink of independence, but Hyde makes the final break when he walks out of Jekyll's life. The move was so powerful that the story and its characters became common currency for any case of split personality or Janus-faced activity. It was the perfect story for the coming century. Mary Shelley's *Frankenstein* had warned the industrializing world about its tendencies to run away with itself, and some combination of Stevenson, his Brownies, and his cocaine had now written the story that would allow the twentieth century to express its dilemmas, contradictions, tensions, splits, writ large in the two-faced spectacle of a culture at war with the very stuff that kicked it into life.

> For God's sake don't let that Coca-Cola thing out—
> William Burroughs, *Nova Express*

In its early days, Coca-Cola was a combination of sugar, coca leaves, kola nuts, and several secret flavorings. Not forgetting the bubbles so crucial to its success: they were made possible by Joseph Priestley's 1772 *Directions for Impregnating Water with Fixed Air*, which described the production of an "exceedingly excellent sparkling water" by introducing carbon dioxide into water.

The soda went on sale in 1886 and was advertised as the perfect lift for a "turbulent, inventive, noisy, neurotic new America." The words *tonic* and *refreshment* had an inevitable appeal for a generation living in a culture of rapid economic, technological, and social change—change that made Americans "the most nervous people in the world," as an early advertisement for the drink declared before listing the maladies ("any nerve trouble . . . mental and physical exhaustion, all chronic and wasting diseases . . .") and sufferers ("merchants, bankers, ladies, and all whose sedentary employment causes nervous prostration") to which coca wine could bring relief.

The coca wine from which Coca-Cola developed was first produced by John Pemberton, a doctor who was addicted to morphine. "We did not know at the time what was the matter with him," wrote one of his contemporaries, "but it developed that he was a drug fiend." It was on the basis of his own attempts to be rid of morphine that Pemberton became convinced that coca was "the very best substitute for opium . . . It supplies the place of that drug, and the patient who will use it as a means of cure may deliver himself from the pernicious habit without inconvenience or pain." Pemberton hailed Coca-Cola, which was first marketed as French Wine Coca, as a "great blessing" to "the unfortunate who are addicted to the morphine or opium habit, or the excessive use of alcoholic stimulants," and declared that "thousands proclaim it the most remarkable invigorator that ever sustained a wasting and sinking system."

Pemberton's studies of coca were extensive. He was convinced that the most effective coca leaves were not necessarily those with the highest cocaine content and that, although cocaine was the most active ingredient, coca users preferred leaves in which cocaine was balanced with other chemicals. Although Coca-Cola was consequently made with coca leaves, there are suggestions that its cocaine content may have been intensified by the kola nut's caffeine. And the Coca-Cola kick was substantial: every bottle once contained the equivalent of a small, but respectable, line of cocaine.

By the end of the century, the cocaine connection that had made so many beverages so popular was becoming a liability. The drug's failing reputation had damaged the market for all commodities associated with cocaine and coca leaves. Except, of course, for one: by the time cocaine was made illegal, Coca-Cola was squeaky-clean.

Not least because coca was so integral to its name, the idea of removing cocaine from Coca-Cola had horrified the company when first suggested. But in 1902, the Coca-Cola Company quietly started to use decocainized leaves, and the strategy turned out to be a great success. Withdrawal was barely noticed, and even in the absence of the cocaine alkaloids, Coca-Cola continued to be marketed as a refreshing tonic, a panacea that would always keep its drinkers coming back for more. It still is, and they still do. Coca-Cola went on to become the world's most popular soda, its most recognizable name, its leading brand.

The company feigned amnesia about cocaine and denied that its drink ever had a drug connection: the name, it said, was "meaningless but fanciful and alliterative" and had no connection with the real thing. But Coca-Cola would be nowhere if coca had not kicked it into life, and as Coke, the link could hardly be more direct.

By the time Coca-Cola celebrated its centenary, the Coca-Cola Company had become one of America's top-ten corporations, selling nearly half of all the soft drinks in the world and spending some four billion dollars every year on marketing. And it was advertising that allowed Coca-Cola to survive without cocaine. Advertisements filled the gap left by the drug, compensating for the loss of an ingredient that had once allowed the drink to sell itself. Advertisements were the hook with which Coca-Cola became the first addictive commodity to contain no addictive substance. In effect, the drink became a virtual cocaine, a simulated kick, a highly artificial paradise. Twentieth-century consumer culture learned much from this sleight of invisible hand.

Images, songs, jingles, and the famous Coca-Cola logo were the new ways of ensuring that the drink would always be "within an arm's reach of desire." The Coca-Cola Company had few qualms about exploiting the connection between coke and sex. Images of Mama Coca as "a goddess of love with coca leaves in her hand" had always been used to sell coca-related drinks, and many of the early Coca-Cola advertisements used variations on the Mama Coca theme. When co-caine disappeared from the formula, the company traded on the risqué image it had now acquired. One 1908 advertise-ment used a bare-breasted girl holding a Coca-Cola bottle; an-other pictured "a young woman in black lingerie reclining on a tiger-skin rug with an expression of exhausted bliss. She held an empty glass, a Coca-Cola bottle on the table beside her. The caption: 'Satisfied.' "

Later images were far more clean and wholesome. Mama Coca's ancient associations with adultery had been wiped out by the Catholic Church when it tried to collapse her into its own female deity. The Coca-Cola Company now pulled the same trick: the "Atlanta virgins," fresh-faced clones of the girl next door, who figured in many later promotions and adver-tisements for Coca-Cola, conjured up an image of "sex with-out the sweat," just as they sold Coca-Cola without coke.

A pause for refreshment. The commercial break. Using the hook of advertising to offset the absence of cocaine, Coca-Cola learned how to exploit all the drug's advantages without run-ning into trouble with the law. And Coca-Cola has led adver-tising ever since. In 1914, the company owned more than five million square feet of American wall space, all of which was plastered with Coca-Cola script. The company erected the first billboards and was responsible for the first "spectacu-lars"—neon signs erected in city centers of the world. Coca-Cola even paved the way for modern methods of market research when, in 1927, consumers were tempted by a prize of ten thousand dollars to say which of the drink's advertised qualities they most preferred. In the 1930s, Coca-Cola was promoted on the radio, and advertisements in the cinema and later on television gave the drink an even wider audience.

Coca-Cola's cultural, economic, and political influence has been immense. The logo is ubiquitous, and in some parts of the world, the drink itself is more readily available than fresh water. There are signs of it everywhere: big neon bottles pour-ing neon Coke in Mexico City; fluorescent glasses filling with

fluorescent bubbles in Saigon. Coca-Cola has come to symbol-
ize America and all that America represents. When Coca-Cola
started bottling in France, there was great resistance to what
the French Communist Party defined as "Coca-Colonization,"
a term that has since come to encapsulate the globalizing tendencies of Western capital.

> It seemed alive. It sparkled intensely. It was like noth-
> ing else in Nature, unless it be those feathery crys-
> tals, wind-blown, that glisten on the lips of crevasses.
> Aleister Crowley, *Diary of a Drug Fiend*

The Coca-Cola story repeated itself in another strange case.
Having learned of the drug as a medical student in Vienna,
Sigmund Freud became one of cocaine's earliest, most enthusiastic, and most influential advocates. He fell in love with the
drug as soon as he acquired his first batch of cocaine from
Merck and, in 1884, declared that he was "busy collecting the
literature for a song of praise to this magical substance." This
song was published later the same year.

"Über Coca," the first of several articles Freud wrote on the
drug, earned him both fame and fortune—or at least a degree
of notoriety and enough money to marry his fiancée, Martha
Bernays. It reported on the use of both coca and cocaine as
aids to the treatment of a variety of conditions, including di-
gestive disorders, anemia, and asthma, and extolled their
ability to deal with "the most diverse of psychic debility—
hysteria, hypochondria, melancholic inhibition, stupor and
similar maladies." Freud also mentioned the anesthetic properties of cocaine, but, much to his later regret, this was one application he failed to pursue. It was one of his colleagues, the
eye specialist Carl Koller, who explored the drug's potential
as a local anesthetic. When Koller presented his findings to a
conference in Heidelberg in 1884, he made his name and established cocaine as a powerful and effective numbing agent.
After the triumphs of general anesthesia, it was now possible

to perform certain operations without the patient being unconscious. Later experiments with the spinal injection of cocaine revolutionized both pain relief and surgical techniques,
and the drug became widely used in dentistry. Novocain, a
synthetic variation on the cocaine theme, is still the staple diet
of the dentist's syringe.

Freud's preferred engagement with the drug was inspired
by benign American reports of its use in the treatment of addiction to alcohol and opiates. Like Pemberton—who also had
an interest in eye surgery and had once performed an operation without anesthesia—Freud was convinced that treating
"morphine addiction with coca does not result merely in the
exchange of one kind of addiction for another—it does not
turn the morphine addict into a *coquero*; the use of coca is only
temporary." As soon as he had the opportunity, Freud
prescribed cocaine to his close friend and mentor Ernst von
Fleischl in the hope that it might relieve his addiction to morphine.

These medical applications of cocaine were hardly Freud's
only interest in the drug. Freud enthused about "the stimula-
tive effect of coca on the genitalia" in "Über Coca," and one of
his letters to Martha, also written on cocaine, forewarned her
of the pleasures she could expect from "a wild man with cocaine in his body." What really inspired Freud was the drug's
ability to induce a sense of "exhilaration and lasting euphoria,
which in no way differs from the normal euphoria of the
healthy person." This is one of the drug's most seductive, subtle, even insidious qualities. "One is simply normal," Freud
declared, "and soon finds it difficult to believe that one is under the influence of any drug at all."

When Siegfried Bernfeld described Freud's writing on the
drug, he wrote of the "subtle, one might say tender, protective
attitude toward his subject, cocaine." Freud laced his paper
with what Bernfeld calls "a very persuasive undercurrent" of
enthusiasm for the drug, indulging in unusually rich descriptions of, for example, "the most gorgeous excitement" in-

duced by what he describes as a "gift" of cocaine. Ernest Jones also commented on the "remarkable combination of objectivity with a personal warmth" that Freud displays in the pages of his "song of praise." "Über Coca," Jones wrote, was composed as if Freud "were in love with the content itself."

Freud's affection for the drug was again on show when he described a party at Charcot's house in 1886. He was nervous and excited about attending such a high-powered gathering. He trimmed his beard, set his hair, wore immaculate white gloves, and took a "little cocaine, to untie my tongue." The evening turned out to be a great success. Freud thought he "looked rather fine" and enjoyed himself immensely. The following day he relished the chance to tell Martha of his achievements—"or, rather," as he added in parentheses, "the achievements of cocaine." But if Freud had so enjoyed himself that night, the drug couldn't see him through every evening. The next time he went to such a party on cocaine, his verdict was quite different: "It was so boring that I nearly burst," he told Martha. "Only the bit of cocaine prevented me from doing so." But certain fantasies have to be maintained: "Please don't tell anyone how boring it was. We shall always talk about the first evening only."

This second letter to Martha is unusually meandering, confused, and insecure. "The bit of cocaine I have just taken is making me talkative," he explained apologetically. He rambled on about his "wretched self" in such a fit of self-deprecation that he even described his qualities in terms of "the absence of outstanding intellectual weaknesses." He then related a recent evening on which his colleague Josef Breuer had told him "that hidden under the surface of timidity there lay in me an extremely daring and fearless being. I had always thought so," Freud admitted, "but never dared tell anyone." Even now his words embarrassed him. "Here I am," he wrote, "making silly confessions to you, my sweet darling, and really without any reason whatever unless it is the cocaine which makes me talk so much."

In these early years of his medical career, Freud's intellectual energies were concentrated on the physiology and functions of the brain. Specializing in neuropathology and other aspects of neurology, he explored the diagnosis and treatment of neural disorders and developed new means of examining the brain by staining nerve tissue to allow its cells and fibers to be perceived. He even experimented with the electrical stimulation of the brain as a therapeutic technique. Freud's interest in cocaine was concurrent with this neurological research. Like any psychoactive substance, the drug was a direct means of affecting thoughts, emotions, and behavior; it was a kind of inner engineering of the personality, a direct stimulation of the brain. The strength and immediacy of its effects must have confirmed Freud's early conviction that states of mind and patterns of behavior had some basis in neurochemistry.

Freud was, of course, faced with waves of reports on cocaine's ability to induce psychosis, addiction, and delirium tremens of the kind previously associated only with alcoholism. The drug that was supposed to be a remedy for so many other addictions and pathologies seemed to be causing more trouble than it cured. But "Über Coca" had made his name, just as cocaine had made Coca-Cola's. Freud was proud of the work he had done, and he continued to praise a drug that was regarded with increasing suspicion by the medical establishment. In "Craving for and Fear of Cocaine," Freud's last essay on the subject, published in 1887, he continued to recommend the drug. Boldly contradicting the widespread view that cocaine was highly toxic and addictive, Freud argued that morphine addicts were alone in being vulnerable to the ill effects of the drug: "All reports of addiction to cocaine and deterioration resulting from it refer to morphine addicts, persons who, already in the grip of one demon, are so weak in will power, so susceptible, that they would misuse, and indeed have misused, any stimulant held out to them. Cocaine has claimed no other, no victim of its own." Freud was soon to be proved very wrong. A year into his treatment for morphinism, von Fleischl was injecting something like a gram of cocaine each day. He had also resumed his use of morphine.

When von Fleischl died of cocaine poisoning in 1891, Freud insisted that he had started to inject himself against Freud's advice. But in 1885, Freud had been "unhesitatingly" happy to "advise cocaine being administered in subcutaneous injections of 0.03–0.05 grammes per dose without minding an accumulation of the drug." Although Freud denied that this had ever been the case, it seems von Fleischl was only acting on his young doctor's advice.

After the death of von Fleischl, Freud's association with the drug became increasingly untenable. A number of reports about cocaine psychosis and addiction appeared in the 1890s, and the drug began to acquire an air of disrepute that Freud, as a young doctor, could not afford to share. Even Freud was now persuaded that "the chemical method of defence against suffering . . . although the most potent, was for that reason dangerously noxious." If the daring and fearless being Breuer had observed in Freud was to be explored, it would be through analysis, not drugs.

When Freud began to work with Josef Breuer, with whom he published *Studies on Hysteria* in 1895, he became increasingly interested in hypnosis as a means of opening patients to both therapeutic suggestion and the cathartic effects of exploring their memories while in this trancelike state. Induced by suggestion rather than any direct tinkering with the brain, hypnosis functioned as a noninvasive, drug-free means of achieving particular states of mind, suspensions between sleep and waking life.

Hypnosis had almost as many detractors and technical limitations as cocaine, and although Freud used it for several years, he spent much of the 1890s on the hunt for more effective therapies. In 1895, he returned to neurology and wrote "Project for a Scientific Psychology," a work now widely dismissed as "an astonishing production." According to James Strachey in his introduction to Freud's later writings on the unconscious in *On Metapsychology*, this essay "purports to describe and explain the whole range of human behaviour, normal and pathological, by means of a complicated manipulation of two material entities—the neurone and 'quantity in a condition of flow,' an unspecified physical or chemical energy. The need for postulating any unconscious mental processes was in this way entirely avoided."

Increasingly dissatisfied with the physiological basis of much research in his field, Freud began to describe his work in terms of psychic analysis, and by 1896 he had renounced neurology and hypnosis and started to develop a new drug-free therapy: psychoanalysis, the talking cure. And publicly, at least, he had given up cocaine.

By the time Freud published *The Interpretation of Dreams* in 1900, "a strange transformation had occurred: not only had the neurological account of psychology completely disappeared, but much of what Freud had written in the 'Project' in terms of the nervous system now turned out to be valid and far more intelligible when translated into mental terms. The unconscious was established once and for all." Freud had effectively completed his long journey from neurological to psychological research, and although, twenty years later, it turned out to be a return trip, he had for now moved from the brain to its mental states, from the treatment of the body to that of the mind. His insistence that the patient lie down on his famous couch was the only remnant of his earlier attention to the body.

As a substitute for morphine and cocaine, a drug-free means of relieving stress and pain, psychoanalysis was timely therapy for a culture trying to kick the habits of the century. It was the perfect solution for what was supposed to be a drug-free century. But Freud's move away from "medicinal magic" was no clear-cut rejection of cocaine. It may be, as Gilles Deleuze and Félix Guattari suggest in *A Thousand Plateaus*, that the "cocaine episode marked a turning point that forced Freud to renounce a direct approach to the unconscious," but for all the guilt that rode his affection for the drug, Freud had many reasons to feel fond of it. And if the drug was in his dreams, it also continued to inform the more oblique approaches to the mind he now began to take. Freud quit cocaine in an atmosphere of impending drug control, but he was neither willing nor able to forget the heights to which cocaine had taken him.

Cocaine had given Freud a problem, a solution, and a goal. The drug had shown him his own hidden Hyde and allowed him to talk about it too: the drug untied his tongue and allowed him to make those "silly confessions" to Martha about both his "wretched self" and his "daring and fearless being," the desiring wolf that lurked inside his shy sheepskin. And if Jekyll takes the powders to fatal extremes, Freud believed that cocaine made it possible to reconcile these aspects of his character. The drug had relieved his anxieties, rescuing him from what were sometimes crippling depressions and giving him a taste of what he called "the normal euphoria of the healthy person," which had eluded him so often in the past; it had introduced him to the possibility of feeling "simply normal." Freud had praised it less for its positive effects than for its ability to remove negatives: its mood, he suggested, is "due not so much to direct stimulation as to the disappearance of elements in one's general state of well-being which cause depression." And when he moved into psychoanalysis, these were precisely the results he sought. Cocaine had shown him that such states were possible, and now he would pursue them with his own therapy.

Psychoanalysis became as fashionable, addictive, and expensive as cocaine. What began as his own search for a drug-free cure, some new method to occupy his mind, became a drug-replacement therapy for everyone. Analysis was Freud's "natural" high, a drug-free cure for anxiety, a noninvasive means of attaining the normal euphoria of cocaine.

Just like the Coca-Cola Company, the psychoanalytic estab-lishment quietly overlooked its original blend, the secrets of the formula that gave it a kick start: Freud's essays on coca and cocaine are rarely included in authorized collections of his work. But there is something irrepressible about cocaine. Its appearance in the book that made his name (again), *The Interpretation of Dreams*, is not so easily erased. Freud was famously his own patient, and the very first dream he analyzed, in 1895, was one he had had about a patient called Irma and a certain Dr. M. This was the dream that had convinced him "that dreams really have a meaning and are far from being the expression of a fragmentary activity of the brain." It was also a dream related to cocaine.

> M. said: "There's no doubt it's an infection, but no mat-ter; dysentery will supervene and the toxin will be elimi-nated." We were directly aware, too, of the origin of the infection. Not long before, when she was feeling unwell, my friend Otto had given her an injection of a prepara-tion of propy, propyls . . . propionic acid . . . trimeth-ylamin (and I saw before me the formula for this printed in heavy type) . . . Injections of that sort ought not to be made so thoughtlessly . . . And probably the syringe had not been clean.

"I was making frequent use of cocaine at that time to reduce some troublesome nasal swellings," writes Freud in his analy-sis of the dream, "and I had heard a few days earlier that one of my woman patients who had followed my example had developed an extensive necrosis of the nasal mucous mem-brane. I had been the first to recommend the use of cocaine . . . and this recommendation had brought serious reproaches down on me. The misuse of the drug had hastened the death of a dear friend of mine." This dream convinced Freud that dreams are expressions of wishes unfulfilled in waking life. Like the medical student who oversleeps while dreaming he

is already in the lab, Freud's dream about Irma's injection fulfilled his "wish to be innocent of Irma's illness" and his deep
desire to be considered a conscientious medical practitioner.
In the dream, it is not Freud but his colleague Otto who uses
the syringe irresponsibly.

Cocaine had made its mark: it was always on his mind.
There were other dreams in which Freud found himself remembering this old lover: "I had written a monograph on a
certain plant. The book lay before me and I was at the moment turning over a folded coloured plate. Bound up in each
copy there was a dried specimen of the plant, as though it had
been taken from a herbarium."

On awakening, Freud recalls that "he really *had* written
something in the nature of a *monograph on a plant*, namely a
dissertation on the *coca-plant*, which had drawn Carl Koller's
attention to the anaesthetic properties of the plant." Freud
was so proud of his role in this development that the dream
even prompted him to fantasize about being treated with his
own discovery:

> On the morning of the day after the dream—I had not
> had time to interpret it till the evening—I had thought
> about cocaine in a kind of day-dream. If ever I got glau-
> coma, I had thought, I should travel to Berlin and get my-
> self operated on, incognito, in my friend's house, by a
> surgeon recommended by him. The operating surgeon,
> who would have no idea of my identity, would boast
> once again of how easily such operations could now be
> performed since the introduction of cocaine; and I should
> not give the slightest hint that I myself had a share in the
> discovery.

As it happens, Freud, Koller, and Leopold Königstein, another
doctor to whom Freud had suggested the anesthetic properties of cocaine, were all present when the drug was used in
the course of an operation to treat Freud's father's glaucoma.

Freud's "Dream of the Botanical Monograph" "carries the subject that was raised in the earlier dream a stage further." Like the dream of Irma's injection, it "turns out to have been in the nature of a self-justification, a plea on behalf of my own rights." Freud was still trying to defend his association with cocaine. "Even the apparently indifferent form in which the dream was couched turns out to have had significance," he wrote. "What it meant was: 'After all, I'm the man who wrote the valuable and memorable paper [on cocaine],' just as in the earlier dream I had said on my behalf: 'I'm a conscientious and hard-working student.' In both cases, what I was insisting was: 'I may allow myself to do this.'"

> Sherlock Holmes took his bottle from the corner of the mantelpiece, and his hypodermic syringe from its neat morocco case. With his long, white, nervous fingers he adjusted the delicate needle, and rolled back his left shirt-cuff. For some little time his eyes rested thoughtfully upon the sinewy forearm and wrist, all dotted and scarred with innumerable puncture-marks. Finally, he thrust the sharp point home, pressed down the tiny piston, and sank back into the velvet-lined armchair with a long sigh of satisfaction.
>
> Arthur Conan Doyle, *The Sign of Four*

Freud acknowledged that it was the "poets and philosophers before me" who had "discovered the unconscious. What I discovered was the scientific method by which the unconscious can be studied." But even Freud's new methodology was lost in the mists of drug-induced time. Running back through his own story, the detective sees himself emerging from the mists of Wilkie Collins's opiated mind, pacing the streets in Poe's twilight zone, even stirring with the life-like figures of De Quincey's animated dreams. He sees the Dark Interpreter, "originally a mere reflex of my inner nature," gaining an autonomy of his own and slipping into reality: "This dark being the reader will see again in a further stage of my opium experience; and I warn him that he will not always be found sitting inside my dreams, but at times outside, and in open daylight."

Until "The Final Problem," Arthur Conan Doyle's detective, Sherlock Holmes, was often to be found injecting morphine or cocaine. The syringe is not as famous as his pipe and violin, but it plays a large part in his life. "Which is it today?" asks a weary Watson when Holmes injects himself in *The Sign of Four*, "Morphine or cocaine?" "He raised his eyes languidly from the old black-letter volume which he had opened. "It is cocaine," he said, "a seven-per-cent solution. Would you care to try it?'"

In "A Scandal in Bohemia," Watson describes Holmes "alternating from week to week between cocaine and ambition." On one occasion, when Watson asks what problems are absorbing him, Holmes replies, "None. Hence the cocaine. I cannot live without brain-work." He is even more forthcoming in *The Sign of Four*:

> My mind rebels at stagnation. Give me problems, give me work, give me the most obtuse cryptogram, or the most intricate analysis, and I am in my proper atmosphere. I can dispense then with artificial stimulants. But I abhor the dull routine of existence. I crave for mental exaltation. That is why I have chosen my own particular profession, or rather created it, for I am the only one in the world.

Holmes turned to drugs when there were no other solutions to be found. Problems, puzzles, intricate analyses become interchangeable with cocaine.

"The Final Problem" is the story with which Conan Doyle intended Holmes to meet his death. It relates the events that led the detective to the Reichenbach Falls in Switzerland, where in 1891 he supposedly died at the hands of his archenemy, Professor Moriarty: " 'You have probably never heard of Professor Moriarty?' said he. 'Never.' 'Ay, there's the genius and the wonder of the thing!' he cried. 'The man pervades London and no one has heard of him. That's what puts him on a pinnacle in the records of crime.' "

Holmes describes Moriarty as "the Napoleon of crime" and "the organizer of half that is evil and of nearly all that is undetected in this great city. He is a genius, a philosopher, an abstract thinker. He has a brain of the first order. He sits motionless, like a spider in the centre of its web, but that web has a thousand radiations, and he knows well every quiver of each of them." As intelligent, analytic, and undetectable as the detective himself, Moriarty is Holmes's evil twin, his perfect counterpart in the underworld, his Mr. Hyde, his own dark side. And while his agents are often caught, "the central power," Moriarty himself, is "never so much as suspected. This was the organization which I deduced, Watson, and which I devoted my whole energy to exposing and breaking up." It reads like a paranoid fantasy. Maybe that's exactly what it is. Holmes's career has "reached its crisis" at this point, as has his use of morphine and cocaine. Watson thinks he looks "paler and thinner than usual," and Holmes tacitly agrees: "I have been using myself up rather too freely."

Conan Doyle's relationship with drugs is more obscure. But there are some revealing clues. "I must admit that in ordinary life I am by no means observant," he wrote. "I have to throw myself into an artificial frame of mind before I can weigh evidence and anticipate the sequence of events." Conan Doyle had studied drugs and certainly had access to both morphine and cocaine. Even if he didn't use them, his "copy of *The Essentials of Materia Medica and Therapeutica* has some impressive marginalia," as Richard Lancelyn Green wrote in his introduction to *The Uncollected Sherlock Holmes*.

Holmes's meeting with Moriarty at the Reichenbach Falls was presumed to be a final showdown between the two men. In the story that was supposed to contain Holmes's last adventure, "The Final Problem," Conan Doyle intended to leave little doubt that Holmes has been killed by Moriarty. But "The Final Problem" wasn't final at all. Conan Doyle's attempt to kill off Holmes met with such public outrage that he made the detective reappear in 1894. In *The Return of Sherlock Holmes*, the detective turns up in London with news of Moriarty's death. He is full of enthusiasm for his new enemy, Colonel Moran, "the second most dangerous man in London," and he has also lost his craving for cocaine: " 'Holmes!' I cried. 'Is it really you? Can it indeed be that you are alive? Is it possible that you succeeded in climbing out of that awful abyss?' "

Sherlock Holmes is the most famous detective, but he was by no means the first. Conan Doyle was particularly keen to acknowledge Poe's influence on Holmes: "Dupin is unrivalled," he declared. "It was Poe who taught the possibility of making a detective story a work of literature." Conan Doyle stated that although any later detective writer "may find some little development of his own . . . his main art must trace back to those wonderful stories of Monsieur Dupin."

Although he began as a figment of Conan Doyle's imagination, Holmes readily assumed a life beyond his author. Holmes's methods have been famously adopted by police and thieves alike, and his adventures have multiplied in the hands of other writers. In one of these additional stories, Sherlock Holmes spends the period between "The Final Problem" and *The Return of Sherlock Holmes* not in Tibet and Persia, as Conan Doyle had related, but in Vienna in the company of Sigmund Freud. Drawn to each other by their shared interests in detection and cocaine, Holmes and Freud teach each other everything they know. Freud learns his analytic skills from Holmes, and Holmes learns to free himself from cocaine. Under Freudian analysis, so the story goes, the detective's use of drugs is discovered to be grounded in his hatred for Moriarty, the evil genius, his absolute adversary, the diabolical source of the crimes that Holmes must solve. Professor Moriarty is

Sherlock's own dark twin, Jekyll's Hyde again, the personifi-
cation of cocaine.

Disowned by true defenders of the Baker Street canon, and
ignored by those for whom fiction and fact are clearly defined,
the story does make its own strange kind of sense. Freud had
lost von Fleischl in 1891, and he was well known for his interest in addiction—if not, as yet, his ability to deal with it. And
he would have been an ideal companion for the detective at
this point: Holmes and Watson have drifted apart, and the detective needs a new doctor. And both men had discovered a
profound relationship between drugs and analysis. Holmes
had used cocaine as a substitute for "the most intricate analysis," and both he and Freud went on to use analysis as a substitute for cocaine: the Holmes who returned in 1894, ready to
deal with a new enemy, was as drug-free as Freud the psycho-
analyst. Perhaps they really did teach each other how to stay
on the case.

It is tempting to imagine Holmes and Freud mainlining
coke and discussing the merits of analysis. Even though the
story is as fictional as Holmes himself, the resonance between
the two detectives is quite real. Freud was familiar with Sherlock Holmes; and it is widely accepted that their methods
have some striking similarities. What really connects them is
their common expertise in what the historian Carlo Ginzburg
calls a new method of conjecture that "quietly emerged toward the end of the nineteenth century" and was based on the
intuition that obscure details and remote clues can be more
important than obvious evidence. According to Ginzburg, one
of the most rigorous developments of this method can be
traced to the work of Giovanni Morelli, an Italian art historian
who developed sophisticated means of analyzing paintings
and published his results in 1897. Morelli was convinced that
galleries were full of paintings attributed to the wrong artists,
and his attention to the details of works of art allowed him to
make some surprising discoveries about the origins of several
well-known paintings.

Freud had also noticed Morelli. In "The Moses of Michelangelo," he describes Morelli's method as "closely related to the technique of psychoanalysis. It, too, is accustomed to divine secret and concealed things from despised or unnoticed features, from the rubbish-heap, as it were, of our observations." For Ginzburg, Holmes makes the triangle complete: "The art connoisseur and the detective may well be compared, each discovering, from clues unnoticed by others, the author in one case of a crime, in the other of a painting." Freud, Morelli, and Conan Doyle all had backgrounds in medicine, and this, for Ginzburg, was crucial to Freudian psychoanalysis, the Morelli method, and the "Science of Deduction and Analysis" developed by Conan Doyle. All three methods can be traced to the diagnostic and prognostic techniques in which the three were trained. Sherlock Holmes was certainly influenced by Joseph Bell, a professor who had greatly impressed Conan Doyle as a medical student in Edinburgh. As *The Uncollected Sherlock Holmes* explains, Bell's "strong point was diagnosis, not only of disease, but also occupation and character." Diagnosis, wrote Bell,

> depends in great measure on the accurate and rapid appreciation of small points in which the disease differs from the healthy state. In fact, the student must be taught to observe. To interest him in this kind of work we teachers find it useful to show the student how much a trained use of observation can discover in ordinary matters such as the previous history, nationality, and occupation of a patient.

Such diagnostic skills have other uses too: "The patient," wrote Bell, "is likely to be impressed by your ability to cure him in the future if he sees that you, at a glance, know much of his past. And the whole trick is much easier than it appears at first." Mama Coca turns and smiles in her grave: the drug of the confidence trick is cocaine.

Holmes's method was "founded upon the observance of tri-fles" and the need to "concentrate upon the details." The "lit-tle things," he said, "are infinitely the most important." In *A Case of Identity*, he enthused about "the importance of sleeves, the suggestiveness of thumbnails, or the great issues that may hang from a boot lace." And Freud was always hunting for the matters of great substance that he was convinced were hiding out in the most minor and apparently negligible de-tails, including his famous slips of the tongue. In his *Introductory Lectures on Psychoanalysis*, Freud described an incident in which a companion had forgotten the name of a particular wine. Various possibilities and associations came in his effort to remember the name, and from these suggestions Freud found both the name and the reason why it had eluded him. And "if it is possible in the case of forgetting a name," he con-cluded, "it must also be possible in interpreting dreams to proceed from the substitute along the chain of associations at-tached to it and so to obtain access to the genuine thing which is being held back." In the case of the forgotten name of the wine, it turned out that Freud's companion was trying to re-member a name it shared with an old lover he was trying to forget.

Like all detectives, Freud was aware that objects and events can be charged with energies that retrospectively affect the se-quence of events that has led to them. Present scenes and cir-cumstances are alive with clues, humming with information on this past, and also the future to which it leads. Freud's crit-ics poured scorn on what were often regarded as his far-fetched interpretations of dreams. Like Sherlock Holmes, he was used to having his conclusions greeted with incredulity, and even he acknowledged that "a number of the solutions to which we find ourselves driven in interpreting dreams seem to be forced, artificial, dragged in by the hair of the head." But this didn't alter their validity. Unlikely they may seem, but as Dupin tells them all: "When you have eliminated the impossi-ble, whatever remains, *however improbable,* must be the truth."

The detective was not content with simply solving crimes. Like Sherlock Holmes obsessed with his quest for Moriarty, Freud was convinced that there was some ultimate secret, a basic instinct, or a first crime. To find the truth, to solve the crime, to bring the "genuine thing" into the conscious mind, was also to ask about the processes involved in its repression: "By what forces is it accomplished? and for what motives?" These were questions raised by every special case, and also by the workings of repression itself. Freud's search famously took him to what he considered the most primary of sexual instincts, the libido, whose excesses are repressed by the border guard, screened by the censor at the threshold of the conscious mind. In *The Interpretation of Dreams*, Freud set the scene with Oedipus, the hero of Sophocles' tragedy, who is destined to fulfill the prophecy made by the oracle at his birth: he is fated to kill his father and sleep with his mother. "The action of the play," wrote Freud, "consists in nothing other than the process of revealing, with cunning delays and ever-mounting excitement—a process that can be likened to the work of a psycho-analysis—that Oedipus himself is the murderer of Laïus, but further that he is the son of the murdered man and of Jocasta." Freud was convinced that the power of this tragedy lay in the fact that its audience would recognize the extent to which they shared this fate. Twenty years later, Freud completely changed his mind about some of the most fundamental features of this complex of ideas. But psycho-analysis remains committed to the basic principle that every (male) child harbors this same unconscious desire to compete with his father for his mother's affections. This is the primal repression, the move with which the unconscious itself is opened up. Sex is the secret of every repression and repression itself.

In a robust defense of his techniques, Freud argued that "the path back to the genuine thing is not easily traced." The allusions made in a dream "are connected with the genuine thing by the strangest, most unusual external associations. In all these cases it is a question, however, of things which are *meant* to be hidden, which are condemned to concealment," and because of this "we must not expect that a thing which has been hidden will be found in its own place, in its proper position." By definition, analysis cannot confine itself to the obvious. In a reference prompted by the First World War, Freud argued that analysts must think like border guards searching for contraband documents:

> In their search for documents and plans they are not content with examining brief-cases and portfolios, but they consider the possibility that spies and smugglers may have these forbidden things in the most secret portions of their clothing where they decidedly do not belong—for instance, between the soles of their boots. If the hidden things are there, it will certainly be possible to call them "far-fetched," but it is also true that a great deal will have been found.

Freud took psychoanalytic theory across the Atlantic in 1909, just as America was convening the first international meeting to discuss drug control. And by the end of the First World War, information was not the only contraband likely to be hidden in the soles of boots. Cannabis escaped the first wave of legislation, but opiates, and Freud's cocaine, were now subject to international and national controls, and both the users of the drugs and the enforcers of the laws found themselves hunting for substances that had once been openly for sale. America introduced the Harrison Narcotic Act in 1914, and in Britain the Defence of the Realm Act—which was supposed to be a piece of temporary wartime legislation— was amended in 1916 to include the control of drugs. The kick Cole Porter got from cocaine would quietly be replaced by champagne, and drugs dropped out of public sight and into the culture's new unconscious mind.

Magicians

A long shot, Watson; a very long shot!
Sherlock Holmes, in Arthur Conan Doyle, *Silver Blaze*

Detectives are famously perceptive, attentive to the finest details, the smallest movements, and the slightest clues. Observing everything except the rules. Carlo Ginzburg's *paradigma indiziario,* elaborated in his essay "Moriarty, Freud, and Sherlock Holmes: Clues and Scientific Method," gives priority to circumstantial evidence and incidental clues, casting the historian as a detective who scours his material for clues, looking for evidence even in the most unlikely places and neglected areas, sorting through the junk of history, picking up the skills of the hunter, who "learned to reconstruct the appearance and movements of an unseen quarry through its tracks—prints in soft ground, snapped twigs, droppings, snagged hairs or feathers, smells, puddles, threads of saliva." The word *sleuth*—which once referred to the tracks left by an animal—testifies to these archaic origins of the detective's art.

In his historical research, Ginzburg pursues every faint suspicion and leaves his mind open and responsive to any hints from his material. "It's a matter of kinds of knowledge which tend to be unspoken, whose rules," he wrote, "do not easily lend themselves to being formally articulated or even spoken aloud. Nobody learns how to be a connoisseur or a diagnostician simply by applying the rules. With this kind of knowledge there are factors in play which cannot be measured—a whiff, a glance, an intuition." This is not the inside knowledge of an elite but a kind of "low intuition," a universal openness to movement, difference, sensation: "the heritage of the Bengalis . . . of hunters, of mariners, of women. It forms a tight link between the human animal and other animal species."

Ginzburg's paradigm gave him "an acute awareness of the awkward problems of method involved in the study of popular culture through sources produced by the learned; oral culture through written texts; and the views of the unorthodox via the investigations of the inquisitors who were trying to suppress them." Although the voices of the powerless are ignored and silenced by such materials, they are often the historian's only source of information, and all the detective can do is scour it for clues, subtle indications of the lives and events it excludes, echoes of the voices that couldn't get a word in at the time.

Ginzburg's most impressive attempt to listen to such voices is his monumental study of the witches' Sabbath, *Ecstasies*, a vast and speculative work of extraordinary complexity. He begins, like a detective, with the scene of the crime, a simple description of the Sabbath that takes all its elements at face value: "Male and female witches met at night, generally in solitary places, in fields or on mountains. Sometimes, having anointed their bodies, they flew, arriving astride poles and broom sticks; sometimes they arrived on the backs of animals, or transformed into animals themselves." There were banquets, orgies, desecrations of the Sacrament, and homages to the devil. "Before returning home the female and male witches received evil ointments made from children's fat and other ingredients."

Convinced that most research had concentrated "almost exclusively on persecution, giving little or no attention to the attitudes and behaviour of the persecuted," Ginzburg wanted to know what had prompted such reports, what was really going on in the minds and lives of the accused. The authors of the *Malleus Maleficarum*, the "classic witch hunters' guide," refused to admit

> that certain wicked women, perverted by Satan and seduced by the illusions and phantasms of devils, do actually, as they believe and profess, ride in the night-time on certain beasts with Diana, a goddess of the Pagans, or with Herodias and an innumerable multitude of women, and in the untimely silence of night pass over immense

tracts of land, and have to obey her in all things as their Mistress, etc.

Did the women really admit to such adventures? Did they believe that they flew on broomsticks and mutated into animals? Was this what they were doing on those sacred nights? Or was the Sabbath just the fantasy of a paranoid Church, whose inquisitors were desperate to distinguish between the mystics' true visions and the witches' stories, which could simply not be true?

Dealing with these questions was a daunting task. Historians of witchcraft "have implicitly or explicitly derived the subject of their research from the interpretative categories of the demonologists, the judges or witnesses against the accused," because the only records of the phenomena are written by the hunters and from their point of view. "The voices of the accused reach us strangled, altered, distorted; in many cases, they haven't reached us at all." What "really happened" has left the scene. Ginzburg set out in the hope of finding "fragments, relatively immune from distortions, of the culture that the persecution set out to eradicate." The prosecution evidence is riddled with gaps: there are holes in the stories the persecutors told. "Hence—for anyone unresigned to writing history for the nth time from the standpoint of the victors— the importance of the anomalies, the cracks that occasionally (albeit very rarely) appear in the documentation, undermining its coherence." Sure enough there was a crack, right there, in his opening description of the Sabbath. He gazed at the scene he had painted, and the "other ingredients" stared back at him.

In medieval Europe, it was widely believed that "animal metamorphoses, flights, apparitions of the devil were the effect of malnutrition or the use of hallucinogenic substances contained in vegetable concoctions or ointments." Inquisitors' reports dating back to the fourteenth century described the use of such ointments and salves, and it is now assumed that the references to witches' brews and flying ointments were based on some real use of psychoactive substances. As well as baby's fat and bat's blood, which was said to aid nocturnal flight, favorite ingredients seem to have included hemlock, monkshood, deadly nightshade, and henbane. In all these plants, there are powerful psychoactive alkaloids: deadly nightshade contains atropine, monkshood contains aconite, and henbane contains hyoscine, present in many other psychoactive plants as well. These properties make them highly poisonous: most of them can kill if they are eaten. Turned into ointments, they can get into the bloodstream through the skin or some bodily orifice, and it is in this capacity that these alkaloids can induce wild hallucinations and trancelike states.

There are limits to their explanatory power, but as Ginzburg argues, "the deliberate use of psychotropic or hallucinogenic substances, while not explaining the ecstasies of the followers of the nocturnal goddess, the werewolf, and so on, would place them in a not exclusively mythical dimension." And the hypothesis opens up the tempting possibility that the witches, like De Quincey, were actually confessing the details of trips induced by their home brews. If their ointments had powerful psychoactive properties, there is every reason to suppose that users would have found themselves transported to what might now be thought of as some tripped-out zone.

Psychoactive ointments and salves would also account for the idea that women used broomsticks as their means of transport to this other world. John Mann quotes several reports to this effect: "In rifleing the closet of the ladie, they found a pipe of oynment, wherewith she greased a staffe, upon which she ambled and galloped through thick and thin." A fifteenth-century account related "that on certain days or nights they anoint a staff and ride on it to the appointed place or anoint themselves under the arms and in other hairy places." The *Malleus Maleficarum* even describes "their method of being transported. They take the ungent which, as we have said, they make at the devil's instruction from the limbs of children, particularly of those whom they have killed before baptism, and anoint with it a chair or a broomstick; whereupon they are immediately carried up into the air, either by day or by night, and either visibly or, if they wish, invisibly." The vaginal membranes are among the most sensitive and permeable regions of the body. One can only imagine the erotic rush that must have been experienced by these women.

But one can actually do a little more than imagine this. Ginzburg's "other ingredients" provide the historical detective with some unusually substantial clues about what might have been happening in the days of the witch craze. What takes the psychoactive substances one step beyond pure speculation is that they are always there to be used again. The cultures and the memories may have faded and died, the rites vanished, and the contexts been transformed, but something of the chemistry remains. The witch-hunt may have been an early war on drugs, but the substances survive. As Mann reports, recent applications of ointments containing henbane and belladonna, or deadly nightshade, have resulted in reports of "wild rides" and "frenzied dancing." Henbane and belladonna are closely related to datura, the highly toxic plant with which Baudelaire's Dr. Moreau had experimented in the nineteenth century. Varieties of datura grow all over the world: in India, its use is closely associated with the Hindu god Siva, and there are countless reports of datura's use as a ritual substance in the Americas. One of the most common daturas is the thorn apple, whose spines are often associated with the fairy tale "Sleeping Beauty" and its fruits with the apple eaten by Eve in the Garden of Eden.

Ginzburg attached particular significance to two other ingredients as well: *Claviceps purpurea,* or ergot, a fungal infection that grows on some species of rye and other grasses when springs and summers are wet and warm, and *Amanita muscaria,* the fly agaric whose red and white livery is still famous for its hallucinatory properties.

> He covers his face with his hands and begins to twirl in a variety of circles. Suddenly, with very violent gestures, he shouts: "Fit out the reindeer! Ready to boat!"
>
> Siberian shaman, in Joseph Campbell,
> *The Hero with a Thousand Faces*

There are some fifty varieties of *Amanita muscaria,* a mushroom that is widely distributed among the birch and fir trees of northern Europe and Asia and also has close relatives in the Americas. According to Valentina Wasson and Gordon Wasson, whose two-volume *Mushrooms, Russia, and History* remains a classic of ethnobotanical—or more precisely, ethnomycological—research, the fungus has been used for thousands of years and can be traced back to the first retreat of the ice cap from the north.

Amanita muscaria was certainly widely used in Siberia, Lapland, and other regions of the far north, where shamans once used it to induce journeys from which they returned with prophecies, solutions, remedies, and songs. These were semi-nomadic people, who followed the seasonal migrations of their deer. When the deer went in search of mushrooms, the herders would go with them. When the deer ate the mushrooms, the herders would drink their urine, consuming the fly agaric's alkaloids after they were processed by the deer. They would also drink each other's urine, and the mushroom could be passed through the bodies of half a dozen people before its potency was lost. Getting pissed is now associated with alcohol—in Britain, at least—but it was the reindeer herders who started the trend. When the Soviet Union organized Siberian reindeer herders into brigades and introduced vodka to the region, much of the cultural infrastructure surrounding the mushroom's use was lost, but there are still communities for which it retains cultural significance.

> After a while she remembered that she still held the pieces of mushroom in her hands, and she set to work very carefully, nibbling first at one and then at the other, and growing sometimes taller and some-times shorter, until she had succeeded in bringing herself down to her usual height.
>
> Lewis Carroll, *Alice in Wonderland*

The fly agaric has influenced far more than modern slang. It is there in countless fairy tales and children's stories, and it is widely suggested that fly agaric is the mushroom that Alice eats in Wonderland. Among the mushroom's most well known effects are the telescopic and microscopic syndromes that play such a central role in the story, and Lewis Carroll—himself a double of Charles Dodgson—had access to several studies of *Amanita muscaria* and, very possibly, to the mush-room itself.

One of the most enduring manifestations of its old sha-manic routes visits the modern world every year when Santa Claus, dressed in red and white, flies through the sky in a sleigh drawn by reindeer bearing gifts from another world.

> It is either through the influence of narcotic potions, of which all primitive peoples and races speak in hymns, or through the powerful approach of spring, penetrating with joy of nature, that those Dionysian stirrings arise, which in their intensification lead the individual to forget himself completely.
>
> Friedrich Nietzsche, *The Birth of Tragedy*

In Britain alone, some thirty thousand people, most of them women, were killed for witchcraft between the late fifteenth century and the 1730s, when the laws were finally repealed. Although the motivations behind this purge of supposed witches were by no means confined to the control of knowledge of the healing and psychoactive properties of fungi, herbs, and plants, the eradication of this knowledge was undoubtedly one of its most enduring effects. In Ginzburg's account of the witch craze, women with such knowledge were particularly vulnerable to prosecution not only because they were "the most marginal of the marginal" members of society, especially when they were unmarried, as were most of the accused, but also because this marginality "reflected in a more or less obscure manner the perception of a proximity between those who generate life and the formless world of the dead and the non-born." Women were already on the borderline between the living and the dead, and, in "a society of the living—it has been said—the dead can only be impersonated by those who are imperfectly integrated into the social body." In cultures whose shamans are male, there is often some sense in which the shamans enter into a state of androgyny or feminization as they cross into their other world: as Joan Halifax reports, Siberian shamans meet spirit guides, who demand that they become "soft man beings."

If the witch-hunters drew the lines around life and death and put an end to return trips to the outer edges of the life-death border zone, these were parameters confirmed and solidified by the institutions of the modern state. Women were no longer allowed to heal the sick or deliver children; all drugs were now entrusted to the care of the Enlightenment's new fraternity; and the shamanic narrative of flight, transformation, and return was abandoned in favor of a new sense of linear time. Now all the stories were supposed to go one way: progress, forward movement, full steam ahead. The Enlightenment imagined itself as a moment of climax, the end of what was retrospectively defined as a long and linear struggle that dated back to the ancient Greeks.

But even this supposedly straight line has a compulsion to repeat itself. Modernity was never really free from its own shamanic past: it was only a matter of time—and not much of it at that—before Coleridge and his generation were exploring these border zones again. And if Athens was imagined as the cradle of what was now defined as Western civilization, even this archaic cradle had been rocked by the very hands that modernity was now determined to deny.

Ancient Greece was familiar with opium, hashish, and, it is thought, many other psychoactive plants and fungi. There are traces of their influence in accounts of the Eleusinian mysteries, stories of Dionysus and his cults, and the legendary oracle that spoke through a priestess at the temple of Apollo at Delphi. The temple of Eleusis was described by Aristides as "a shrine common to the whole earth, and of all the divine things that exist among men, it is both the most awesome and the most luminous. At what place in the world have more miraculous tidings been sung, where have the *dromena* called forth greater emotion, *where has there been greater rivalry between seeing and hearing?*" Initiates to the mysteries were responsible men, sworn never to discuss what had happened and allowed to participate in the rite only once in a lifetime. Accounts of the rite refer to *kykeon*, a potion that included mint and barley and, very possibly, many other ingredients.

> Eleusis was the supreme moment in an initiate's life. It was both physical and mystical: trembling, vertigo, cold sweat, and then a sight that made all previous seeing seem blindness, a sense of awe and wonder at a brilliance that caused a profound silence, since what had just been seen and felt could never be communicated; words were unequal to the task.

Many writers are convinced that this experience could have been induced only by some psychoactive potion, which is widely suggested to have included ergot.

In *The White Goddess,* Robert Graves also traced Dionysus to his psychoactive source, from a vine god back to

> an earlier Dionysus, the Toadstool-god; for the Greeks be-
> lieved that mushrooms and toadstools were engendered
> by lightning—not sprung from seed like other plants.
> When the tyrants of Athens, Corinth and Scyon legalized
> Dionysus-worship in their cities, they limited the orgies,
> it seems, by substituting wine for toadstools; thus the
> myth of the Toadstool-Dionysus became attached to the
> Vine-Dionysus.

And Dionysus's centaurs, satyrs, and maenads "ritually ate a spotted toadstool called 'flycap' [*Amanita muscaria*] which gave them enormous muscular strength, erotic power, deliri-ous visions, and the gift of prophecy."

Ginzburg also found traces of the same shamanic culture in many of the Greeks' legendary rituals. The Orphic legends tell the story of how Dionysus was murdered as a child by the Ti-tans, who cooked him in a pot and roasted him on a spit. In some versions of the story, they devoured him; in others, he came back to life. Graves quotes Plutarch on this theme:

> In describing the manifold changes of Dionysus into
> winds, water, earth, stars and growing plants and ani-
> mals, they use the riddling expressions "render asunder"
> and "tearing limb from limb." And they call the god
> "Dionysus" or "Zagreus" ("the torn") or "The Night Sun"
> or "The Impartial Giver," and record various Destruc-
> tions, Disappearances, Resurrections and Rebirths, which
> are their mythographic account of how those changes
> came about.

Orpheus is similarly said to have been "torn in pieces by a pack of delirious women intoxicated by ivy and also, it seems, by the toadstool sacred to Dionysus."

Fungi and ivy, which is now known only as a highly toxic vine, predate the associations of Dionysus with Bacchus, the god of wine, and possibly much Christian imagery too: there are suggestions that the image of the mushroom predates the cross and that the image of the ivy leaf, which is still visible on the walls of the temple of Apollo at Delphi, lies behind the image of the sacred heart. And Delphi is the source of other traces of ancient Greek uses of psychoactive substances. It is said that the Delphic oracle was transmitted by a priestess who sat "astride a cleft in the earth from which subterranean vapours arose." It is sometimes suggested that the priestess was also inhaling the smoke of smoldering henbane: Ernst von Bibra, from whom Freud seems to have taken much of his information on coca, suggests that "the priests at the Oracle of Delphi administered the prepared seeds of the thornapple to their seers to put them in the desired prophetic ecstasy." In *The White Goddess*, Graves used the possibility that the oracle was carried in these fumes and transmitted through the body of the priestess to support his notion that inspiration was first of all a material event: the "breathing-in by the poet of intoxicating fumes." Only later, he suggested, does it come to be associated with the breath of God or some more secular conception of thin air. It was this same oracle, at Delphi, that gave Oedipus the prophecy that sent him on his tragic way.

In the writings of Pythagoras, Heracleitus, and Parmenides, there are remnants of this ancient world. But by the time Plato wrote Socrates down, in the fifth century B.C., the door to these old cultures had been firmly closed. The cults were disbanded, the temple was destroyed, and Dionysus, as Ginzburg argues, was subsumed by the new tragic figure of Oedipus. Both ancient theology and modern philosophy take some of their most basic structures of reason, truth, and morality from Plato's distinction between the true, eternal world of the forms and the transient dimension of material reality. It is Plato who first insists that truth cannot be found in the here and now, that there are no shortcuts to the infinite:

the *Republic* lays down one true path to enlightenment, the point at which the human soul can finally run free of the body and converge with the ideal, the eternal, the good, the straight lines along which the soul must train itself in readiness for the fatal day when it can escape the confines and corruptions of life on earth. Now the only way was up, toward the light, as far from the underworld as it is possible to get.

This was a complete reversal of the old shamanic story and also a rejection of the body and all the transient processes at work in the material world: in *The Last Days of Socrates,* Plato wrote, "If we are ever to have pure knowledge of anything, we must get rid of the body and contemplate things by themselves with the soul by itself." Knowledge is possible only "if we avoid as much as we can all contact and association with the body, except when they are absolutely necessary; and instead of allowing ourselves to become infected with its nature, purify ourselves from it until God himself gives us deliverance." Only the pure soul can hope to find the truth, and any attention to the body is bound to throw the soul into a realm of illusions and deceptions, fantasies and lies. The warnings have been endlessly repeated, even in the relatively secular terms of modern humanism, in which reason is valued over desire in an effort to sustain the Platonic insistence that the body is a corrupting, even evil, influence on what would otherwise be pure thought. But there always comes a point at which the body "intrudes once more into our investigations, interrupting, disturbing, distracting, and preventing us from getting a glimpse of the truth."

Plato provided the philosophical basis for much of the world's later theology. The world of forms becomes the Christian heaven, and the good, the eternal, the true, becomes personified as God. Now only He can take you there, and only once. For those who stray from the one true path to the light and wander back into the old hallucinatory zone of dark illusion, there are confessors and inquisitors, priests guarding the borders between life and death, and, of course, a day of final judgment.

But if such enlightenment was possible only at the end of a lifetime of hard work, how did Plato come to see the light so soon? It was obvious to Gordon and Valentina Wasson that Plato had "drunk of the potion in the Temple of Eleusis and had spent the night seeing the great vision." Was this the theater of the first drug war? Is it possible that Plato saw the light and effectively determined to keep the secret of its discovery—and repetition—to himself? To deny that the body could be engineered to perceive the infinite in the here and now? Is this also the story of Socrates, who died from a draught of hemlock, his own last trip supposed to be the last for everyone? And Oedipus, from whom Freud takes his idealized image of male identity, sent to his fate by an intoxicated priestess?

Wasson's suggestion that Plato took his inspiration from the mysteries has encouraged speculation about the extent to which psychoactive substances have continued to inform theistic beliefs in a purely immaterial realm, a spiritual home in which the human soul might one day find truth, liberation, enlightenment. There are, for example, suggestions that the notion of transubstantiation has its sources in ancient mushroom cults and that the visions of St. Teresa of Ávila and many other Christian mystics were aided, if not primarily induced, by the accidental or deliberate use of psychoactive substances. It is certainly true that all theistic cultures are wary of the mysticism on which they continue to depend, not least because of its attempt to connect with the absolute in the here and now. Travelers returning with good news from this other world are welcomed back as saints, but those with other stories have been condemned as heretics and, until the eighteenth century, burned as witches. As J. M. Cohen writes in the introduction to *The Life of Saint Teresa*, Teresa of Ávila "pursued her path close beneath the shadow of her Church's dogma, and by continually dwelling on it unconsciously shaped the imagery of her visions and locutions to suit its teaching . . . if her experience taught her one thing and the Church another, she was on the side of authority."

In the *mystical theology*, which I have begun to speak of, the understanding ceases to work because God suspends it . . . What we must not do is to presume or imagine that we can suspend it ourselves.

St. Teresa of Ávila

Ginzburg's inquiry into the emergence of the Sabbath led him to believe that "an important part of our cultural patrimony originates—through channels that largely escape us—from the Siberian hunters, the shamans of Northern and Central Asia, and the nomads of the steppes." *Ecstasies* finds the same stories of animal metamorphosis, inhuman perception, flight, and ecstasy cropping up all along this trail. And while Ginzburg insisted that "no privation, no substance, no ecstatic technique can, by itself, cause the recurrence of such complex experiences," the use of what are often very similar psychoactive plants and fungi recurs all along this route as well. Ginzburg's shamanic trail across the continents and through the centuries was also a long chain of chemical continuities.

As the story of the witches' sabbath began to unravel across space and time, Ginzburg realized the scale of his attempt to understand the phenomenon: "When considering the long trail of research it involved, I remember experiencing a sensation vaguely resembling vertigo." It took him twenty-five years to make the trip. When he wrote up the results of his immense research, laying it out in all its meticulous detail in *Ecstasies*, he wrote of "the deep resemblance that binds the myths that later merged into the witches' Sabbath. All of them work a common theme: going into the beyond, returning from the beyond." The Sabbath seemed to hold the key to an "elementary narrative" that "has accompanied humanity for thousands of years." Why is the story so enduring? "Why this permanence? The answer is possibly very simple. To narrate means to speak here and now with an authority that derives (literally or metaphorically) there and then." The ability to make a return trip to some other world and to live to tell the tale, to participate "in the world of the living and of the dead, in the sphere of the visible and of the invisible," is, he argued, so long standing and ubiquitous that it can even be defined as "a distinctive trait of the human species."

Ginzburg's own story was no exception: "The attempt to attain knowledge of the past is also a journey into the world of the dead." The historian makes the same shamanic trip, a voyage into the twilight zone of faded memories, ghostly archives, hidden clues. He hones the same skills of divination and detection and works with the same keen senses and sharp eyes. And he, too, returns with a changed mind: new perspectives on the scene of the Sabbath with which he had begun. Ginzburg began his inquiries keen to disprove some notion of human nature, but he found himself describing the shamanic story of flight, transformation, and return as "not one narrative among many, but the matrix of all possible narratives."

> There is no branch of detective science which is so important and so much neglected as the art of tracing footprints.
>
> Sherlock Holmes, in Arthur Conan Doyle,
> *A Study in Scarlet*

One of Ginzburg's psychoactive candidates, ergot, was already notorious in Europe. Eating flour made from infected rye can induce ergotism, a syndrome that is thought to have underwritten many outbreaks of unrest and apparent madness in the medieval period, when it was known as St. Anthony's Fire and said to be the source of the visions brought to life in Flaubert's story of the saint's temptation. Ginzburg is by no means the only writer to suggest that the fungus has exerted a great, if unintentional, influence on the ancient and early modern cultures of western, central, and northern Europe. Mann has speculated that the Massachusetts witch craze of the early 1690s may have been induced by ergot: as he pointed out, "the weather pattern was conducive to a good growth of ergot on the local rye." He also suggested that ergot had a hand in the *grande peur,* the "great fear" of 1789 that swept through revolutionary France.

Ergot also has a long history of more deliberate, medicinal uses. Sixteenth-century herbals report its ancient use by midwives as a means of precipitating childbirth, and that so many midwives were condemned as witches substantiates Ginzburg's suggestion that the fungus was well known to them. In some forms, ergotism can lead to gangrenous and fatal infections; in others, it can cause convulsions and hallucinations. 'Some were shaken by extremely painful contractions; others, 'like ecstatics fell into a deep sleep: when the seizure was over, they awoke and told of various visions.'" As Ginzburg observed, all this was once attributed "to a supernatural cause. Today we know that certain species of *claviceps purpurea* contain, in varying quantities, an alkaloid— ergonovine—from which lysergic acid diethylamide (LSD) was synthesized in 1943."

> These substances have formed a bond of union between men of opposite hemispheres, the uncivilized and the civilized; they have forced passages which, once open, proved of use for other purposes; they produced in ancient races characteristics which have endured to the present day, evidencing the marvellous degree of intercourse that existed between different peoples just as certainly and exactly as a chemist can judge the relations of two substances by their reactions.
>
> Louis Lewin, *Phantastica*

Toward the end of the First World War, a Swiss chemist, Werner Stoll, began to research the pharmacological properties of ergot. His work led to the isolation of the alkaloid ergotamine in 1918, and, by the 1930s, ergot had yielded a number of medicinal compounds for use in both obstetrics and the treatment of migraine. One of Stoll's junior colleagues at Sandoz, the Swiss pharmaceutical firm for which he worked, was equally intrigued by ergot's medicinal potential. Albert Hofmann knew it had "a fascinating history, in the course of which its role and meaning have been reversed: once dreaded as a poison, in the course of time it has changed to a rich storehouse of valuable remedies," and in the late 1930s, he began to analyze a series of chemicals derived from the fungus.

These were the days of "bucket chemistry," when chemists searched through vast combinations of chemicals, hunting for some clue or indication of therapeutic potential. Hofmann was convinced that ergot had a future as fascinating as its past and sifted through hundreds of compounds in the search for useful substances. He paid little attention to the twenty-fifth in a series of lysergic acids when he first synthesized it in 1938. But five years later, a "peculiar presentiment—the feeling that this substance could possess properties other than those established in the first investigations" drew him back to the formula for LSD-25. And one afternoon, as he was working with the compound, Hofmann found himself

> affected by a remarkable restlessness, combined with a slight dizziness. At home I lay down and sank into a not unpleasant intoxicated-like condition, characterized by an extremely stimulated imagination. In a dreamlike state, with eyes closed (I found the daylight to be unpleasantly glaring), I perceived an uninterrupted stream of fantastic pictures, extraordinary shapes with intense, kaleidoscopic play of colors. After some two hours this condition faded away.

The intensity of these effects convinced Hofmann that he must have been exposed to some strong chemical, but the episode was shocking and mysterious. In *LSD, My Problem Child*, he asked:

> How had I managed to absorb this material? Because of the known toxicity of ergot substances, I always maintained meticulously neat work habits. Possibly a bit of the LSD solution had contacted my fingertips during crystallization, and a trace of the substance was absorbed through the skin. If LSD-25 had indeed been the cause of this bizarre experience, then it must be a substance of extraordinary potency. There seemed to be only one way of getting to the bottom of this. I decided on a self-experiment.

A more deliberate experiment with LSD-25 confirmed Hofmann's initial impression. "I thought I had died," he later wrote. The effects of the chemical were so powerful that "I lost all control of time; space and time became more and more disorganized and I was overcome with fears that I was going crazy." Hofmann knew he was dealing with a unique substance of remarkable strength. Werner Stoll called it "A New Hallucinatory Agent, Active in Very Small Amounts" in the title of a 1947 report. But it was difficult to know what to do with a drug whose effects were so disturbing and profound. There were certainly no obvious medicinal uses for LSD. Hofmann's experiences with the chemical did, however, leave him in no doubt that its extraordinary powers might be of some psychiatric and even philosophical interest.

> Of greatest significance to me has been the insight that I attained as a fundamental understanding from all of my LSD experiments: what one commonly takes as "the reality," including the reality of one's own individual person, by no means signifies something fixed, but rather some-

thing that is ambiguous—that there is not only one, but that there are many realities, each comprising also a different consciousness of the ego.

The synthesis of LSD excited interest in other hallucinogens. *Teonanactl*, a mushroom whose name translates as "flesh of the gods," had been found by Roberto Weitlaner and Richard Evans Schultes in the Oaxaca region of Mexico in the 1930s. But it was not until the early 1950s that serious research on the mushroom was conducted by Valentina Wasson and Gordon Wasson, whose visits to María Sabina, the shaman who had introduced them to the drug in 1955, left them in no doubt that "the magical powers attributed to the mushrooms actually existed and were not merely superstition." These trips were followed by several attempts to extract the active chemicals from the mushrooms in both the United States and France. Eventually the mushrooms found their way to Sandoz, where Hofmann, keen as ever to experiment, tried them on himself. "Thirty minutes after my taking the mushrooms," he wrote,

the exterior world began to undergo a strange transformation. Everything assumed a Mexican character. As I was perfectly well aware that my knowledge of the Mexican origin of the mushroom would lead me to imagine only Mexican scenery, I tried deliberately to look on my environment as I knew it normally. But all voluntary efforts to look at things in their customary forms and colors proved ineffective. Whether my eyes were closed or open, I saw only Mexican motifs and colors. When the doctor supervising the experiment bent over me to check my blood pressure, he was transformed into an Aztec priest and I would not have been astonished if he had drawn an obsidian knife.

After an hour and a half or so, "the rush of interior pictures, mostly abstract motifs rapidly changing in shape and color, reached such an alarming degree that I feared that I would be torn into this whirlpool of form and color and would dissolve. After about six hours the dream came to an end."

By 1958, Hofmann had isolated two of the mushroom's compounds, psilocybin and psilocin, the same alkaloids that crop up in the magic mushrooms that grow across the British Isles and in many other parts of northern Europe in the autumn. With their chemical structures determined, it was now possible to synthesize these compounds without recourse to the mushrooms themselves. With this move, Hofmann later wrote, "The demystification of the magic mushrooms was accomplished. The compounds whose wondrous effects led the Indians to believe for millennia that a god was residing in the mushrooms had their chemical structures elucidated and could be produced synthetically in flasks." But was this a great scientific advance? Had anything been solved? "Just what progress in scientific knowledge was accomplished by natural products research in this case? Essentially, when all is said and done, we can only say that the mystery of the wondrous effects of teonanactl was reduced to the mystery of the effects of two crystalline substances."

One element of this mystery was the apparent similarity of these substances with LSD-25 and its related alkaloids. These compounds not only induced similar effects but also were remarkably close in terms of their chemical structures. In 1960, when Hofmann experimented with the seeds of morning glory, a variety of convolvulus, he found some even stronger and stranger links. Morning glory was radically different from the fungi with which Hofmann had worked, and it was widely assumed that chemical configurations tended to be specific to particular orders of the plant kingdom. To Hofmann's amazement, and many other chemists' disbelief, the major active principles of morning glory seeds turned out to be identical to the alkaloids crucial to the psychoactivity of ergot and LSD.

Hofmann felt that his work had "now formed a circle, one could almost say a magic circle." His early syntheses of lysergic acid amides from ergot had led to his work on LSD, which had led in turn to the isolation of psilocybin and psilocin and then to the discovery of the same lysergic acid amides in the morning glory seeds. Hofmann's magic circle had many other turns to take: the connections between ergot, psilocybin, and morning glory alkaloids were the first of many links to be established between a number of apparently very different hallucinogenic plants and fungi, whose extraordinary distribution pays scant attention to the distance between distinct geographic regions, species of plants, and all the categories and classifications with which the modern world understands organic life. The connections seem to know as few bounds as the visions these substances induce.

Psilocybin, ergot, and, by implication, LSD turned out to be closely related to a number of short-acting tryptamines, including DMT (N,N-dimethyltryptamine), DET, and 5-methoxy-DMT. These are powerful psychoactive chemicals that are ineffective when ingested orally, because the enzyme monoamine oxidase (known as MAO) destroys their molecular structure when they are absorbed in the stomach. But they can be smoked, with dramatic, intense, and, as their designation suggests, remarkably short-lived effects. The first of these tryptamines had been isolated in the 1930s, long before their connections with ergot and its many relatives were understood, and synthetic versions of DMT and its relatives were also produced at Sandoz by Albert Hofmann. But the plants in which they are found have ancient shamanic uses in Colombia, Venezuela, and many other parts of the Americas, where they are still used for the diagnosis of disease, prophecy, and divination. The use of snuff containing these compounds was reported by early Spanish travelers and Jesuit priests. "They have another abominable habit of intoxicating themselves through the nostrils with certain malignant powders which they call Yupa," wrote one eighteenth-century priest of the Otomac Indians in the Orinoco region. "Before a battle, they would throw themselves into a frenzy with Yupa, wound themselves and, full of blood and rage, go forth to battle like rabid jaguars."

> The hallucinogen drugs shift the scanning pattern of "reality" so that we see a different "reality"—There is no true or real "reality"—"Reality" is simply a more or less constant scanning pattern.
>
> William Burroughs, *Nova Express*

Some half-dozen species of hallucinogenic plants and fungi are native to Europe, but the Americas play host to scores of them. All of them are known to cultures in which the shamanic return trip is a continual refrain: stories of journeys that transform travelers, reconfiguring their bodies, remixing their minds, and returning them with news from some other world. Early European adventurers were wary of these drugs. The Church was positively hostile, and the conquistadores were interested only in fauna that could be turned to some religious or economic advantage. Hallucinogens did not fit the bill. Many Spanish chroniclers and botanists recorded native uses of these mushrooms, cacti, vines, and herbs, but the Church did its best to eradicate their use in the Americas as it had done at home. Ayahuasca, or yage, for example, was regarded with great distrust: known as "the vine of the soul," it is so closely associated with prophetic and divinatory powers that when its active alkaloid was first isolated, it was dubbed telepathine. "All medicine men," wrote Burroughs in *Naked Lunch*, "use it in their practice to foretell the future, locate lost or stolen objects, to diagnose and treat illness, to name the perpetrator of a crime."

It was an inconspicuous cactus, peyote, for which the Church reserved its most vehement and often violent condemnations. Peyote was described as an "infernal abuse" and a "diabolic root" by churchmen who reported that people on the drug would "lose their senses, see visions of terrifying sights like the devil and were able to prophesy the future." Richard Rudgley quotes another seventeenth-century report:

> Inasmuch as the use of the herb or root called Peyote has been introduced into these Provinces for the purposes of detecting thefts, or divining other happenings, and of foretelling future events, it is an act of superstition condemned as opposed to the purity and integrity of our Holy Catholic Faith. This is certain because neither the said herb nor any other can possess the virtue or inherent quality of producing the effects claimed, nor can any cause the mental images, fantasies, and hallucinations on which the above stated divinations are based.

There were logistic reasons for this distrust as well: the Spanish believed that peyote allowed its Indian users to "report mutinies, battles, revolts and death occurring 200 or 300 leagues distant, on the very day they took place, or the day after." Peyote, it was said, operated as a "rapid communications service," as if short-circuiting the space-time grid known to the Europeans. In spite of the best efforts of the Church, peyote is still used, and many of the rites associated with its ancient use are still practiced, by the Huichol, the Tarahumara, and many other Central American peoples. In 1960, the Native American Church, which uses peyote as a sacrament, won the legal right to include peyote buttons and mescaline in their religious ceremonies.

> When I eat *hikuri*, the world becomes radiant with glowing colour. Káuyumarie, the Little Deer, comes to me to show me how it all is. When you hear me chanting sacred songs, it is not I who sing but

Káuyumarie who is singing into my ear. And I transmit these songs to you. It is he who teaches us,
shows us the way. This is how it is.

Matsúwa, Huichol shaman, in Joan Halifax,
Shamanic Voices

According to a follower of "the Tipi way," a member of the
Californian Washoe tribe quoted in *The Drug User,* peyote

> makes your eyes like X-ray so you can see what's inside
> things. You can see inside a person and see if he is in
> good health or he got some sickness in there. It makes
> your mind like a telegram. You can send your thoughts
> far away to some other person and that person can send
> messages to you. It works like electricity.

As it happens, it was only with the development of the X ray,
the telegram, and electricity that the Western world really began to tune in to these plants and their properties. Weir
Mitchell and Havelock Ellis were among a number of prominent writers who tried peyote, or mescaline, in the closing
years of the nineteenth century. Parke-Davis and Company
distributed peyote buttons as early as 1887, and Louis Lewin
isolated several alkaloids from the cactus before mescaline, its
most active compound, was isolated in Germany by Arthur
Heffter in 1897.

William James, dissuaded by nausea, said he would take its
visions "on trust," but both Mitchell and Ellis published influential accounts of their experiences with mescaline, in which
they praised its aesthetic, intellectual, and metaphysical qualities. "The visions never resembled familiar objects," wrote Ellis. "They were extremely definite, but yet always novel; they
were constantly approaching, and yet constantly eluding, the
semblance of known things." He described them as "living
arabesques," which "grew and changed without any reference
to the characteristics of those real objects of which they

vaguely reminded me, and when I tried to influence their course it was with very little success." They did exhibit

> a certain incomplete tendency to symmetry, as though the underlying mechanism was associated with a large number of polished facets. The same image was in this way frequently repeated over a large part of the field; but this refers more to form than to colour, in respect to which there would still be all sorts of delightful varieties, so that if, with a certain uniformity, jewel-like flowers were springing up and expanding all over the field of vision, they would still show every variety of delicate tone and tint.

The drug spread through the bohemian quarters of America and Europe, inspiring Aleister Crowley, W. B. Yeats, and other members of the Hermetic Order of the Golden Dawn. And mescaline has continued to inspire Europe's artists and writers. The French writer Henri Michaux devoted much of his life and work to the drug, and, in 1954, Aldous Huxley published *The Doors of Perception,* a book that explored the mescaline experience in some depth and was followed a year later by *Heaven and Hell.*

Huxley is also closely associated with another drug: *soma,* the potion used for dubious purposes of social engineering in *Brave New World.* Huxley's use of the term *soma* picks up on one of the most fascinating threads running through the ancient history of drugs. It is mentioned in countless passages of the earliest Aryan texts, the Rig-Veda, which are thought to be some three thousand years old, and although there have been many attempts to identify the plant, or the potion, *soma* has defied even the most determined drug detectives. The Wassons equate it with fly agaric, and Carlo Ginzburg tends to agree. But one of the most compelling suggestions is that *soma* is harmal, or Syrian rue, a plant native to the Middle East with close chemical relations to South America's yage. Among the active alkaloids in yage, which grows across Central and South America, are harmine and harmaline.

Richard Rudgley develops a persuasive chain of associations that links both *soma* and harmal with *hoama*, another enigmatic psychoactive substance, which is mentioned in the Avesta, the Zoroastrian teachings, and *mang*, the potion with which Wiraz undertakes his journeys to heaven and hell on a flying carpet in the *Book of Arda Wiraz*. A beautiful nexus emerges in the course of Rudgley's discussions about Syrian rue: the image of the flying carpet whose instructions are woven into its own design. Not only do the patterns of Turkish and Persian carpets have a striking resonance with those perceptible on yage and its relatives, but the characteristic red dye used in these designs is extracted from harmal.

Soma and *mang* have also been associated with ephedrine, the principal psychoactive element at work in the ancient Chinese herb mahuang, or *Ephedra vulgaris*. Mahuang, which also contains the alkaloid norpseudoephedrine, has been used in China to calm fevers and aid respiration for some five thousand years, and the plant was also found in a Neanderthal burial site in Iraq. Although the plant has few of the properties of which the Vedas speak, Vedic priests refer to the use of *soma* as a stimulant for warriors. Ephedrine is also the active alkaloid in qat, a plant widely used in Yemen and Somalia, where it is chewed or made into tea, and said to predate the use of coffee.

Ephedrine, which has close links to mescaline and to MDA, MDMA, and many more contemporary psychoactive drugs, was first isolated in Japan in the 1880s. A close synthetic relative, phenylisopropylamine, was developed at the same time. MDA was synthesized in 1910, and MDMA was patented in 1914. Although there was little interest in these compounds at the time, these developments marked the emergence of one of the twentieth century's most widely used psychoactive compounds: amphetamine sulfate, or speed.

Pilots

It was as a medicine that speed first became available to the Western world. When the pharmaceutical company Smith Kline & French introduced a nasal inhaler called Benzedrine in 1932, it was hailed as another panacea and marketed with the same sense of indiscriminate enthusiasm that had once sold opiates and cocaine. As Lester Grinspoon wrote:

> Never before had a powerful psychoactive drug been introduced in such quantities in so short a period of time, and never before had a drug with such a high addictive potential and capability of causing long-term or irreversible physical and psychological damage been so enthusiastically embraced by the medical profession as a panacea or so extravagantly promoted by the drugs industry.

There were claims that Benzedrine had dozens of clinical applications, ranging from the treatment of migraine, epilepsy, and postencephalitic Parkinson's disease to colic and hypertension. It was used for the treatment of hyperactive children shortly after its development and widely dispensed as an appetite suppressant and slimming agent. There were also the inevitable suggestions that amphetamines, like so many drugs before them, could be used to treat addictions.

But the majority of Benzedrine prescriptions dispensed the drug as a stimulant and an antidepressant. Speed was a cheap, functional, and legal substitute for drugs with an increasingly bad press, and in this capacity it found a ready market in the depressed days of 1930s America: "Thanks to Benzedrine," wrote Grinspoon, "Americans could look forward not only to freedom from blocked and runny noses, but to a euphoria that would let them temporarily forget about their own personal financial depressions." Speed has served these purposes ever since, and not only in America. Amphetamines are widely used in cough mixtures, expectorants, and inhalers to relieve the symptoms of asthma, common medicinal applications that have always made them easily diverted from their authorized uses and licit economies. Speed is also an easy drug to make, and although it is shipped across continents and traded on the world market, much of it is now produced wherever it is widely used. Such accessibility makes speed cheap and ubiquitous: it is a basic, no-frills commodity, a crude, straightforward high. Speed is the default drug, the bottom line.

Although many amphetamine products had been banned by the end of the 1950s, there were several loopholes in the law. In the United States, methamphetamine, which was first synthesized in Japan in 1919, was not covered by the initial legislation, and amphetamines were easily obtainable by prescription and by mail order for much of the 1960s. The pharmaceutical companies producing amphetamines stood up to attempts to introduce more stringent controls in 1965, and by the 1970s the legal production of amphetamines had exceeded ten billion doses per year. Amphetamines continue to be widely used to control children diagnosed as suffering attention deficit disorder: in 1997, it was estimated that 2.5 million schoolchildren in the United States were being prescribed Ritalin, or methylphenidate, a drug the pharmaceutical industry disingenuously defines as a non-amphetamine.

Speed can energize and stimulate, enhancing performance and perceptions. As the teenagers of the 1950s discovered, it can certainly keep you up all night and even sustain a good fight with the police on Brighton beach. In America, Jack Kerouac took speed until he "felt he was blasting so high that he was experiencing real insights and facing real fears. With benzedrine he felt he was embarking on a journey of self-discovery, climbing up from one level to the next, following his insights . . . benzedrine intensified his awareness and made him feel more clever." It also landed him in the hospital, with thrombophlebitis in his legs, but this did little to dissuade him from his later experiments. "Each of Kerouac's books was written on something and each of the books has some of the feel of what he was on most as he wrote it. *On the Road* has a nervous, tense and benzedrine feel," wrote his biographer Ann Charters. "I heard his typewriter (as I came up the stairs) clattering away without pause," recalled John Clellon Holmes,

> and watched with some incredulity, as he unrolled the manuscript thirty feet beyond the machine in search of a choice passage. Two and a half weeks later, I read the finished book, which had become a scroll three inches thick made up of one single-spaced, unbroken paragraph 120 feet long, and knew immediately it was the best thing he had ever done.

But this is more than a drug of endurance. Large and continuous doses of speed can lead users into a singular world of fragmentation, anxiety, paranoia, psychosis. "Do androids dream of electric sheep?" It was speed that asked this question of Philip K. Dick, giving him the title of the book that was to become *Blade Runner,* a film in which Deckard, detective and assassin, treads a new fine line between human and replicant, the living and the dead, never quite sure which side he is on. His assignment is to track down the replicants, but he is always in danger of hunting himself, too. Their lives are artificial, their memories are implants, their means of perception have been manufactured by scientists working for a vast paranoid machinery, the Tyrell Corporation. "If only you could see what I have seen with your eyes," says one of the hunted to the man who gave him sight. These themes recur in many of Dick's novels and stories, including "We Can Remember It for You Wholesale," later made into the film *Total Recall.* Jekyll and Hyde find a new extreme with Dick's Substance D: it stands for death, he says in *A Scanner Darkly,* which cuts the speeding mind again when its hero becomes a detective assigned to track his own movements and stake out his own life.

> I saw the best minds of my generation destroyed by
> madness, starving hysterical naked,
> dragging themselves through the negro streets at
> dawn looking for an angry fix . . .
> Allen Ginsberg, *Howl*

It was as a military drug that speed really made its presence felt during the Second World War. Soldiers had been fighting under the influence of drugs ever since morphine and syringes were used to dull the pain of the American Civil War and, later, the traumas incurred on the killing fields of the First World War. As the fighting forces of the twentieth century found themselves entangled with advanced technologies of war, drugs became increasingly important to workings of the military machine. Soldiers already shaped and formed by the rigors of military discipline could now be controlled from the inside out. Amphetamines were distributed among the British, German, and Japanese armed forces, and, in Japan, the drug also enjoyed widespread domestic use, boosting industrial output and producing some 200,000 cases of amphetamine psychosis by the end of the war. Amphetamines certainly turned German pilots into living, speeding machines. Speed, then known as "blitz," made the Luftwaffe's pilots as high as the new speeds at which their planes could fly. Already strapped into the cockpit, wired up to devices, and surrounded by controls, pilots were now changed from the inside out, their bodies optimized, their brains attuned to the speeds and heights of flight. The speeding pilots and their speeding planes were way ahead of a game whose self-guiding systems launched the V-2, the cruise missile, and the Cold War rush toward mutually assured destruction. As the fastest-ever moving targets, the Luftwaffe also provided the impetus for the Allied development of the antiaircraft systems from which modern cybernetics emerged. Speed was overtaking itself.

This was war on drugs of a very different kind. Even the leaders were speeding through the war. At one time, Hitler was injecting himself with methamphetamine eight times a day. And Churchill was discovering the joys of speed: "I took your pill at 1 p.m.," he said to his doctor, Lord Moran, whose biographer, Richard Lovell, reported Churchill's use of both amphetamines and barbiturates. "It was a great success. It cleared my head and gave me great confidence." Many later heads of government repeated the prescription when they found themselves struggling to deal with the crises that rocked the world in the postwar years. The British prime minister Anthony Eden did battle with Suez on Benzedrine, and John F. Kennedy sped his way through the Cuban missile crisis in 1962. Perhaps speed even manufactured the crises it was used to solve: think of Kennedy, Eden, even Churchill, all making gross errors of judgment on the drug. And Hitler, racking his brains with all that speed running through his veins, his whole mission fueled by megalomania, feverish fears of conspiracy, and dreams of clean, lean supermen, disciplined and fast.

> This is a game planet. All games are hostile and basically there is only one game, and that game is war. Research into altered states of consciousness—which might result in a viewpoint from which the game itself could be called into question—is inexorably drawn into the game.
>
> —William Burroughs, *Nova Express*

Nick Land described the Vietnam War as "a decisive point of intersection between pharmacology and the technology of violence" in which America's conscript army was " 'wasted' ('blitzed,' 'bombed out') on heroin, marijuana and LSD."

Chasing the dragon through the jungles, firing through a smoke screen of local weed, a trip upriver through the purple haze, a journey to the source of the horror in *Apocalypse Now,* a terrifying web of deceit and illusion in *Jacob's Ladder.* It has been suggested that more than 200 million doses of amphetamine were distributed throughout the U.S. military between 1966 and 1969. U.S. forces first used speed to excess during the war in Korea, where amphetamines had been manufactured and consumed in vast quantities for years. Speedballs—mainlined solutions of heroin mixed with speed or, better still, black-market cocaine—were popular mixtures in the Korean War and were widely used again in Vietnam, where U.S. soldiers took whatever they could get. And there was no shortage of heroin: even the official figures state that 15 percent of Vietnam veterans returned to the United States as heroin addicts, and more soldiers were evacuated from Vietnam for drug-related problems than for war injuries.

> Weapons are tools not just of destruction but also of perception: the history of battle is primarily the history of radically changing fields of perception.
>
> Paul Virilio, *War and Cinema*

Drawn into the modern military machine, drugs evoke some ancient memories of war. "Tied to his machine," writes Paul Virilio,

> imprisoned in the closed circuits of electronics, the war pilot is no more than a motor-handicapped person temporarily suffering from a kind of possession analogous to the hallucinatory states of primitive warfare. In the next scene, he's totally immersed. The trip is now inscribed on silicon, a chip about the size of a microdot, a tab of LSD . . . he undertakes his missions in a simulated world, storming the deserts, flying through an artificial paradise of war.

Virilio looks forward, not so far, to a time when the "presentation of the images from aerial combat will be projected directly into the pilot's eyeballs with the aid of a helmet fitted with optic fibres. This phenomenon of hallucination approaches that of drugs, meaning that this practice material denotes the future disappearance of every scene, every video screen."

By the end of the Second World War, psychoactive drugs had presented the military with a wide range of possible applications. The Germans had experimented with the use of mescaline during interrogations, and on all sides it was clear that drugs were chemical weapons that could keep people quiet, wake them up, and, if necessary, break them down. They could enhance performance, sharpen senses, heighten aggression and self-confidence. They could be used as a means of controlling minds, programming thoughts, and washing brains.

In the early 1950s, all these possibilities were being explored by various sections of the U.S. military and the Central Intelligence Agency. Much of the CIA's drug research was conducted under the auspices of MK-ULTRA, a division of the agency's existing mind-control program, ARTICHOKE, which had already investigated several substances that were—or soon would become—controlled: the CIA was experimenting with morphine, heroin, ether, LSD, mescaline, and cocaine, as well as amphetamines. A CIA agent even accompanied the Wassons on their second trip to Oaxaca. The primary purpose of this work was to find a truth drug. But none of these substances yielded good results. The effects of LSD and mescaline were so unpredictable and volatile that the only useful suggestion they inspired was that they could make interrogation completely ineffective.

Nevertheless, such powerful substances could hardly be abandoned in the new theater of the Cold War. The precedent for military uses of hallucinogens had been set in Germany, and the incentive to stay ahead in even a potential drug arms race was high. Many psychotropic plants, including ergot, were prevalent in Russia, and although the CIA had gained assurances from Sandoz, the Swiss manufacturer of LSD, that sales would not be made to hostile powers, it was widely feared that the USSR was manufacturing LSD or experimenting on other drugs.

If LSD could not be used to elicit the truth, the CIA was impressed by claims that the drug could induce temporary insanity. It certainly seemed to have this effect on its own agents. "Turn your back in the morning and some wise-acre would slip a few micrograms into your coffee," wrote Jay Stevens.

> Case-hardened spooks would break down crying or go all gooey about the "brotherhood of man." Once or twice things went really awry, with paranoid agents escaping into the bustle of downtown Washington. After one spectacular chase the quarry was finally run to ground in Virginia, where they found him crouched under a fountain, babbling about those "terrible monster[s] with fantastic eyes" that had pursued him across Washington.

In a manner reminiscent of the Nazis' medical experiments, the CIA funded, coordinated, and in many cases conducted an amazing number and variety of bizarre and often dangerous experiments on unwitting or ill-informed U.S. civilians. "By this time," wrote Kathy Acker in *Empire of the Senseless*, "the CIA had tested chemicals on themselves to such an extent that they were now either lobotomy cases or insane, they needed new experimentees." Prison inmates and drug addicts, most of them black, were given enormous experimental doses of the drug, often in exchange for heroin or their drug of choice and sometimes on a daily basis for periods of more than six weeks. The CIA also laid some extraordinary traps for unsuspecting members of the public. In Operation Midnight

Climax, visiting businessmen were lured to a brothel as unwitting LSD guinea pigs, observed from behind one-way mir-
rors, and sent off in the morning without explanation.

> I saw my friends in that brothel destroyed by mad-
> ness starving hysterical naked dragging themselves
> through the whitey's streets at dawn looking for an
> angry fix.
>
> Kathy Acker, *Empire of the Senseless*

It was LSD's ability to mimic psychosis—its role as a
psychotomimetic—that provided the justification for this research. The CIA was ostensibly interested in using hallucinogens to perform a kind of chemical brainwashing, disrupting
established worldviews and breaking down integrated sub-
jects to a point at which they could effectively be reprogrammed. This was a line of inquiry that touched on many
different areas of scientific and medical research. LSD awak-
ened interest in neurochemistry and experimental psychiatry, and postwar work on cybernetics and computing had
stimulated research on the intelligence and behavior of both
humans and machines. The CIA's support for a number of
leading academic programs and foundations in these fields
induced a flurry of LSD-related research in the 1950s. As well
as effectively distributing the drug, the CIA made it cheap
and easy to produce. The agency was unwilling to depend on
a foreign company for its supplies of anything, and Sandoz
LSD, produced from ergot, was also an expensive chemical.
By 1954, at the CIA's request, the Indianapolis pharmaceutical
company Eli Lilly was producing a cheap, synthetic, and
American LSD. Although it cannot be given all the credit for
the availability of LSD, the CIA can certainly be said to have
encouraged easy access to the drug. This meant that every
user of LSD had passed, "unawares, through doors opened by
the Agency. It would become a supreme irony that the CIA's

enormous search for weapons among drugs . . . would wind up helping to create the wandering, uncontrollable minds of the counterculture."

CIA operatives supplied the drug to academic programs and individuals, and they in turn filtered it into the wider world. Frank Fremont-Smith, head of the Macy Foundation, which organized a series of CIA-sponsored conferences on LSD and neuropharmacology, was given LSD by Harold Abramson, who also gave some to the anthropologist Gregory Bateson, who gave some to the poet Allen Ginsberg . . . Just as Coleridge had implicitly passed his habit on in the nineteenth century, LSD spread itself around the intellectual and bohemian worlds of the 1950s and 1960s.

> The music vibrated through my body as if I were one of the instruments and I felt myself becoming a full percussion orchestra, becoming green, blue, orange. The waves of the sounds ran through my hair like a caress. The music ran down my back and came out of my fingertips. I was a cascade of red-blue rainfall, a rainbow, I was small, light, mobile.
>
> Anaïs Nin, *Diaries, 1947–1955*

LSD is often taken lightly now, but in the 1950s and 1960s, the drug was an uncharted journey, an exploration of its own effects. And it offered plenty to explore. Tasteless, colorless, odorless, and potent in extremely small quantities, LSD-25 remains one of the world's most remarkable and intriguing chemicals.

When Humphry Osmond coined the term *psychedelic* for LSD and the other hallucinogens known to the 1950s, he intended to inscribe them as means for the exploration of the hidden extremities of the human psyche: it was to "fathom hell or soar angelic" that one took "a pinch of psychedelic." The term emphasized LSD as a soul-searching drug of inner exploration: *psychedelic* means "to make the soul visible."

There were other words suggested, such as Aldous Huxley's rather inelegant *phanerothyme*, which carries the same meaning. Had it not been such a poor marketing ploy, *psychotomimetic* might have been the most appropriate term. Just as morphine had bottled the dreams of the nineteenth century, LSD seemed to be twentieth-century psychosis distilled.

> "If you started in the wrong way," I said in answer to the investigator's questions, "everything that happened would be a proof of the conspiracy against you. It would all be self-validating. You couldn't draw a breath without knowing it was part of the plot."
>
> Aldous Huxley, *The Doors of Perception*

A certain Alfred Hubbard was one of the first to provide the vocabulary of dose, set, and setting that became so integral to the 1960s trip. He also gave William Burroughs his first taste of LSD. Hubbard had learned his practices from the shamanic guides of Central and South America, and he drew from them in his attempts to develop the use of images, objects, words, music, and perfumes to induce not merely a propitious general environment in which to take the drug but specific emotional responses and engagements at different stages of the trip. Certain images, he knew, would convey specific messages to particular explorers, and this was not simply a matter of some intended representation: a patch of color might be absorbed as a guardian figure; a particular sound might calm or excite.

By 1960, a vast international network of chemists, psychologists, psychiatrists, anthropologists, and philosophers had been experimenting with LSD, peyote, and their chemical relatives. Many psychiatrists took LSD to experience some moment of the madness once confined to their patients. "To take a dose of LSD," wrote Huxley in *The Doors of Experience,* is to have the experience of being more or less crazy, but this will make quite good sense because you *know* you took the dose of LSD. If, on the other hand, you took the LSD by accident, and then find yourself going crazy, not knowing how you got there, this is a terrifying and horrible experience. This is a much more serious and terrible experience, very different from the trip which you can enjoy if you know you took the LSD.

In Britain, R. D. Laing began his pioneering experiments with hallucinogenic drugs at Kingsley Hall, where he used LSD to take schizophrenic patients through their madness and out the other side. "We can no longer assume that such a voyage [schizophrenia] is an illness that has to be treated," he wrote in *The Politics of Experience.* "Can we not see that this voyage is not what we need to be cured of, but that it is itself a natural way of healing our own appalling state of alienation called normality?"

LSD was by no means universally welcomed by psychologists and psychiatrists. Therapy had been here before, with Freud, and until the introduction of LSD, pharmacological approaches to neurosis and psychosis had been subsumed by the psychoanalytic insistence that minds be treated, not bodies and brains. And the Freudians were not alone: "I am profoundly mistrustful of the 'pure gifts of the Gods,'" wrote Carl Jung in 1954. "You pay dearly for them." In any case, he argued, the world was already crazy enough: there was no shortage of material to investigate without adding drugs to the mix and "no point in wishing to know more of the collective unconscious than one gets through dreams and intuition. The more you know of it, the greater and heavier becomes your moral burden . . . Do you want to increase loneliness and misunderstanding? Do you want to find more and more complications and increasing responsibilities? You get enough of it."

Anaïs Nin expressed misgivings, too. "The one who wrestles his images from experience, from his smoky dreams, to create, is able then to build what he has seen and hungered for. It does not vanish with the effects of the chemical," she wrote. "But when I discuss this with Huxley, he is rather irritable: 'You're fortunate enough to have a natural access to your subconscious life, but other people need drugs and should have them.'" Nin decided to "go on in my own way, which is a disciplined, arduous, organic way of integrating the dream with creativity in life, a quest for the development of the senses, the vision, the imagination as dynamic elements with which to create a new world . . . What can be more wonderful than the carrying out of our fantasies, the courage to enact them, embody them, live them out instead of depending on the dissolving, dissipating, vanishing quality of drug dreams." Perhaps, as Carlo Ginzburg suggested in *Ecstasies*, women have a preexisting sympathy with the worlds their male counterparts explore on drugs.

Huxley had such faith in LSD that he died with his wife by his side and a large dose of the drug running through his mind. But Arthur Koestler decided to stick to alcohol. "It warms one and brings one closer to people," he said. "Mushrooms whirl you inside, too close to yourself . . . I solved the secret of the universe last night, but this morning I forgot what it was." Not unlike Baudelaire, Koestler "felt this was buying one's visions on the cheap." The second time he took psilocybin, Timothy Leary recalled in *Flashbacks*, Koestler said: "This is wonderful, no doubt. But it is fake, ersatz. Instant mysticism. There is no quick and easy path to wisdom. Sweat and toil are the price." He talked, but his companions were off on journeys of their own.

"What did he say?" asked Olson from a million miles away.

"Something about sweat and toil," I said.

Leary's answer to Koestler was as unequivocal as Huxley's to Nin: "Rejecting drugs as a tool would be like rejecting the microscope because it makes seeing too easy. I think people de-serve every revelation they can get." Leary was one of the most notorious members of this new generation of explorers. His interest in psychedelics had been aroused by psilocybin mushrooms, but it was his work with LSD that brought both him and the drug notoriety. Convinced by Neal Cassady, Jack Kerouac's old friend, that he was taking his research too seri-ously by conducting it in the clinical conditions of Harvard Medical School, Leary established a psychedelic resort at Zi-huatanejo in Mexico—Hotel Nirvana, he called it—"where people got high safely and respectably."

Leary and his colleague Richard Alpert were sacked from Harvard in 1963, but "I didn't want to be a professor any-way," said Leary, who was working with Alpert and Ralph Metzner on a translation of *The Tibetan Book of the Dead*, which they hoped would provide a new guidebook for their tripping contemporaries. "We felt that we were involved in a fascinat-ing historical event," wrote Leary in his autobiography, "the first research project in which experimentally induced mysti-cal experiences were being woven into the fabric of daily work and play. We saw ourselves as pioneers developing modern versions of the traditional techniques for philosophic inquiry and personal growth."

I was beginning to understand dimly the enormity of the spectrum of vocabularies used by organisms to commu-nicate with each other. In this timeless environment, hy-persensitive to the signals from my memory banks and my chattering hormones, and alerted by commands from DNA control templates cunningly buried in my cells, I recognized that everything was information. Everything was shouting, "Hey, look at me, I'm here. Open up. I have a message . . . " Everything I put in my mouth—the spoon, a swallow of water, every bite of food, every sexy-smooth lick—contaminated me with data.

Leary was the most vociferous explorer of these dimensions, but one of the bravest was John Lilly. His adventures with LSD and isolation tanks, which were poorly represented in Ken Russell's movie *Altered States*, allowed him to develop an entirely new understanding of "cosmos with all of its infinite variations" and to produce some detailed maps and guides to the spaces he explored. "It is all too easy to preach 'go with the flow,'" Lilly wrote in *The Centre of the Cyclone*. "The main problem is identifying what the flow is, here and now . . . Without clear maps one cannot even see the flow, much less go with it. Even when one truly goes with the flow one had better touch shore or bottom once in a while to be sure one isn't floating in the stagnant waters of secure beliefs." Lilly's main publication, *Programming and Metaprogramming the Human Biocomputer*, remains one of the most fascinating products of this wave of psychedelic research. When academic licenses for such experiments were withdrawn in the late 1960s, Lilly started working with dolphins, pioneering research into their systems of communication, learning, and intelligence.

If the criminalization of LSD interrupted authorized research, it served only to confirm the impression that the drug was dangerously subversive. Leary's famous injunction to "turn on, tune in, and drop out" inspired the young and filled their guardians with fear: in 1963, an agent of the Food and Drug Administration had told Leary that the "people in law enforcement—and believe me, they have the power—can't wait for these drugs to be illegal so they can bust your ass." When Leary tried to convince him of the wisdom of legalizing drugs, the agent said it all sounded great except that "President Johnson has made it very clear he wants a drug-free America."

Not everyone was convinced that LSD was so full of revolutionary potential. "Drugs are an excellent strategy against society," wrote Jeff Nuttall, "but a poor alternative to it." Political activists and tripping hippies often shared nothing more than mutual distrust. Revolutionaries ascribed tripped-out talk of inner revolution to bourgeois indulgence and escapist fantasy. Jack Kerouac, who took LSD just once, was "sure that it had been introduced to America by the Russians as part of a plot to weaken the country," and there were many suggestions, not so improbable, that the drug had been deliberately popularized by the CIA in an effort to depoliticize its 1960s users and undermine their ability to organize, coordinate, or simply think straight. "At the immediate risk of finding myself the most unpopular character of all fiction—and history is fiction," wrote Burroughs in the guise of Inspector J. Lee in *Nova Express*, "throw back their ersatz Immortality—It will fall apart before you can get out of The Big Store—Flush their drug kicks down the drain—They are poisoning and monopolizing the hallucinogen drugs—learn to make it without chemical corn."

Whatever the significance of the trips it induced, LSD certainly made its mark on Western culture in the late 1960s. The drug ran through the music, the colors, the patterns and designs of those days. It brought love to West Coast summers, washing California in Day-Glo light; it inspired Vietnam War protests, crazy warehouse parties, vast festivals, trips to Mexico, and trails to India. LSD challenged all accepted notions of sanity, normality, and identity, presenting itself as a solution to the madness and alienation of what Nuttall defined as "bomb culture," an era that believed it was about to disappear into a mushroom cloud and was filled with demands for total revolution.

Opiates had calmed and numbed the nineteenth century; cocaine came on line with electricity; speed had let the twentieth century keep up with its own new speeds. For Marshall McLuhan, it seemed obvious that hallucinogens were performing some similar cultural role. "Drug taking," he wrote in the late 1960s, "is today inspired by the penetrating information environment." Trippers were seeking some kind of integration with the "feedback pattern of our new electric environment . . . The impulse to use hallucinogens is a kind of empathy with the electronic environment," as well as "a way of repudiating the old mechanical world." McLuhan saw the new "cool" multimedia of the 1960s—television and early computing, both as addictive and hallucinatory as the interior technologies of drugs—shaping the entire sensorium of a generation whose predecessors' senses had been extended one by one with what McLuhan defined as the "hot" mediations of, for example, the camera and the radio.

> It is not uncommon for people on these trips, especially with new chemical drugs, as opposed to organic ones, to develop the illusion that they are themselves computers. This, of course, is not so much a hallucination as a discovery. The computer is a more sophisticated extension of the human nervous system than ordinary electric relays and circuits.
>
> Marshall McLuhan and Quentin Fiore,
> *War and Peace in the Global Village*

In *An Essay on Liberation,* published in 1969, Herbert Marcuse also described the emergence of a "new sensibility" that underlay the revolutionary impulses of the day. "Today's rebels want to see, hear, feel new things in a new way," he wrote. "They link liberation with the dissolution of ordinary and orderly perception," and any notion of political revolution would have to be a liberation of desire as well. "The 'trip,' " wrote Marcuse,

> involves the dissolution of the ego shaped by the established society—an artificial and short-lived duration. But the artificial and "private" liberation anticipates, in a distorted manner, an exigency of the social liberation: the revolution must be at the same time a revolution in perception which will accompany the material and intellec-

tual reconstruction of society, creating the new aesthetic environment. Awareness of the need for such a revolution in perception, for a new sensorium, is perhaps the kernel of truth in the psychedelic search.

Drugs were artificial, private, and short-lived, but they also fueled the dreams that revolution could bring true.

Marcuse's interest in the possibility that drugs anticipated revolutionary desire ran all the way back to Baudelaire, whose poetry and essays on hashish exerted a profound influence on one of Marcuse's most influential predecessors, Walter Benjamin.

Benjamin was one of several German intellectuals who experimented with mescaline, opium, and hashish in the years between the wars. His early participation in what became known as critical theory found him chasing a secular version of the intoxication of religious ecstasy, "a *profane illumination*," as he wrote in his essay on surrealism, "a materialistic, anthropological inspiration to which hashish, opium or whatever else can give an introductory lesson (but a dangerous one . . .)." Benjamin imagined revolution as a moment of shared intoxication, a modern expression of a wild and ancient energy, running through the proletariat. The German language gave Benjamin the benefit of the word *Rausch*, which does far more work than the English *trip* and suggests a passionate rush, a rapturous journey, an exhilarating trip. And this would be the rush of revolution, an injection of what Benjamin described as "the intoxication of cosmic experience" into the new consciousness of the revolutionary mass.

Benjamin was an early member of the Frankfurt School of critical thinkers, whose syntheses of Marx and Freud had an enormous influence on the theorists of the 1960s. He might have thought his dream was coming true with the events of Paris in 1968, when such moments of elation hit the streets and the slogans said it all: "Power to the imagination." The writing on the wall: "Take your desires for reality." The demand was for a revolution of everyday life: not only the state and the economy but thinking and perception, love and desire, art and design, space and time. "Run, comrades, the old world is behind you!" This intoxication may well have resonated with Baudelaire's illuminations and Rimbaud's disordering of the senses, but it lived independently of poets or drugs, running through the veins of a people linked by the euphoria of rebellion.

Benjamin's essay "Hashish in Marseilles" is suffused with Baudelaire's experience of hashish. Benjamin described the drug's "immense dimensions of inner experience, of absolute duration and immeasurable space," and the sense that a "wonderful, beatific humour dwells all the more fondly on the contingencies of time and space." Hashish gave Benjamin the feeling that the world of things and objects was not mute and inert but carried its own energy and liveliness. The drug made the dullest objects shine and gave Benjamin a sense of empathy, an affection for everything: "One becomes so tender, fears that a shadow falling on the paper might hurt it." He sat overlooking a square that seemed to have "a tendency to change with everyone who stepped on to it," as if the details of its architecture spoke to the people who traversed it. Benjamin left Marseilles convinced that the world of objects has memories, associations, a life of its own, an aura that hashish could render perceptible. The drug had made its point perfectly: hashish was a lump of psychoactive stuff, an object with its own unmistakable effects, a piece of material with something to say.

> And so, a piece of broken plaster, picked at random from the ruin of a building . . . for example . . . becomes under the eye of the hashish smoker the repository of an aesthetic secret just as vivid and individual as the secret in the sculptured grain of a

Japanese Netsuki, with its intricate carving out of some lustrous semi-precious metal.
Alexander Trocchi, "Trocchi on Drugs"

This notion of aura was probably Benjamin's most influential thought. "To perceive the aura of an object we look at," he wrote, "means to invest it with the ability to look at us in return." Hashish was one way of achieving this effect, but it was the work of art in which Benjamin invested his hopes for this sense of aura. The work of art returns the viewer's gaze when it evokes the same intimations of beauty, wonder, inner truth. Benjamin's fears that photography and film were stealing the authentic soul of the work of art, expressed in his famous essay "The Work of Art in the Age of Mechanical Reproduction," had an enduring impact on the work of the Frankfurt School and generations of later cultural theorists.

Baudelaire's delayed effect on the thinking and politics of the 1960s was one of many answers to the question Flaubert had posed to him as he railed against the effects of hashish, opium, *excesses*: "How do you know what will come of it all later?" In the wake of the events of 1968, a generation of philosophers—including Gilles Deleuze, Félix Guattari, and Michel Foucault—moved beyond the syntheses of Marx and Freud cultivated by the Frankfurt School. Critiques of alienation and repression, and all the old interests in authenticity and liberation, were now subsumed by an onslaught on modern culture that ran far beyond desires for "profane illumination" or attempts to "see the soul" in which both the political theorists and the psychedelic explorers of the 1960s had invested. Although Deleuze and Guattari took drugs in directions utterly distinct from those pursued by Benjamin, they, too, developed the notion that drugs could provide some "introductory lessons" in the achievement of extensive and enduring change. They had little interest in Benjamin's "anthropological" concerns: Deleuze and Guattari's work was instead a recognition that humanist investments in liberation were obstacles to more immediate experiments with the body and its organization, which is also to say the thinking mind and the categories of logic and morality with which it has been territorialized. If philosophy is concerned with ideas, this was not philosophy at all but experimentation, a pragmatic attempt to explore space and time stretched out on a plane that "knows nothing of differences of level, orders of magnitude, or distances. It knows nothing of the difference between the artificial and the natural," Deleuze and Guattari wrote in *A Thousand Plateaus*. "It knows nothing of the distinction between contents and expressions, or that between forms and formed substances." As Deleuze and Guattari developed their onslaught on modernity's categorized, classified world, with its oedipalized, well-organized individuals and its belief in the importance of its own ideas, it was modernity's long years of drug experimentation from which they drew some of their most incisive lines of thought.

Ghosts

As a young child, I wanted to be a writer because writers were rich and famous. They lounged around Singapore and Rangoon smoking Opium in a yellow pongee silk suit. They sniffed cocaine in Mayfair and they penetrated forbidden swamps with a faithful native boy and lived in the native quarter of Tangier smoking Hashish and languidly caressing a pet gazelle.

William Burroughs, "Literary Autobiography"

When Coleridge forgot the words to "Kubla Khan," he inspired generations of writers to experiment with drugs. And at the end of the 1970s, there was no shortage of writing on drugs for Deleuze and Guattari to read. But writing is a form of capture, and drugs are never easily tied down. "Opium enables one to give form to the unformed, it prevents, alas, the communication of this privilege to anyone else," wrote Jean Cocteau in *Opium*. Hashish made writing too much like hard work for Baudelaire: if the drug could inspire its users, they would still find themselves trapped in what he defined in *Les Paradis artificiels* as "a vicious circle. Let us grant for a moment that hashish gives, or at least augments, genius—they forget that it is in the nature of hashish to weaken the will; so that what hashish gives with one hand it takes away with the other . . . it gives power to the imagination and takes away the ability to profit by it." Worse still, the drug will always taunt its users with Baudelaire's daunting question: "What is the sense of working, tilling the soil, writing a book, fashioning anything whatsoever, when one has immediate access to paradise?" Aldous Huxley knew the problem well. "Though the intellect remains unimpaired and though perception is enormously improved," he wrote in *The Doors of Perception*, "the will suffers a profound change for the worse. The mescalin taker sees no reason for doing anything in particular and finds most of the causes for which, at ordinary times, he was prepared to act and suffer, profoundly uninteresting. He can't be bothered with them, for the good reason that he has better things to think about."

> Reading what I have written, now, then, I have a familiar feeling that everything I say is somehow beside the point. I am of course incapable of sustaining a simple narrative . . . with no fixed valid categories . . . not so much a line of thought as an area of experience . . . the immediate broth; I am left with a coherence of posture[s].
>
> Alexander Trocchi, "Trocchi on Drugs"

All writing is addiction, and all writers are hooked. "Stories are my refuge," wrote Robert Louis Stevenson. "I take them like opium." Even the most straight and sober of writers know what it is to find themselves entranced, possessed, suspended, and abandoned in the worlds their words assemble on the page. Drink talks easily, as Baudelaire observed. But drugs and written words are matters of profound, sometimes isolating, solitude, the stuff of very private investigations that are never easily shared. Drugs take writers to extremes with which they are all too familiar: sentenced to find words for what seem to be intensely subjective and wordless worlds, weary and frustrated by the inexpressible, condemned to claustrophobic panic when the words run dry, and yet endlessly compelled to try, hunting through the bookshelves and the streets in a desperate search for inspiration, stimulation, any kind of fix.

> The addict feels better if he knows that some alien substance is coursing through his blood stream.
> William Burroughs, *Naked Lunch*

Give these writers drugs, and all the lines connect. Not necessarily with any great success: too much excitement and the words run fast and loose, the thoughts can't be contained, the ideas dissipate. Characters and authors lose their plots. Words break down, letters flicker on the screen, theories decompose, notes trip each other up, plans are trodden. "Under hashish it can sometimes be difficult to sustain a thought," wrote Alexander Trocchi. "The mind can be like a grasshopper." And hashish took him wandering "like a sleepwalker, into many pastures . . . all experimental, all hypothetical, and at times, when one is most intensely under its influence, one can explore a sense of panic, confronted by the absurdity of every alternative." Fitz Hugh Ludlow's pen "glanced presently like lightning in the effort to keep neck and neck with my ideas," and eventually his "thought ran with such terrific speed that I could no longer write at all."

> The whole thing was . . . *the experience* . . . this certain indescribable *feeling* . . . Indescribable because words can only jog the memory, and there is no memory of . . . *The experience* of the barrier between the subjective and the objective, the personal and impersonal, the *I* and the *not-I* disappearing . . . that feeling!
>
> Tom Wolfe, *The Electric Kool-Aid Acid Test*

And yet they all kept trying, and they still do: Jean Cocteau, Antonin Artaud, Henri Michaux, Alexander Trocchi, William Burroughs . . . Coleridge had written a preface for them all. Not that they were equally impressed by him. Artaud's conception of theater as a shamanic adventure, a theater of cruelty, owes everything to his suspension of disbelief, but "Coleridge was a weakling," declared Artaud. "He got scared." The "crime of the ancient mariner is that of Coleridge himself," not because he turned to opium as a means of intensifying or exploring but because he used it as a means of escaping what for Artaud were the horrors of reality. For this, Artaud despised him with a vengeance:

> For not having been believed when he came bearing the gift of his insane mucus, Gérard de Nerval hanged himself from a streetlamp; and for not having been able to adapt himself to his mucus, the Count de Lautréamont died of fury; and in the face of all this, what did Samuel Taylor Coleridge do? He transformed the mucus that was taken from him into opium, and so he took laudanum till the day he died.

Coleridge had turned his back on the true darkness of reality, assuming the role of a guilt-ridden priest who "ended up forgetting everything," so that he could tell his pretty tales of Xanadu. Coleridge protected his own interests, his own life; he didn't sacrifice himself for poetry but kept himself alive at its cost. Was there an alternative? Artaud thought so, even when his own writing dived into depths of incommunicable madness. Better to write howls and numbers than sing of maidens in paradise.

> No doubt I shall go on writing, stumbling across tundras of unmeaning, planting words like bloody flags in my wake.
>
> Alexander Trocchi, *Cain's Book*

All these writers find themselves used, sometimes used up by their drugs, driven to distraction, crazy by their dreams, endlessly rehearsing the same lamentations of weakness and despair, joining in the same predictable chorus of confession and regret. "I have cultivated my hysteria with delight and terror," wrote Baudelaire in "My Heart Laid Bare," before he woke up to "the morrow! The terrible morrow!"

"Thus there is a confederacy amongst users," wrote Trocchi in *Cain's Book*, "loose, hysterical, traitorous, unstable, a tolerance that comes from the knowledge that it is very possible to arrive at the point where it is necessary to lie and cheat and steal, even from the friend who gave one one's last fix." Never trust a junkie, as even junkies say. This perverse alliance, a dishonor among thieves, forms a link between opiated writers that has extended across time and space: Coleridge, Collins, Poe . . . all of them chasing their own and each other's dragons, as if they were compelled to repeat the same compulsion to repeat, making the journey over and again through scenes already played out in advance. Writing on drugs has evolved and mutated like a contagion, each writer reading the others' work, repeating their adventures, and also their mistakes, endlessly rehearsing the same refrain. The same old story, time and again. "I have done it hundreds of thousands of times in this room," says John Jasper in *The Mystery of Edwin Drood*, "hundreds of thousands of times. What do I say? I did it millions and billions of times. I did it so often, and through such vast expanses of time, that when it was really done it seemed not worth the doing, it was done so soon." Coleridge, De Quincey, Baudelaire . . . until Burroughs finally realizes the eternal loop they are all on: "I am not an addict, I am *the* addict."

> Certain organisms are born to become prey to drugs. They demand a corrective, without which they can have no contact with the outside world. They float. They vegetate in the half-light. The world remains unreal, until some substance has given it body.
>
> Jean Cocteau, *Opium*

Opium had set these scenes, but they were to repeat themselves with many other drugs. *A Scanner Darkly* ends with a shocking list of Philip K. Dick's own dead or injured speeding friends:

> They were like children playing in the street. They could see one after the other of them being killed—run over, maimed, destroyed—but they continued to play anyhow. We really all were very happy for a while, sitting around not toiling but just bullshitting and playing, but it was for such a terribly brief time, and then the punishment was beyond belief: even when we could see it, we could not believe it.

The same story, time and again. In *A Thousand Plateaus*, drug users are "considered as precursors or experimenters who tirelessly blaze new paths of life" but always run to the same dead ends: "They either join the legion of false heroes who follow the conformist path of a little death and a long fatigue. Or, what is worse, all they will have done is make an attempt only non-users or former users can resume and benefit from, secondarily rectifying the always aborted plane of drugs, discovering through drugs what drugs lack." In this sense, drugs can demonstrate nothing more than their own ineffectiveness, continually forcing their users to "fall back into what they wanted to escape."

Deleuze and Guattari repeatedly warn of "the dangers of a too-sudden, careless destratification" of the organized body and its ordered thoughts. *Caution*, "the art of dosages," is the word of the day. Take a dose of care with everything: "You have to keep enough of the organism for it to re-form each dawn." It becomes a matter of losing, and keeping, control, perhaps, sometimes, to just the right degree. This is Arthur Rimbaud's intoxicated quest for a *"rational* derangement of the senses," Coleridge's desire to *"choose* to be deceived," and Poe's attempt to walk the fine line between fact and fantasy, truth and lies, fact and fiction, reality and make-believe. Many of these writers found themselves trapped in Nietzsche's double bind: "You can have the choice: either *as little pain as possible,* in short painlessness," he wrote in *The Gay Science,* "or *as much pain as possible* as the price of an abundance of subtle joys and pleasures hitherto rarely tasted!" But there are always alternatives, the chance of a third option that cuts straight through this double bind. Poised on the border, addiction is not the only repetition that lies in wait for the writer on drugs. There are other patterns and recurring themes, calls that echo through the work of them all.

> On both sides of the wound, we invariably find that the schism has already happened (and that it had already taken place, and that it had already happened that it had already taken place) and that it will happen again (and in the future, it will happen again): it is less a cut than a constant fibrillation. What repeats itself is time.
>
> Michel Foucault, "Theatrum Philosophicum"

"And now, in another life," wrote Ludlow,

I remembered that far back in the cycles I had looked at my watch to measure the time through which I had passed. The impulse seized me to look again. The minute-hand stood halfway between fifteen and sixteen minutes past eleven. The watch must have stopped; I held it to my ear; no, it was still going. I had travelled through all that immeasurable chain of dreams in thirty seconds. "My God!" I cried, "I am in eternity."

Cocteau "used to sleep interminable sleeps lasting half a second," and De Quincey "sometimes seemed to have lived for 70 or 100 years in one night; nay, sometimes had feelings representative of a millennium passed in that time, or, however, of a duration far beyond the limits of any human experience."

And it was De Quincey's Dark Interpreter who told him just

how narrow, how incalculably narrow is the true and actual present. Of that time which we call the present, hardly a hundredth part but belongs either to a past which has fled, or to a future which is still on the wing. It has perished, or it is not born. It was, or it is not. Yet even this approximation to the truth is infinitely false. For again subdivide that solitary drop, which only was found to represent the present, into a lower series of similar fractions, and the actual present which you arrest measures now but the thirty-sixth millionth of an hour . . .

Modern, historical time is linear and inevitably proves fatal to the rite; the past is irreversible and will never return. The ultimate meaning of the use of drugs in our time is thus clearer now: it is a criticism of linear time and a nostalgia for (or a presentiment of) another sort of time.

Octavio Paz, *Alternating Current*

Tripping at six o'clock: "A significant improvement," wrote Michaux in *Infinite Turbulence* after several hours of acceleration. "A relative but definitive slackening of speed. I still advance at the speed of hundreds of (conscious) moments a minute." But this was easier to bear than the extremities of "speeds and slownesses without form, without subject, without a face" he had encountered on other trips. Mescaline, he wrote, "is accelerative, repetitive, agitating, accentuator, overthrower of all reverie, interrupter. Demonstration of the discontinuous." Even the speeds themselves are continually shifting, discontinuous, uneven, "as though under the effect of an unexpected gear-shift or of a chain reaction." Runaway velocities are marked by interruption and disturbance, "extreme acceleration, the speeding-up of released arrows"; movements that, "however rapid and extraordinarily speeded-up they may be, must periodically be interrupted, must cease and come to a complete halt, in order to suddenly set off again." And if once "you were unaware of such turbulence" and "all was apparently immobile," now infinite turbulence is inescapable. And after "eight hours, that is to say a century," with mescaline, the fabric of the time continuum is never quite the same. Even when the world settled down again, Michaux couldn't stop "thinking, thinking, these variations, these variations of intensity, of speed, these variations."

Michaux described the "streaming that went through me" as "something so immense, unforgettable, unique, that I thought, that I did not stop thinking: 'In the state I'm in, a mountain, for all its unintelligence, a mountain with its waterfalls, its ravines, its runoff slopes, would be better able to understand me than a man.'" One mescaline encounter was, he wrote, "so absolutely horrible, horrible in its essence, I can't find any way of saying it and I feel like a counterfeiter when I try."

If Michaux felt like a counterfeiter when he tried to write on mescaline, writers on drugs are never far away from the fear of being read as counterfeiters, too. When Carlos Castaneda's stories of shamanic adventure with his guide Don Juan were exposed as fictions long after they appeared as matters of anthropological fact, the air of dispute and disrepute surrounding all these writers was magnified. Even Michaux, one of the most fearless of the twentieth century's writers on drugs, made some efforts to cover his tracks and assure his readers of his sobriety. "Those who go in for unified explanations may be tempted to judge all my writings as the work of a drug addict from now on," he wrote at the end of *Miserable Miracle,* insisting that he was "more the water-drinking type. Never alcohol. No stimulants, and for years no coffee, no tobacco, no tea. From time to time wine, and very little of that. All my life, very little of everything people take. Take and abstain. Abstain, above all. Fatigue is my drug, as a matter of fact." Lacing these words with irony, he added, "I was forgetting: twenty-five years ago or more, I must have tried ether seven or eight times at the most, laudanum once, and twice alcohol (frightful)." The illegality of drugs demands such reticence, but this is only the most prosaic of the many problems such writers face. Drugs inspire profound, sometimes debilitating, fears of losing face, authority, respectability. Even the nineteenth century's most outspoken writer "hesitated about the propriety of allowing this, or any part of my narrative, to come before the public eye, until after my death." On the first page of *Confessions of an English Opium-Eater,* De Quincey has this to confess: "It is not without an anxious review of the reasons, for and against this step, that I have, at last, concluded on taking it."

When Coleridge's "Kubla Khan," Shelley's *Frankenstein,* and Robert Louis Stevenson's *Strange Case of Dr. Jekyll and Mr. Hyde* were published as transcripts of their dreams, did this make their writers into authors or transcribers, perhaps even fraudsters or plagiarists, misrepresented as the authors of their work? Were they simply sidestepping their responsibilities, as if to make themselves unaccountable for the work they had produced? Don't blame me, blame the dreams, the drugs, the little people, the Dark Interpreters: *"They* wheeled in mazes; *I* spelled the steps," wrote De Quincey of his three Sorrows. *"Theirs* were the symbols,—*mine* are the words." All he did was write them down.

All writers on drugs become ghostwriters for their drugs. Or perhaps their drugs are ghostwriting them. "The days glide by strung on a syringe with a long thread of blood," wrote Burroughs in *Naked Lunch*: "I am forgetting sex and all sharp pleasures of the body—a grey, junk-bound ghost. The Spanish boys call me El Hombre Invisible—the Invisible Man."

Even the most eloquent writers have found themselves writing out of character on drugs. On LSD, Anaïs Nin encountered "another Anaïs, not the one which was lying down weeping, but a small, gay, light Anaïs, very lively, very restless and mobile." The old Anaïs thought she "could capture the secret of life because the secret of life was metamorphosis and transmutation," but this other Anaïs knew that

it happened too quickly and was beyond words. Comic spirit of Anaïs mocks words and herself. Ah I cannot capture the secret of life with WORDS.

Sadness.

The secret of life was BREATH. That was what I always wanted words to do, to BREATHE. Comic spirit of Anaïs rises, shakes herself with her cape, gaily, irresponsibly, surrenders the abstruse difficulties. NOW I KNOW WHY THE FAIRY TALES ARE FULL OF JEWELS.

Such multiplicity makes a mockery of modern attachments to the authority of authors and their texts. Shamanic cultures that use psychoactive drugs are far more familiar with the notion that the substances have more to say than their users. Some Siberian peoples believe that fly agarics constitute a separate tribe, whose members guide humans through the worlds of the future and the past and teach them new languages, stories, and songs. "Fly agaric men" and "amanita girls" figure in many historical and contemporary accounts of their use. Psilocybin mushrooms have this same sense of personality, and all the tryptamines introduce the elfin, cartoon characters described as "the machine elves of cyberspace" by Terence McKenna, who has published a number of influential discussions of DMT and its relatives. As well as giving their users messages, ayahuasca, peyote, and psilocybin mushrooms are all said to call their hunters to the places where they grow. In *Psychedelics Encyclopedia,* Heinz Kusel reported that "a Campa Indian in my boat, when we were drifting far from shore, was 'called' by ayahuasca, followed the 'call,' and later emerged from the forest with a sampling of the fairly rare liana that today is cultivated by the ayahuasquero in secret spots."

Hallucinogens are not the only drugs with attitude. Cocaine introduces its own powerful sense of duplicity and multiplicity, as both Freud and Stevenson discovered. "Opium, not the Opium-Eater, is the hero" of De Quincey's tale, and the hero in a thousand other guises too: "my only friend," said Wilkie Collins as "another Wilkie Collins" worked with him through the night. "It's my life, it's my wife," sang Lou Reed as he spent another perfect day with heroin. And Burroughs often had occasion to remember "my old friend, Opium Jones." In *The Job,* he recalls:

> We were mighty close in Tangier 1957, shooting every hour fifteen grains of methadone per day . . . I never changed my clothes. Jones liked his clothes to season in stale rooming-house flesh until you can tell by a hat on the table a coat hung over a chair that Jones lives there. I never took a bath. Old Jones didn't like the feel of water on his skin. I spent whole days looking at the end of my shoe just communing with Jones. Then one day I saw that Jones was not a real friend that our interests were in fact divergent.

The morning went by in a blur, but at one point he was vaguely aware of being surrounded by soldiers and policemen in the Indian's hut. Jack panicked, thoughts of Burroughs and filthy Mexican jails came to his mind, but the police only wanted some of his marijuana.

Ann Charters on Jack Kerouac

Thoughts of Burroughs, sick of heroin by the time he finished writing *Junkie*: "I am ready to move on south and look for the uncut kick that opens out instead of narrowing down like junk." Burroughs found his uncut kick not with peyote but with ayahuasca, yage, in Mexico. "Images fall slow and silent like snow . . . Serenity . . . All defences fall . . . everything is free to enter or to go out . . . Fear is simply impossible . . . A beautiful blue substance flows into me." In a passage of his letters on yage that later found its way into *Naked Lunch*, he wrote, "Yage is space-time travel . . . The room seems to shake and vibrate with motion . . . The blood and substance of many races, Negro, Polynesian, Mountain Mongol, Desert Nomad, Polyglot Near East, Indian—new races as yet unconceived and unborn pass through the body . . . Migrations, incredible journeys through deserts and jungles and mountains."

Burroughs's yage experience was to color his writing as much as, if not more than, his use of heroin. The Composite City he had seen on yage became Interzone, "with its glut of nylon shirts, cameras, watches, sex and opiates sold across the counter," the tangled urban space that sprawls through nearly all his books. It was a city "where all human potentials are spread out in a vast silent market," a world of "combinations not yet realized," a city filled with "a haze of opium, hashish, the resinous red smoke of Yage, smell of the jungle and salt water and the rotting river and dried excrement and sweat and genitals." Yage had shown him a world of "combinations not yet realized," followers "of obsolete unthinkable trades doodling in Etruscan, addicts of drugs not yet synthesized."

As yet unborn; still to be realized; not yet synthesized: yage seemed to let the future flood into its past, taking Burroughs ahead of himself but also elsewhere, as if off the time tracks altogether, to a "place where the unknown past and the mergent future meet in a vibrating soundless hum . . . Larval Entities waiting for a Live One . . ."

> Through hashish I have been able to live in an absolutely poly-relational present: all relations in this state are tentative, hypothetical . . . no certainty beyond the sudden utter certainty of the moment is imaginable. The state of mind, too, can be a critical one; razor-like, one finds oneself sensitive to the slightest equivocation in a man's demeanour.
> Alexander Trocchi, "Trocchi on Drugs"

Burroughs's *Interzone* is spaced-out on hashish as well: "Fights start, stop, people walk around, play cards, smoke *Kief*, all in a vast, timeless dream." Yage was far more intense, but hashish took Burroughs to this same untimely multidimensional space: "Hashish affects the sense of time so that events, instead of appearing in an orderly structure of past, present and future, take on a simultaneous quality, the past and future contained in the present the moment." Hashish allowed Trocchi "to live in an absolute poly-relational present: all relations in this state are tentative, hypothetical . . ." Burroughs heard all these qualities in Arab music, which "has neither beginning nor end. It is timeless. Heard for the first time, it may appear meaningless to a Westerner, because he is listening for a time structure that isn't there." And he found them in the cities of the hashish-smoking world: "Tangier seems to exist on several dimensions. You are always finding streets, squares, parks you never saw before."

But once you've seen the world laid out, the naked lunch, the soft machine, the future and the past converge in front of you, what do you do with such material? Burroughs's multidimensional spaces and times could hardly be fashioned into straightforward narratives. Hashish demanded novel kinds of writing, not lyrical ballads or melodic story lines but some written match for Arab music, a city like Tangier, an interzone like Interzone.

> That night I had a vivid dream in colour of the green jungle and a red sunset I had seen during the afternoon. A composite city familiar to me but I could not quite place it. Part New York, part Mexico City and part Lima which I had not seen at this time. I was standing on a corner by a wide street with cars going by and a vast open park down the street in the distance. I can not say whether these dreams had any connection with Yage. Incidentally you are supposed to see a city when you take Yage.

And with the "blood and substance of many races" running through his veins, who would be writing such a story anyway? Who is Burroughs when he writes on drugs? What happens to the author as the drugs take effect?

> I'm a martyr to this fucking typewriter—a man as basically unmechanical as I am should never buy used machinery—but before I'll ask help from the Commander I'll write with blood and a hypodermic needle.
>
> William Burroughs, *Interzone*

Someone threw Burroughs a solution: "What to do with all this?" asked Brion Gysin: "Stick it on the wall along with the photographs and see what it looks like. Here, just stick these two pages together and cut it down the middle. Stick it all together, end to end, and send it back like a big roll of music for a pianola. It's just material, after all. There is nothing sacred about words." Encouraged by his ally Gysin, who was convinced that writing was "fifty years behind painting," Burroughs did just this, cutting and folding his writing into arrangements that escaped his authority. Poets, wrote Gysin, "are supposed to liberate the words—not to chain them in phrases. Who told poets they were supposed to think? Poets are meant to sing and to make words sing. Poets have no words 'of their very own.' Writers don't use their own words. Since when do words belong to anybody. 'Your very own words.' Indeed! And who are you?" Cut this up, and this is what he learns: "And words not to chain. Posed to liberate the supposed to think? Told poets they were Poets to make words own their words. Very own. Writers' 'very own words' belong to anybody. You and you."

"You'll soon see," said Gysin, "that words don't belong to anyone. Words have a vitality of their own and you or anybody can make them gush into action." Burroughs agreed. "You can't call *me* the author of those poems, now, can you? I merely undid the word combination, like the letter lock on a piece of good luggage, and the poem made itself."

"I am acting as a map maker, an explorer . . . and I see no point in exploring areas that have already been thoroughly surveyed." Burroughs becomes an element of what he defined in *The Third Mind* as the "Burroughs machine, systematic and repetitive, simultaneously disconnecting and reconnecting—it disconnects the concept of reality that has been imposed on us and then plugs normally dissociated zones into the same sector—eventually escapes from the control of its manipulator; it does so in that it makes it possible to lay down the foundation of an unlimited number of books that end by reproducing themselves." The writing machine assembles itself, and new sectors are added to interzone. This attempt to get beyond a writing that simply records, reports, and represents heads, with Deleuze and Guattari, to a point at which there "is no difference between what a book talks about and how it is made." Poe wrote backward, from effect to cause; Michaux abandoned grammar; Artaud abandoned words; Burroughs cut them up and folded them away. Cocteau kept a diary but used it to say, "One must at all costs cure oneself of the tire-some habit of writing. The only possible style is thought made flesh. Read official reports, the writing of mathematicians, surveyors." Ada Lovelace wrote in the machine code of her "opium system," but that's another story, of a kind.

> The ideal for a book would be to lay everything out on a plane of exteriority of this kind, on a single page, the same sheet: lived events, historical deter-minations, concepts, individuals, groups, social for-mations.
>
> Gilles Deleuze and Félix Guattari, *A Thousand Plateaus*

If Michaux was no stranger to the profound sense of isolation that awaited him when he failed to articulate such fine-tuned perceptions, he was also one of the most determined and per-sistent of them all. Even when it seemed impossible to capture its atmosphere and describe its effects, Michaux kept trying, taking every chance and grabbing at anything that might al-low him to communicate his moments with mescaline. For years, he let it take him to a turbulent, molecular zone of speeds and vibrations, a dimension of everything in general and nothing in particular from which he tried to broadcast to the world. Sometimes his impatience with poetry comes through in his rejections of elegance and style—an exception-ally brave move to make in French. When he tried to express the magnitude and multiplicity of one experience, he wrote, "As if there was an opening, an opening like a gathering to-gether, like a world, where something can happen, many things can happen, where there's a whole lot, there's a swarm of possibilities, where everything tingles with possibilities."

Frustrated by the demands and limitations of the written word, Michaux sometimes turned to painting and drawing. His mescaline paintings are among his most powerful expres-sions of the drug's effects, and the original text of *Miserable Miracle* was "easier to feel than to read, as much drawn as written" before it was cleaned up for publication. Even when he stuck to words, Michaux found himself moving far beyond the conventions of poetry and prose: "Quickly thrown out, in jerks, in and across the page, interrupted sentences—their syllables flying, shredded, torn apart—would go charging, diving, dying." To challenge the rules of syntax and grammar is brave in any language. It is even more audacious to do it in French, a highly structured language that tends not to lend itself to such extravagant experiments. Michaux also wrote with little regard for those elements of French literary culture that place great emphasis on language as a privileged thing in itself. He was interested in the written word only insofar as he could use it to demonstrate, rather than describe.

Michaux's words were devices and techniques for extending and exploring the worlds opened up by his drugs. "Perhaps Michaux has never tried to express anything," wrote Octavio Paz. "All his efforts have been directed at reaching that zone, by definition indescribable and incommunicable, in which meanings disappear. A centre at once completely empty and completely full, a total vacuum and a total plenitude." Mescaline took Michaux to "a space of countless points" in which his thinking could run at "full speed, in all directions, into the memory, into the future, into the data of the present, to grasp the unexpected, luminous, stupefying connections." Time lengthened and shortened, stretched and compressed, sped up, slowed down, and sometimes stole away, running off into spatiality. Michaux was convinced that his drug-induced experience was more than a matter of "mere hallucination." And his writing was not just an attempt to get his adventures onto the page: he was not a correspondent, like Baudelaire, but an engineer after Coleridge and Poe. Writing was his way of continuing to open mescaline's "virtual space in the image of reality." He was always trying to add to the effects of his drugs, to continue the experiments they kicked off in his mind. "Hashish doesn't just make pictures. It commits acts," he wrote. "Mescaline never imitates nature. It is not familiar with nature. It engineers its own compositions."

Michaux took all his drugs as journeys, voyages through virtual dimensions with their own cartographies. "In the grasp of that afternoon," he wrote in *By Surprise,* "I had received the great gift of another world. I had landed there and it had enveloped me, it had included me. *Terra incognita.*" Like many explorers of these regions, he was a great traveler around the world as well, taking trips to Ecuador and many other parts of Central and South America, fusing his real journeys with his voyages to the unknown lands of mescaline. Although De Quincey's horror of life beyond his shores had confined him to England, his journeys through opiated space were often walks through London, wanderings in which he lost his sense of time and found himself in "such knotty problems of alleys, such enigmatic entries, and such sphynx's riddles of streets without thoroughfares, as must, I conceive, baffle the audacity of porters," he wrote in *Confessions of an English Opium-Eater.* "I could almost have believed, at times, that I must be the first discoverer of some of these *terra incognita.*" Flaubert, Nerval, Gautier, and Baudelaire traveled in the world they called the Orient, and Baudelaire's hashish-induced meanderings through Paris gave modernity its first flaneur. Artaud roused himself from European narcosis and traveled to Mexico, where he took peyote with the Tarahumara Indians in the 1930s; Burroughs followed in his tracks and also wandered off to North Africa; the 1960s "hippie trail" terminated in Goa and Kathmandu. All these trips—on drugs, in search of drugs, instead of drugs—converge with the notion of psychogeography developed by the situationists, with whom Trocchi worked for a brief period in the 1960s. Today's psychedelic explorers follow Hofmann, the Wassons, and the CIA to Central America in search of the cultures and the plants in which the tryptamines and their relatives occur.

All these explorations can easily tip back into elitist, purist, even old colonial desires. Both De Quincey and Cocteau wanted to distinguish their use of opium from the experiences of those they disdainfully called amateurs, and, just as many travelers refuse to see themselves as tourists, there are still drug explorers who elevate themselves above day-trippers with return tickets. But the most recreational drug users can be profoundly affected by their Friday-night adventures, just as package vacations can sometimes change lives. Like all journeys, drugs can override the motives and intentions with which they are begun.

And many of them come with instructions of their own. EAT ME, says the piece of cake to Alice. When Michaux took mescaline, he swallowed its advice as well. "It is," he wrote, "an exploration. Through words, signs, sketches. Mescaline is the explored." Or was this a case, asked Octavio Paz, of "the poet Michaux explored by mescaline?" He certainly experienced mescaline as a "reversal of power," after which it is "the turn of ideas, images and impulses to have force and power over him, to hold him in their grip, to modify him." His sense of self-control, his autonomy, was lost. His ideas were no longer his own, and the 'Self, the arbiter, the controller, the master of ideas, he who habitually decides and commands, is powerless."

When he forgets himself to this extent, he goes to pieces, breaks down, falls to bits: "The subject, divided, also feels multiplied. He is at a crossroads where a hundred savage currents intersect, he is pulled at in opposing directions, in lightning states of alienation." Michaux never lost this sense of multiplicity. "There isn't one me," he once wrote. "There aren't ten me's. There is no me. ME is only a position of equilibrium. An average of 'me's,' a movement in the crowd."

> "Who are you?" said the Caterpillar.
> This was not an opening for a conversation. Alice replied, rather shyly, "I—I hardly know, sir, just at present—at least I know who I was when I got up

this morning, but I think I must have been changed several times since then."

"What do you mean by that?" said the Caterpillar sternly. "Explain yourself!"

"I can't explain myself, I am afraid, sir," said Alice, "because I'm not myself, you see."

"I don't see," said the Caterpillar.

Lewis Carroll, *Alice in Wonderland*

With so many questions about who is writing what and whether it is possible to write at all, it is hardly surprising that the history of writing on drugs is littered with abandoned projects and incomplete reports. Walter Benjamin had high hopes of writing on the drugs he used, not just hashish, but as Gershom Scholem wrote, "A book on this subject was among his projects that remained unfinished. Naturally he did not want to content himself with the notes and descriptions that have been preserved but wished to probe the philosophical relevance of such perceptions from an altered state of consciousness, which he regarded as more than mere hallucination." Even the prosaic attempt simply to report on the histories and effects of drugs plunges writers straight into a hallucinatory world where nothing is quite as it seems. 'So far as my 'studies' are concerned," wrote Ernst Jünger in a 1940s letter to Albert Hofmann, "I had a manuscript on that topic, but have since burned it. My excursions terminated with hashish, that led to very pleasant, but also to manic states, to oriental tyranny . . ." In the 1960s, Alexander Trocchi made plans for a book called *Drugs of the Mind*. It, too, failed to see the light of day. Deadlines passed, contracts lapsed, and, by the early 1970s, Trocchi had abandoned the idea. As Andrew Wilson wrote when introducing Trocchi's notes for this work, it is "perhaps unsurprising that the book was never published." The project was ambitious, and, to its author, the "idea of a finished text or object was anathema; perhaps *Drugs of the Mind* could only have existed in Inner Space."

But Baudelaire's insistence that "what hashish gives with one hand it takes away with the other" was turned around by many later writers on drugs. "It has been my experience," wrote Jünger to Hofmann, "that creative achievement requires an alert consciousness, and that it diminishes under the spell of drugs. On the other hand," he added, "conceptualization is important, and one gains insights under the influence of drugs that indeed are not possible otherwise." Opium, wrote Trocchi, "is a very neutral drug; beyond the delightful sense of relaxation it can impose on the user, the ecstatic intensity in *being*, and the resultant cool, it opens no doors, neither into heaven or hell." It put everything in abeyance, left the "perennial in parenthesis," and made him "able to sustain a flow. That I should need heroin is possibly a weakness, but then it was not I who boasted of being strong." Jünger burned one manuscript, but after many years he did publish an analysis of drugs, as well as *Heliopolis: Rückblick auf eine Stadt* (Heliopolis: Retrospective on a city), which relates the adventures of Antonio Peri, a drug researcher who spins off from Flaubert's St. Anthony and is described by Jünger as "a purely sedentary man, who explores the archipelagos beyond the navigable seas, for which he uses drugs as a vehicle. I give extracts from his log book. Certainly, I cannot allow this Columbus of the inner globe to end well—he dies of a poisoning. *Avis au lecteur.*" But he has some great adventures on the way.

> He captured dreams, just like others appear to chase after butterflies with nets. He did not travel to the islands on Sundays and holidays and did not frequent the taverns on Pagos beach. He locked himself up in his studio for trips into the dreamy regions. He said that all countries and unknown islands were woven into the tapestry. The drugs served him as keys to entry into the chambers and caves of this world. In the course of the years he had gained great knowledge, and he kept a log book of his excursions. A small library adjoined this studio, consisting

partly of herbals and medicinal reports, partly of works by poets and magicians. Antonio tended to read there while the effect of the drug itself developed . . . He went on voyages of discovery in the universe of his brain.

"We have been aided, inspired, multiplied," wrote Deleuze and Guattari at the beginning of *A Thousand Plateaus*. "We had hallucinatory experiences, we watched lines leave one plateau and proceed to another like columns of tiny ants." This is how the plateaus of their book composed themselves as they tried to make their writing a matter of "surveying, mapping even, realms that are yet to come." When Deleuze and Guattari took Carlos Castaneda's shamanic journeys with his guide Don Juan, they took his books as neither fact nor fiction but in their own pragmatic terms: "So much the better if the books are a syncretism rather than an ethnographical study, and the protocol of an experiment rather than an account of an initiation." Whether fictional or real, Don Juan had guided Castaneda to the point at which "experimentation has replaced interpretation, for which it has no use."

And yet Deleuze still feared the charge of inauthenticity, artifice, fraudulence, irresponsibility. "What will people think of us?" he asked when Michel Foucault published some remarks on opium and LSD in a 1970 essay on Deleuze's *Logic of Sense*. Drugs take all authority away, and even more than poets, professors of philosophy were supposed to be straight, not endlessly repeating the same mistake: "always to start over again from ground zero, either going on the drug again or quitting, when what they should do is make it a stopover," a way station on another trip to the point at which " 'to get high or not to get high' is no longer the question, but rather whether drugs have sufficiently changed the general conditions of space and time perception so that non-users can succeed in passing through the holes in the world and following the lines of flight at the very place where means other than drugs become necessary." But Deleuze and Guattari's book looked

back on the history of writing on drugs and saw a discontinuous program of research that "has left its mark on everyone,
even non-users." Antonin Artaud, they wrote, might not have
succeeded for himself, but "it is certain that through him
something has succeeded for us all." Even the most sober individual lives in a world in which drugs have already had
profound effects.

Undaunted by Deleuze's reservations, and the countless
failures that preceded him, Foucault raised the possibility of
writing "a study of the culture of drugs or drugs as culture in
the West from the beginning of the nineteenth century. No
doubt it started much earlier," he said in an interview with
Charles Raus, "but it would come up to the present, it's so
closely tied to the artistic life of the West." Foucault died in
1984, just two years after these comments had been made and
before he had a chance to start his research. The world lost
out, and so did he. A book on drugs would have made the
perfect complement to his existing portfolio of research on
madness, disease, crime, and sexuality, and it is easy to imagine the enthusiasm with which he would have embarked on
this research. The tangled and evasive history of drugs, their
effects and their side effects on the modern world—all this
would have allowed him to explore many of his favorite
philosophical themes and historical issues. Although he
hardly needed an excuse, a book on drugs would have also
given him a chance to indulge far more than his academic interests: "I don't know if he injected," said Daniel Defert, but
his drugs were "stronger than mere alcohol or hashish."

Perhaps Foucault was always writing on drugs and didn't
need to write the book at all. The figure of the addict walks
silently through the corridors of his hospitals, his asylums,
and his prison cells, and drugs are implicit in all his work,
bound up with his studies of medicine, psychiatry, and the
penal code, his studies of the shifting definitions and treat-
ments of sickness, insanity, and crime. The use and control of
drugs take Foucault's overriding theme—the deployment of

the body as an instrument of power, resistance, and experiment, and the continually shifting distinctions between its proper and improper uses, the activities sanctioned by its culture and those defined as illegitimate—to some of its most intimate and substantial extremes. If all his studies deal with material histories of the body, drugs are the point at which they converge.

> One might trace the history of the limits, of those obscure actions, necessarily forgotten as soon as they are performed, whereby a civilization casts aside something it regards as alien. Throughout its history, this moat which it digs around itself, this no man's land by which it preserves its isolation, is just as characteristic as its positive values.
>
> Michel Foucault, *Madness and Civilization*

Although Foucault's last work was centered on sexuality, one of its aims was to escape the psychoanalytic insistence that sex is the point of everything, the ultimate pleasure and the most secret self, the true source of one's identity, and, for the late twentieth century, something repressed that must be freed again. Foucault was convinced that the modern world had been duped by Freudian beliefs in repression and post-Freudian beliefs in the liberation of desire. And although his *History of Sexuality* is full of prohibitions and repressions, ways of "saying no to all wayward or unproductive sexualities," he was convinced that sex had always been surrounded by rules and laws that have worked "as mechanisms with a double impetus." The identification of the male homosexual at the end of the nineteenth century was a repression of sorts, but it was also one that produced what has now become a wild world of clubs, bars, fetishes, identities, and trends; highly sophisticated and heterogeneous sexes and sexualities: "Pleasure and power do not cancel or turn back against one another; they seek out, overlap, and reinforce one another.

They are linked together by complex mechanisms and devices of excitement and incitement." The laws and rules are "not boundaries not to be crossed, but *perpetual spirals of power and pleasure.*"

Foucault's critique of sexuality does not map precisely onto the drug world, but there are some striking parallels. Even when De Quincey made a career of his opium eating, taking drugs was still perceived as an activity, not a lifestyle or an identity, and although it might be possible to define him retrospectively as an addict, there was no such role to play in his day: not until the late nineteenth century did the addict emerge as a new identity, an individuated outsider born at the same time as the homosexual, both of them figments of a modern imagination that needed to define its own normality, drawing the boundaries around the upright, productive, and reproductive members of twentieth-century society. Just as cocaine was removed to make Coca-Cola a new kind of real thing, so the addict was removed from the social body to assure the non-using population of its own free agency.

> Opium desocializes us and removes us from the community. Further, the community takes its revenge. The persecution of opium addicts is an instinctive defence by society against an antisocial gesture.
>
> Jean Cocteau, *Opium*

Burroughs: not a man, but a soft machine, writing both *Junkie* and *Queer* in a twentieth century through which homosexuality and addiction have stalked each other, finding a tragic connection with the spread of HIV in the last twenty years of the century. Foucault's death, itself set in motion by some exchange of infected bodily fluids, connected him with the fatal network that now connected these undergrounds.

By the turn of the century, using drugs was something only addicts were supposed to do, just as gay sex was confined to homosexuals. Occasional flirtations with life beyond the straight lines of normality were no longer legitimate options. This was a confinement of desire, an attempt to channel pleasure into productive and reproductive behavior. But it had a wide variety of other effects, too. Any hint of some illicit deployment of the body and its pleasures was enough to dispatch vast swathes of the population into a new category, and also a new underground with its own signs and secret gestures, cryptic messages, dress codes, glances, clubs, street corners, covert actions, whispered promises, and hidden deals. Kiss the dealer for your rock; slip the money in your sock. Cities gained new maps, geography of stolen pleasures, a new commerce of desire. Sex and drugs are both entangled in these spirals of power and resistance, regulation and escape, and there is nothing to be freed or liberated at work in either of them: no long-lost leather fetishist, no repressed past in which ecstasy could be freely bought in the clubs of the world or peyote buttons could be found in Amsterdam. If attempts to confine sexuality "produced and determined the sexual mosaic," the confinement of drugs has also produced and multiplied the thrills it chased. "Modern society is perverse," stated Foucault, "not in spite of its puritanism or as if from a backlash provoked by its hypocrisy; it is in actual fact, and directly, perverse."

> The needle junkie is a magician who can work the conjuring trick of making a hole and simultaneously fixing it.
>
> Marek Kohn, *Narcomania*

"Michel always considered the process of thinking to be an experiment," wrote Deleuze in his book on Foucault. And drugs were one of many ways in which Foucault explored the possibilities inherent in "the body and its pleasures," to use his phrase. This was both an intellectual inquiry and a personal passion: "I think I have real difficulty in experiencing pleasure," he once said. "I think that the kind of pleasure I would consider as the *real* pleasure would be so deep, so intense, so overwhelming that I couldn't survive it. I would die." These words, recorded in David Macey's biography, aptly titled *The Lives of Michel Foucault,* are the words of an explorer, someone bound to seek out that pleasure. "I'm not able to give myself and others those middle-range pleasures that make up everyday life," said Foucault. 'Such pleasures are nothing for me and I am not able to organize my life in order to make room for them."

As Burroughs knew, "Junk suspends the whole cycle of tension, discharge and rest. The orgasm has no function in the junky. Boredom, which always indicates a discharged tension, never troubles the addict. He can look at his shoes for eight hours. He is only roused to action when the hour glass of junk runs out." But there are other drugs that take the body just as far from its deployment as a reproductive being without simply destroying its pleasures and desires: Foucault also used drugs that, he said, were "really important for me because they are the mediation to those incredibly intense joys that I am looking for and that I am not able to experience, to afford by myself." Even orgasm seemed a limiting and pale imitation of the far more expansive pleasures Foucault found in his favorite drugs. The belief that sex could be free one day had diverted attention away from the possibilities presented by drugs and many other means of experimenting with the body and its pleasures. "The apologia for orgasm made by the Reichians still seems to me to be a way of localizing possibilities of pleasure in the sexual," he wrote, "whereas things like yellow pills or cocaine allow you to explode and diffuse it throughout the body; the body becomes the overall site of an overall pleasure."

> Who can long remain body-crazed, and not at times use unworthy means of making his Body the fit instrument of his mind?
>
> Samuel Taylor Coleridge, *Notebooks*

Foucault's experiments with the body were also experiments in thought, willful attempts to lose the plot laid down by philosophical convention, to get to a point at which, as he wrote in "Theatrum Philosophicum," "Thought becomes a trance; and it becomes worthwhile to think." These are dangerous adventures in unmapped, unmanned worlds. The risks are great, and the price can be high. "The entrenched camp where man may be said to dwell, the fortified area wherein he manoeuvres his ideas falls apart," wrote Henri Michaux. *Infinite Turbulence* describes trance as "a vicious state in comparison with the normal. Even a saint (although his only drug has been that of asceticism and exhaustion) knows that there is something monstrous here, something which seems to be a perversion of nature." This was an encounter with what Michaux called "an unlimited, soaring, exalting evil, which is not opposed to the good, but to the ideal, to the celestial, which is the ideal reversed."

> A kind of order or apparent progression can be established for the segments of becoming in which we find ourselves; becoming-woman, becoming-child; becoming-animal, -vegetable, or -mineral; becomings-molecular of all kinds, becomings-particles. Fibres lead us.
> Gilles Deleuze and Félix Guattari, *A Thousand Plateaus*

Mescaline was Michaux's "God-extractor," his soul destroyer: "Pollution of the angel in man." And like Michaux, Foucault craved such pollution. For him, this was thinking at its most worthwhile: a thinking that might find a way to cut through the familiar categories that organize and classify the self and the world. It was a loss of logic, an abandonment of will, an escape from his own masculinity, and, in all these respects, a dangerous game: "Don't do it with a sledgehammer," wrote Deleuze and Guattari in *A Thousand Plateaus*. "Use a very fine file . . . invent self-destructions which have nothing to do with the death drive. Dismantling the organism has never meant killing yourself, but rather opening the body to connections that presuppose an entire assemblage, circuits, conjunctions, levels and thresholds, passages and distributions of intensity, and territories and deterritorializations measured with the craft of a surveyor." Foucault knew that such attempts to think without a map were perilous: "We court danger in wanting to be freed from categories," he wrote in "Theatrum Philosophicum." It is easy enough to escape their grasp but much harder to deal with the world they leave behind. Without the old parameters, Foucault finds himself absorbed into an "amorphous fluidity," immersed in the "boundless monotony" of a shapeless, meaningless reality: "No sooner do we abandon their organizing principle than we face the magma of stupidity. At a stroke we risk being surrounded not by a marvelous multiplicity of differences, but by equivalences, ambiguities, the 'it all comes down to the same thing,' a leveling uniformity, and the thermodynamism of every miscarried effort."

The fear of getting absolutely lost in this unsupported, insupportable state, trapped forever in an unformed world devoid of structure and distinction, is enough to dissuade most people from venturing too far. "For the unprepared," wrote Leary, Metzner, and Alpert in their psychedelic version of *The Tibetan Book of the Dead*, "the discovery of the wave-nature of all structure, the *Maya* revelation, is a disastrous web of uncertainty." The "subject staggers around, grasping at electron-patterns, striving to freeze them back into the familiar robot forms," and feeling "ultimately tricked. A victim of the great television producer. Distrust. The people around you are lifeless television robots. The world around you is a façade, a stage set. You are a helpless marionette, a plastic doll in a plastic world."

Leary and his colleagues were convinced that further was the only way to go. Michaux agreed: mescaline, he wrote, "creates many unpleasant surprises for those who, whilst in the throes of dispossession, are called back by their possessive natures." There are dangers for those who "still refuse to give themselves absolutely, as they should, in such a way so as to no longer be there, for that which is stands in the way." And the rewards could be impressive. Michaux's mescaline brought more of everything. The mind expands; it takes more in.

> The ability to separate out, to gauge, increases in the eye (which can see the most delicate reliefs, insignificant wrinkles), in the ear (which can hear the slightest sound from far away and is hurt by loud noises), in the understanding (an observer of non-apparent motives, of the underside, of the most distant causes and consequences that ordinarily go unnoticed, of all kinds of interactions, too numerous at other moments to be grasped simultaneously), and above all in the imagination (where visual images flash by, with unheard-of intensity, far above "reality," which weakens and diminishes)—and finally, importantly, in paranormal faculties, which sometimes reveal the gift of clairvoyance and divination to the subject.
>
> Henri Michaux, *Darkness Moves*

When Aldous Huxley later used the drug, there were no hallucinations of the obvious sort the literature had led him to expect: no "faces or forms of men or animals. I saw no landscapes," he wrote, "no enormous spaces, no magical growth and metamorphosis of buildings, nothing remotely like a drama or parable. The other world to which mescaline admitted me was not the world of visions; it existed out there, in what I could see with my eyes open." And even the screen on which they might have appeared seemed to collapse before him: "Ninety minutes into the experience," wrote Jay Stevens, "Huxley felt himself pass through a screen, at least that is what it seemed like."

But the doors of perception, rips in the screen, holes in the walls of reality, can open onto terrible fears, appalling visions, an abyss from which the voyager returns broken, if at all. Antonin Artaud encountered all the dangers, and extreme results, to which Foucault and Michaux referred when he took peyote with the Tarahumara. "Friable is the word for it—I was; and not just in some places, but through and through," he wrote. "I was, in the literal sense of the word, bewitched." The effects far outlived the drug's sojourn in his bloodstream. "After waiting twenty-eight days," he wrote, "I had still not come to myself—I should instead say: *come out* into myself." And there was worse to follow, a loss of control that found him "being hoisted on and off my horse like a broken robot," a confrontation with the "invincible organic hostility" in which "it was *me* that did not want to continue."

After his first experiment with mescaline, René Daumal "was 'unhinged' for several days, cut adrift from what is customarily called 'the real.' Everything seemed to me an absurd phantasmagoria, no logic could convince me of anything, and, like a leaf in the wind, I was ready to obey the faintest interior or exterior impulse." Daumal's advice, in "A Fundamental Experiment," was unequivocal: "The cry: 'It's I, I who am at stake' should frighten the curious who think they might like to perform the same or a similar experiment. I warn them now, it is a terrifying experience, and if they want more precise information on its dangers, they can ask me in private." But he was more than willing to insist on them:

> I do not mean the physiological dangers (which are great); for if, in return for accepting grave illness or infirmity, or for a considerable shortening of the span of physical life, one could attain to a *single* certainty, the price would not be too high. I am not speaking, moreover, only

of the dangers of insanity or of damage to the mind, which I escaped by extraordinary good luck. The danger is far graver.

Most turn back before it is too late. "Having once seen the danger," wrote Daumal, "I stopped repeating the test." Jünger wrote to Hofmann: "My practical studies in this field are far behind me. These are experiments in which one sooner or later embarks on truly dangerous paths, and may be considered lucky to escape with only a black eye." Others were determined not to turn back too soon. Artaud refused to renounce the "dangerous disassociations it seems Peyote provokes," for they were precisely what he "had for years sought by other means." This was, he wrote, a course to which "I knew my physical destiny was irredeemably attached."

Foucault was persistent, too. The bland, blind chaos of a world stripped of its categories was just the start, the beginning, not the end, of a journey that might take him somewhere new. Foucault learned to deal with his cluelessness, to

persist in his confrontation with stupidity, to remain motionless to the point of stupefaction in order to approach it successfully and mime it, to let it slowly grow within himself (this is probably what we politely refer to as being absorbed in one's thoughts), and to await, in the always unpredictable conclusion to this elaborate preparation, the shock of difference.

Faced with the blank immensity of an undifferentiated reality, Foucault had to sit and stare it out, dealing with the overwhelming ignorance that is his only possible response and opening himself to the possibility that something might propel him from this limbo into a reconfigured world. This is what he was waiting for: "the sudden shift of the kaleidoscope, signs that light up for an instant, the results of the thrown dice, the outcome of another game."

Foucault insisted that drug-induced perceptions were not to be judged in terms of truth and illusion, fact and fiction, whether their effects were real or not. "Drugs—if we can speak of them generally," he wrote in "Theatrum Philosophicum," "—have nothing at all to do with truth and falsity; only to fortunetellers do they reveal a world 'more truthful than the real,'" and it is "useless to seek a more substantial truth behind the phantasm, a truth to which it points as a rather confused sign." Drugs would not take him to the world laid bare. But this was no problem for Foucault, who wasn't looking for the truth anyway. His thinking was far more than an attempt to tell the difference between fact and fiction, the true and the false, real and artificial worlds. This was no longer a search for the infinite, an attempt to sneak a preview of heaven, a moment of bliss, or even some authentic experience: this was an exploration of reality, a journey through a world of thoughts, perceptions, and events that are not simply sitting there, waiting to be judged, but emerge and unfold as the trip is made. Like drugs themselves, their effects have to be taken on their own terms, "freed from the restrictions we impose upon them, freed from the dilemmas of truth and falsehood and being and non-being," and "allowed to conduct their dance, to act out their mime, as 'extra-beings.'" Like the detectives of the opiated past, these "extra-beings" have long made a habit of coming true.

Drugs couldn't make it happen for Foucault, but they did have a role to play: "perhaps, if it is given to thought to confront stupidity, the drugs, which mobilize it, which color, agitate, furrow, and dissipate it, which populate it with differences and substitute for the rare flash a continuous phosphorescence, are the source of a partial thought—perhaps." Foucault described LSD as a shortcut between and beyond the categories of illusion and reality, the false and the true. It induced an accelerated thinking that "no sooner eliminates the supremacy of categories than it tears away the ground of its indifference and disintegrates the gloomy dumbshow of stupidity" to the point at which he encounters a "univocal and acategorical mass" that is not only "variegated, mobile, asymmetrical, decentered, spiraloid, and reverberating, but causes it to rise, at each instant, as a swarming of phantasm-events." The processes speed up: structures are displayed, shattered, and surpassed in swift succession, and "as it is freed from its catatonic chrysalis, thought invariably contemplates this indefinite equivalence transformed into an acute event and a sumptuous, apparelled repetition." And opium, he wrote, "ensures a weightless immobility, the stupor of a butterfly that differs from catatonic rigidity," and "far beneath, it establishes a ground that no longer stupidly absorbs all differences, but allows them to arise and sparkle as so many minute, distanced, smiling, and eternal events."

> Drugs are nihilistic: they undermine all values and radically overturn all our ideas about good and evil, what is just and what is unjust, what is permitted and what is forbidden. Their action is a mockery of our morality based on reward and punishment.
>
> Octavio Paz, *Alternating Current*

Judgment is left in abeyance. The usual criteria need not apply. This is both the threat and the promise drugs can make. Just as repetition can fall into an addictive trap, so suspended disbelief can leave a vacuum where once there was a sense of right and wrong. But Foucault's careful genealogies of modern power are underwritten by the conviction that it is only such dispassionate and suspended states from which the workings of the world can be perceived. There is a cool ambivalence in all his work, a refusal to allow his thinking to fall back into the censorious positions of philosophical discourse. And if drugs tend to put aside the West's modern, even ancient, attempts to judge everything in terms of the really real and the truly true, they also introduce the only perspective from which they themselves can be understood. "Drugs have now become a part of our culture," said Foucault in his interview with Charles Raus. "Just as there is good music and bad music, there are bad drugs and good drugs. So we can't say we are 'against' drugs any more than we can say we're 'against' music."

> That is one of the virtues of the drug, that it empties such questions of all anguish, transports them to another region, a painless theoretical region, surprising, fertile, and unmoral. One is no longer grotesquely involved in becoming. One simply is. I remember saying to Sebastian before he returned to Europe with his new wife that it was imperative to know what it was to be a vegetable, as well.
>
> Alexander Trocchi, *Cain's Book*

Dancers

If Coleridge's opium gave the English language the word *intensify*, heroin gave it another word: "The perceiving turns inwards," wrote Trocchi in *Cain's Book*. "The eyelids droop, the blood is aware of itself, a slow phosphorescence in all the fabric of flesh and nerve and bone; it is that the organism has a sense of being intact and unbrittle, and, above all, inviolable. For the attitude born of this sense of inviolability some Americans have used the word 'cool.'" These Americans were jazz musicians, and *cool* was one of the most sonorous terms to come out of the moment in which jazz picked up a needle and became bebop just before the war. Marijuana was the drug of jazz in the 1930s, and although its prohibition in 1937 hardly interrupted its use, illegality did change the atmosphere surrounding the drug and, not least, the nature of its sources and suppliers when grass was thrown into the underground circuits that already carried heroin and cocaine. Heroin was a predominantly white drug when Charlie Parker started using it, often, in his short life, to excess. Jill Jones quotes the line that summed up the state of the art in the 1950s: "Jazz was born in a whiskey barrel, grew up on marijuana and is about to expire on heroin." Just like Charlie Parker himself, who died in his mid-thirties, leaving cool jazz and bebop washing through the soundscapes of the world: his "sense of rhythm, challenging, dangerous and always confident, is now heard in music everywhere." After Parker, waves of musicians chased his cool. Billie Holiday's was only one of the beautiful voices to sing itself into the cool, cool, cold of death.

Even in the modern world, which has forgotten so much of the rhythm and the rhyme of sound, drugs have made music in ways that are far more compelling and immediate than all the convoluted routes on which they have changed words. LSD was the Beatles' "Lucy in the Sky with Diamonds" and Jimi Hendrix's "Purple Haze," and the raw kicks of glue and speed ran through punk. And then came the reggae explosion, which had been cooking in Jamaica for years before Bob Marley popularized the association among reggae music, Rastafarianism, and ganja, grass. In the early 1960s, the stars were Lee "Scratch" Perry, widely acknowledged to be one of the first and best of the sound engineers who have now become so crucial to dance music, and Jimmy Cliff, whose music was popularized by *The Harder They Come*, in which Ivan, the innocent young hero from the country, finds himself selling ganja and asking: "Who making all the money?" It's a film with some great music, a flashback sense of circularity, and some telling dialogue: "Look, I know you use the trade as a form of control," says the commissioner of police to his detective, "but I can't explain that officially."

By the late 1970s, England was dreaming on Jamaican grass, Lebanese hashish, the Iranian heroin that gave the Stranglers "Golden Brown," and its own brands of speed, which the band Dexy's Midnight Runners dropped into its name. Hallucinogenic drugs were largely confined to the edges of the underground, and cocaine was rare and expensive. Ten years later, everything had changed.

> These metaphysicians of natural chaos dance, restoring every iota of sound, each fragmentary perception, as if it were ready to return to its origins, able to wed movement and sound so perfectly it seems the dancers have hollow limbs to make sounds of woodblocks, resounding drums and echoing instruments with their hollow, wooden limbs.
>
> Here we are suddenly in the thick of a metaphysical struggle and the rigid aspect of the body in a trance, tensed by the surging of the cosmic powers attacking it, is admirably expressed in that frenzied dance full of angular stiffness, where we suddenly feel the mind's headlong fall begins.
>
> They seem like substantial waves, dashing their crests into the deep, and rushing from all points of the horizon to hurtle themselves into an infinitesimal portion of a quivering trance—to cover the void of fear.
>
> Antonin Artaud, *The Theatre and Its Double*

MDMA was rediscovered in the 1960s by Alexander Shulgin, still one of the world's most famous and adventurous researchers of new and ancient psychoactive drugs. The intensely pleasurable effects of MDMA and some of its near relatives, such as MDA and MDEA, made them popular as recreational drugs on the West Coast in the late 1960s, and MDMA's particular calming, empathetic tendencies allowed it to be sold as a respected therapeutic aid until it was added to the long list of controlled substances in 1985. MDMA, variously known as ecstasy, X, or E, has been described as an empathogen, an entactogen, a drug of empathy and touch. For

Simon Reynolds, it was "the remedy for the alienation caused by an atomized society."

But it was not until the late 1980s that the drug came into its own. Something of the spaces it opened up seemed to resonate with that other new dimension that had crept in with *Neuromancer*: cyberspace. Something of the precision with which it seemed to work, the vast expanses, that pixilated haze—it seemed as if ecstasy had been waiting for the age of intelligent machines.

Ecstasy multiplies and magnifies senses, perceptions, emotions, sounds, and images, connecting everything on plateaus that seem to run forever through space and time. It can also introduce a cool lucidity in which what are normally perceived as knotty problems present themselves on vast and serene planes that allow them to be perceived with unusual clarity. Shulgin has reported that his own research into the molecular structure of compounds such as MDMA has been greatly enhanced by his use of the drug itself: MDMA gives a calm sense of spatiality that has allowed him to contemplate its molecular structure from angles that would otherwise elude him.

"With its mildly trippy, pre-hallucinogenic feel," wrote Reynolds, "Ecstasy makes colours, sounds, smells, tastes and tactile sensations more vivid . . . The experience combines clarity and a limpid, soft-focus radiance. Ecstasy also has a particular physical sensation that's hard to describe: an oozy yearn, a bliss-ache, a trembly effervescence that makes you feel like you've got champagne for blood." Hard to describe, but easy to synthesize: MDMA displays "a uniquely synergistic/synaesthetic interaction" with both the fast, frantic tension and the languid peace of the sounds the drug inspired.

> By assembling modules, source elements, and elements for treating sound (oscillators, generators, and transformers), by arranging microintervals, the

synthesizer makes audible the sound process itself,
the production of that process, and puts us in contact with still other elements beyond sound matter.
Gilles Deleuze and Félix Guattari, *A Thousand Plateaus*

Writing on drugs has always been chasing the effects such
music can achieve. Like jazz, dance music's repetitive beats
had little to do with the representations and accompaniments
of song. This was music as a matter of modifying states of
mind, perceptions, bodies, brains; music that became almost
as immediate as drugs themselves; music that remembered
the techniques of dance and drumming, rhythm and trance,
and anticipated the sense that music has more to do with
sound and frequency than with melody and meaning. In
Britain, the BBC complained about the few drug references it
noticed in the music it now felt obliged to broadcast, but such
moves had already become irrelevant: that game was up. Ecstasy didn't have to be mentioned by name: the drug *was* the
music, and the music was a means of engineering and exploring its effects. Coleridge's word came into its own. The dance
music of the 1990s "gradually evolved into a self-conscious
science of intensifying MDMA's sensations. House and techno
producers have developed a drug-determined repertoire of effects, textures and riffs that are expressly designed to trigger
the tingy rushes that traverse the Ecstatic body."

This was not a means of escaping the body but a way of let-
ting the body escape the structures and boundaries that keep
it organized. In the first wave of the drug's popularity, it felt
as if it was melting everybody down. And if music had once
been an accompaniment to the effects of drugs like LSD,
dance music learned how to enhance and intensify these visceral, rhythmic, bodily effects of MDMA. "Organized around
the absence of crescendo or narrative progression, rave music
instils a pleasurable tension, a rapt suspension that fits perfectly with the sustained pre-orgasmic plateau of the MDMA
high." This was Artaud's theater, Michaux's "virtual space,"

Burroughs's cut-up, folded wordless world, his Arab music, and his cities too: Tangier, Interzone, "where the unknown past and the mergent future meet." De Quincey's opiated dreams anticipated the technologies of perception that came after him, Poe's opiated mind gave him a kind of artificial intelligence, and MDMA's dream trippers had a preview of virtual life in cyberspace. The nineteenth century's search for the moment between life and death was now strung out across a plane of suspended disbelief. And the music was produced as Lautréamont had hoped poetry would be written one day, "not by one, but by all." Hooks and licks, the old riffs of jazz, random mutations, accidents, mistakes, reappearing in a starless meshwork of continuous evolution: sounds, DJs, dancers, engineers. The old hierarchies kept rearing their heads, but, at its best, this club scene hosted a mutating network that broke down all the old identities and reassembled them on a new plane of its own.

MDMA's users neither trip nor dream. They are immersed, entranced, possessed, as nameless as the planes to which the drug takes them, as faceless and anonymous as the warm airs and cool clear breezes washing through the skin. They are dancers, rhythms, speeds, and beats, disorganized and dispersed beyond their own individuation, overwhelmed by their own connectivity. This is a world of rhythm, repetition, an oceanic sound that, as Deleuze and Guattari wrote, "invades us, impels us, drags us, transpierces us. It takes leave of the earth, as much in order to drop us into a black hole as to open us up to a cosmos. It makes us want to die."

MDMA is one of the most influential inside tracks of the digital, sampled, cybernetic world that came on-line in the late 1980s. It steals identity away, but it also throws its users into new connective tissues of dance, movement, rhythm, sound, and there's none of the terror encountered by Daumal, Michaux, Artaud, Poe: the drug makes it all feel easy and taste so nice. MDMA takes the fear of death away. It was the interior technology for the digital age, the wetware for the software revolution, the molecular adjustment that allowed a generation to explore the new machine interface. It also made that generation fearless about drugs, willing, eager to try everything. Ketamine hydrochloride, for example, a surgical anesthetic first synthesized in 1963 and now manufactured by Parke-Davis, the first American producer of cocaine, can take its users to dimensions whose elaborate intensities far outshine even the most fearful of the "fearful realities" that played in the theater of De Quincey's mind. The extraordinary visions that seem to generate in the absence of so much normal bodily sensation take the nineteenth century's anesthetic revelations to new extremes. MDMA's mellow and welcoming effects introduced the mainstream world to the whole pharmacopoeia of psychoactive drugs: LSD, speed, cocaine, even crack and heroin were now thrown into the recreational mix. Consumption became conspicuous.

> Not that we needed all that for the trip, but once you get locked into a serious drug collection the tendency is to push it as far as you can.
> Hunter S. Thompson, *Fear and Loathing in Las Vegas*

The underground came up for air. And the music went along with this new polydrug use. Jungle and drum 'n' bass gave a keen black breakbeat edge to what had been the clean white sounds of techno and house, making "the music feel treacherous" and transforming it into "a rhythmic psychedelia." It is, wrote Reynolds, "a non-verbal response to troubled times, a kind of warrior-stance. The resistance is in the rhythms. Jungle is the metabolic pulse of a body reprogrammed and rewired to cope with an era of unimaginably intense information overload."

The music and the books became too numerous to name. But one wave of writing seemed to feel this rush of music coming on: cyberpunk, a genre in which what Bruce Sterling defined as the "powerful theme of mind-invasion" played a crucial part: "brain-computer interfaces, artificial intelligence, neurochemistry—techniques radically redefining the nature of humanity, the nature of the self." After Dick's paranoia, the acid wit of Thomas Pynchon's patterned prose, and the subtle drug inflections of J. G. Ballard's cool dark words, cyberpunk anticipates a world in which drugs are enhanced or replaced by even more immediate and precise means of modifying brains and changing minds: Richard Kadrey's *Metrophage*, Neal Stephenson's *Snow Crash*, Pat Cadigan's *Synners*, and William Gibson's novels, in which Poe's detective and his science fictions converge on a world of simulated stimulations, multiplicitous identities, and the "larval hum" of Burroughs's "drugs not yet synthesized."

> "A detailed neurochemical response to your first question would be very lengthy."
> "What was its purpose?"
> "With regard to you?"
> She has to look away from the ruby eyes. The chamber is lined with panels of ancient wood, buffed to a rich gloss. The floor is covered with a fitted carpet woven with circuit-diagrams.
> "No two lots were identical. The only constant was the substance whose psychotropic signature you regarded as 'the drug.' In the course of ingestion, many other substances were involved, as well as several dozen sub-cellular nano-mechanisms, programmed to restructure the synaptic alterations . . ."
> William Gibson, *Neuromancer*

With the cybernetic spaces of the new millennium, the hallucinations become consensual, no longer left to private eyes and poets to detect. Spaces and events once possible only through chemistry began to emerge on electronic nets, and all the diverse elements of drug-induced experience—addiction, stimulation, narcosis—have become ubiquitous in the postmodern world. If Tilden's extract of hashish once seemed to put the world on the tip of Ludlow's tongue and De Quincey could buy happiness with a penny's worth of laudanum, variations of their fantastic worlds are now accessible with or without drugs. The same addictive simulations now come free with the latest versions of Hasan Sabbah's worlds: the marble-floored, gold-plated, video-walled gardens and fountains of the shopping mall; the virtual worlds available on-line. Baudelaire's tortuous debates about the validity or the artifice of his hashish experience have been overtaken by the simulacra of a digital age that cares little for such distinctions. Coleridge's Xanadu is spread out on the Net, whose virtual landscapes are neither true nor false, factual or fictional, but simply there.

> "That's a hypercard. I thought you said Snow Crash was a drug," Hiro says, now totally nonplussed.
> "It is," the guy says. "Try it."
> "Does it fuck up your brain?" Hiro says. "Or your computer?"
> "Both. Neither. What's the difference?"
> Neal Stephenson, *Snow Crash*

Gray Areas

Like Sherlock Holmes, who declares his intention to devote his "declining years to the composition of a textbook which shall focus the whole art of detection into one volume," Sigmund Freud planned to write up the theoretical basis for psychoanalysis in a book that was to be called *Preliminaries to a Metapsychology*. Only a few of the papers that were to appear in this book have survived, but two of them, "Beyond the Pleasure Principle," published in 1920, and "The Economic Problem of Masochism," which appeared in 1924, present ideas that are quite different from Freud's earlier convictions about the pleasure principle. These essays were written in the wake of a war that had made it difficult to sustain the idea that the human organism was driven by the avoidance of unpleasure, or pain. It now seemed as if "there *might* be such a thing as primary masochism," wrote Freud, "a possibility which I had contested at that time."

One of Freud's motivations for this new line of inquiry was the shell shock suffered by the soldiers of the First World War. Freud defined "as 'traumatic' any excitations from outside which are powerful enough to break through the protective shield" that surrounds the living organism, making a "breach in an otherwise efficacious barrier" that protects it against unwanted stimuli. In complex organisms, including human beings, this shield is refined into the sense organs of Freud's "perceptual system," by means of which "samples of the external world" are absorbed. This system is the "borderline between outside and inside," the body's interface with the outside world. Anything that storms this border will traumatize the system, sending it into a state of shock.

Soldiers diagnosed with what were then called war neuroses suffered from what would now be called flashbacks to the traumatic circumstances in which they had experienced some overwhelming fright, and this seemed to suggest that there were some "mysterious masochistic trends" at work, some deep-seated desire to repeat the traumas of the past. There appeared to be a "compulsion to repeat," a pattern of behavior that was difficult to explain in terms of the quest to minimize pain. Freud found himself confronting the mysteries of "a new and remarkable fact, namely that the compulsion to repeat also recalls from the past experiences which include no possibility of pleasure, and which can never, even long ago, have brought satisfaction even to instinctual impulses which have been repressed."

Freud now began to argue that the organism was continuously pulled in two directions, with the sexual instincts striving for life and another tendency that could easily "give the appearance of a 'daemonic' force at work," which he now explained in terms of a struggle waged by all the other instincts "to restore an earlier state of things." It was "as though the life of the organism moved with a vacillating rhythm. One group of instincts rushes forward so as to reach the final aim of life as swiftly as possible; but when a particular stage in the advance has been reached, the other group jerks back to a certain point to make a fresh start and so prolong the journey." It now seemed as if the organism was engaged in a continuous double movement that gave its life instincts the task of prolonging what was now an overriding, or a powerful, drive to die. The two instincts serve each other, and the life of the organism as a whole becomes a quest "to make ever more complicated detours before reaching its aim of death," to take increasingly "circuitous paths to death." What keeps life living is not so much its desire for life itself as the fact that "the organism wishes to die in its own fashion." Even Freud was shocked by these lines of thought: "It cannot be so," he said, although he was convinced that he had unearthed a new and fascinating problem. "If pain and unpleasure can be not simply warnings but actually aims, the pleasure principle is paralysed—it is as though the watchman over our mental life were put out of action by a drug."

This, Freud knew, was the limit of psychoanalysis. He now found himself discussing not an idealized notion of the unconscious but the timeless, deathless planes of microbiological life that persist within and regardless of the lives and deaths and reproductive cycles of organized, multicellular life. This took him back to the vocabulary and the interests he had left behind with the nineteenth century. It was a return to the body, the brain, the anatomy of what was now described as an organism with its own economy rather than an ego with an unconscious. All the activities, tensions, and tendencies at work in the organism now took their character not from the structured image of a house with adjoining rooms but from a new conception of the organism as an open system, a complex and dynamic economy composed of several conflicting but mutually sustaining impulses: "The *Nirvana* principle expresses the trend of the death instinct, the *pleasure* principle represents the demands of the libido, and the modification of the latter principle, the *reality* principle, represents the influence of the external world." If he had once believed that the organism was committed to maintaining its own stability, minimizing pain and unpleasure, he was now convinced that there was some more positive desire for disturbance, even pain, at work in even the most life-affirming systems. Sex was not the secret: there was no secret. Life was a nexus of conflicting and mutually supporting desires.

It has often been suggested that Freud's addiction to tobacco—which contributed to several cancers during his lifetime and, eventually, to his death—had more of a hand in these developments in his research than the mass destruction of the First World War. Freud was driven to distraction by his attempts to stop smoking, and this addiction was probably his compulsion to repeat par excellence. Although his work on the death instinct is, like his early work on cocaine and the brain, glossed over by many of his followers, it was a fascinating move that Freud knew was ahead of its time. "We must be patient and await fresh methods and occasions of research," he wrote. "The deficiencies in our description would probably vanish if we were already in a position to replace the psychological terms by physiological or chemical ones."

Freud had abandoned such notions as the neurone and the chemical energy to which he referred as "quantity in a condition of flow" when he left his neurological research behind in the 1890s. But his later works marked a striking return to these neurological ideas, which it now seemed he had abandoned only for want of a more detailed understanding of the brain. And if they harked back to his early attempts to develop what James Strachey described as a "highly complicated and extraordinarily ingenious working model of the mind as a piece of neurological machinery," they also have a powerful resonance with recent neuroscientific research.

> Ever pop coke in the mainline? It hits you right in the brain, activating connections of pure pleasure. The pleasure of morphine is in the viscera. You listen down into yourself after a shot. But C is electricity through the brain, and the C yen is of the brain alone, a need without body and without feeling. The C-charged brain is a berserk pinball machine, flashing blue and pink lights in electric orgasm. C pleasure could be felt by a thinking machine, the first stirrings of hideous insect life.
>
> William Burroughs, *Naked Lunch*

Textbook diagrams of the human brain still tend to give the impression that it is a discrete and fixed entity located in the skull. But the brain is an immensely complex and distributed system, a vast communications network, an immense mesh of cells and fibers, pathways, circuits, humming with junctions, messages, and messengers. It is plastic, dynamic, and finely tuned, a system of such staggering complexity that it struggles even to think about itself. Some of its regions have been explored, but most of it remains completely obscure.

The brain also extends far beyond the organ in the head. Although it is often imagined as a collection of large and distinct areas, the central nervous system is much more interconnected than such imagery suggests. It is also difficult to say precisely where it begins and ends: the central nervous system includes the spinal cord, which is protected by bone, and the cranial nerves, which carry information to and from the eyes, the nose, the skin, and other sensory organs. Several of the brain's most important regions—including the cerebellum, the thalamus, and the hypothalamus—are involved in a variety of other crucial regulatory, sensory, and motor controls.

186

In addition to the major regions of the central nervous system, the networks that make up the peripheral nervous system deal with the body's voluntary and involuntary movements and processes. The somatic system controls voluntary movement. Although it has most of its neurons in the central nervous system, its axons extend from the spinal cord to muscles, joints, and the skin. The neurons of the autonomic nervous system, which controls involuntary processes, are widely distributed throughout the body. And the movement and processing of food are conducted and monitored by the so-called little brain, the enteric part of the autonomic nervous system, a semiautonomous neural system embedded in the lining of the stomach, the intestines, the pancreas, and the esophagus.

The most important and mysterious region of the central nervous system is the cerebral cortex, with what Oliver Sacks has described as its "hundred million cells, twenty cell types, six layers, an infinity of connections both intrinsic and extrinsic." It is composed of a thin sheet of neurons lying just under the surface of the cerebrum and covering the forebrain. In an adult human, this sheet extends to something like eighteen square inches, folded and wrinkled to fit inside the skull. This large surface area has a crucial and as yet largely unknown role in the higher functions of human intelligence and consciousness. Some of its areas can be attributed to motor and sensory functions, but most of it is simply designated as "associative," and hardly anything is understood about what it does and how it works. The growth of the cortex is thought to account for much of the growth of the human brain, which has undergone a rapid expansion in the last three million years—a remarkably short time, given that humans began to emerge some fifteen million years ago. And the more the cortex has expanded, the more unmapped associative areas it has gained.

Neurons are the basic cells of the brain. They were first observed in the late nineteenth century by the anatomist Camillo

Golgi, who discovered how to identify neurons in the midst of a mass of brain tissue but refused to believe that the brain could be, like the rest of the body, composed of such cells. It was widely thought that the brain must be made of some very different stuff until Santiago Ramón y Cajal established the existence of neurons at the turn of the century and some level of continuity between the cells of the body and brain was accepted.

Although they are cells, neurons are very different from those at work in the body as a whole. They have developed a highly specialized and sophisticated means of communication: each neuron has a nucleus and a multiplicity of fibers on which it can transmit, conduct, and receive information from other cells. It has dendrites, on which it receives information from other cells, and an axon, the fiber on which it transmits information to other cells. Toward the end of the axon, it divides into several other fibers. Each of these new branches ends with an interface, a synapse.

Synapses are crucial elements of the brain's communications systems. They are also numerous: because a particular neuron can have many thousands of synaptic connections with other neurons, there are trillions of them at work in the human brain. These are the terminals, the input-output ports, the gateways through which neurons can communicate. A communicating neuron first sends out an electrical signal to its axon terminal, and the arrival of this signal, an action potential, gives the membrane of the terminal a positive charge. Once the signal has been received, it opens channels that allow calcium ions to flood into the axon, where they trigger the release of a neurotransmitting chemical. This is the messenger dispatched with a message for the next cell. It jumps the tiny gap between the transmitting synapse of the first neuron and the receiving synapse of the next. When this gap, the synaptic cleft, has been crossed, the neurotransmitter binds to its receptors on the other side. It fits these receptors like a key in a lock. It opens the ion channels on the new membrane and dispatches its message to the cell. Once the neurotransmitter has done its work, it then has to be cleared away so that others can follow in its wake. Some of it disperses, and most is removed by a process of re-uptake, which allows it to be reabsorbed into the first axon terminal.

There are also many different types of neurons in the nervous system as a whole. Motor neurons communicate with muscles and glands. Sensory neurons carry information from the body to the nervous system. Within the brain itself, there are principal neurons, large cells whose axons extend beyond their own region, and interneurons, which confine their communications to their immediate vicinity. And neurons are not the only cells at work in this network. Glias, which do not transmit or receive information, are even more numerous than neurons. Some of them are responsible for increasing neuronal conductivity; others form the blood-brain barrier that protects the brain from toxins in the bloodstream. They may also be involved in clearing up the debris when neurons die and taking up unnecessary or excessive chemicals at the synapses, but as with so much of the brain, much of their activity is unknown.

Synaptic transmission is one of the nervous system's most important activities. The English physiologist Charles Sherrington identified the synapse in 1897, and there were some early suggestions that muscarine, one of the elements of *Amanita muscaria*, could activate the vagus nerve of frogs. But it was not until the 1920s that the nature of the transmissions it facilitates was identified as chemical. The possibility that information was carried between neurons by specific chemicals was first raised by the German pharmacologist Otto Loewi, who speculated that the cells in the brain might talk to one another with "little whiffs of scent." And then, in 1921, he had a powerful dream:

The night before Easter Sunday of that year I awoke, turned on the light, and jotted down a few notes on a tiny slip of thin paper. Then I fell asleep again. It occurred to me at six o'clock in the morning that I had written down something most important, but I was unable to decipher the scrawl. That Sunday was the most desperate day in my whole scientific life. During the next night, however, I awoke again, at three o'clock, and I remembered what it was. This time I did not take any risk. I got up immediately, went to the laboratory, made the experiment on the frog's heart, and at five o'clock the chemical transmission of the nervous impulse was conclusively proved.

Loewi was amazed by the dream source of his discovery. "Careful consideration in daytime would undoubtedly have rejected the kind of experiment I performed," he wrote. "Yet the whole nocturnal concept of the experiment was based on this eventuality, and the result proved to be positive, contrary to expectation." He would have been even more astounded by the later news that the chemical of which he dreamed was itself responsible for stimulating dreams themselves.

What Loewi had discovered with his experiment on the frog was that there was chemical transmission of information from the vagus nerve to the heart. Soon after Loewi's discovery, Henry Dale defined this chemical messenger as acetylcholine, and the two men shared a Nobel Prize for this work in 1936.

Acetylcholine was the first of many chemical neurotransmitters to be identified during the following decades. Although they have crucial roles to play in the central nervous system, many of these chemicals are at work in all the body's communications networks: the central nervous system, the autonomic nervous systems, the somatic motor system, and the endocrine system. Glutamate, for example, is an amino acid that, as one of the building blocks of protein, is abundant in neurons and all the body's cells. Acetylcholine is a synthesis of acetyl, which is present in all the body's cells, and choline, an element of many different foods. Serotonin, which has an impact on the regulation of emotions, moods, body temperature, and sleep patterns, is a neurotransmitter and a hormone—a chemical transmitter at work in the rest of the body as well as the brain. Serotonin can be synthesized from tryptophan, an amino acid found in bananas and many other protein-rich foodstuffs. Tyrosine, also present in such foods, is an amino acid that is converted into dopa, from which dopamine, adrenaline—or epinephrine—and noradrenaline —or norepinephrine—can then be synthesized. The peptides, which are involved in the alleviation of pain and, by implication, the experience of pleasure, are strings of amino acids synthesized by neurons and also in the endocrine system. You can even feel it in your bones: of all these elements, it is calcium that plays some of the most universal and crucial roles in neurotransmission. The multifunctionality of so many of these chemicals, their ability to work as both neurotransmitters and hormones, suggests that it is difficult to draw the line between processes at work in the brain and those in the rest of the body. The obvious dividing line is the blood-brain barrier, the cellular coating that prevents many substances that are carried or absorbed by the bloodstream from getting into the workings of the brain, but even this is by no means an absolute divide. There are also suggestions that interneuronal transmissions are not confined to synapses but occur at a distance too. Such remote, or parasynaptic, communications introduce a far more complex and even more distributed notion of the brain and its activities.

> The body is no longer the obstacle that separates thought from itself, that which it has to overcome to reach thinking. It is on the contrary that which it plunges into or must plunge into, in order to reach the unthought, that is life.
>
> Gilles Deleuze, *Cinema 2*

By the 1970s, neurochemical research had begun to reveal the whole human nervous system as a living laboratory, a vast system of chemical processes continuously engaged in the manufacture, synthesis, and distribution of a vast range of its own means of chemical communication and regulation. It is now well known that the activities of these chemicals are closely related to experiences of extreme pleasure, euphoria, depression, the body's ability to respond to pain and stress, arousal and excitement, the workings of memory, and indeed all the body's normal and extreme processes, activities, and states. And these are the chemical activities that can be interrupted, waylaid, blocked, or excited by the introduction of psychoactive drugs. All psychoactive drugs contain chemicals that allow them to pass as the brain's neurotransmitters, mimicking their chemical structures and behaviors so well that the brain's receptors accept them as its own. Nicotine, for example, so closely resembles acetylcholine that certain acetylcholine receptors welcome it in. The molecular structure of LSD is so similar to serotonin that it interferes with the brain's own serotonin circuitry.

All psychoactive drugs work in very different and specific ways. Compounds that are recognized by some receptors of a certain neurotransmitting chemical may not be accepted by others. Nicotine, for example, is not recognized by all the acetylcholine receptors and acts only on those in the skeletal muscle, which are consequently known as the nicotinic receptors. The other acetylcholine receptors, which are located in the heart, respond to muscarine but have no effect on the nicotinic receptors. Some neurotransmitting chemicals, including opiates, activate other molecular processes in the neurons with which they communicate, triggering second-messenger effects that in this case alter the cell's ability to synthesize particular proteins. And if the molecular construction of particular receptors can influence the workings of certain drugs, there are many different ways in which psychoactive drugs can affect synaptic activity.

Many of the psychoactive effects of these drugs are consequences of the brain's attempts to cope with the influx of new
chemicals. Neurochemical transmissions can be excited or depressed by different drugs: LSD is thought effectively to silence the brain's serotonin circuits, although there is some
considerable doubt about whether this drug and the other
tryptamines are agonists or antagonists at these sites. Amphetamines are assumed to stimulate the release of dopamine,
and other psychoactive substances work by prolonging the
action of neurotransmitting chemicals in the synaptic cleft, in-
tervening in the postsynaptic processes that normally clear
the chemicals away. Cocaine is thought to block the re-uptake
of dopamine; and, as well as stimulating dopamine release,
amphetamines block the re-uptake of both dopamine and
noradrenaline. The actions of many of these chemicals add to
the difficulties of distinguishing between the body and the
brain. Only about 2 percent of any dose of mescaline crosses
the blood-brain barrier and works directly on the central nervous system: the rest of it heads for the liver, which suggests
either that just a small percentage of the compound is sufficient to produce its dramatic effects or that even this most apparently cerebral drug does most of its work outside the
brain. This is also the case with LSD, a substance that mysteriously disappears from the central nervous system shortly after it is taken, even though its effects can last for many hours.

> Opium is the only vegetable substance which com-
> municates the vegetable state to us. Through it, we
> get an idea of that other speed of plants.
>
> Jean Cocteau, *Opium*

If psychoactive substances function as messengers in the human brain, it seems they gave it this message too. With the
same neat circularity that psychoactive drugs seem to introduce into everything, much of this chemistry was uncovered
in the course of research into psychoactive drugs.

Concerned about heroin addiction among returning soldiers from Vietnam, Richard Nixon appointed Jerome Jaffe to head research into drug abuse in 1971, and Jaffe asked a friend, Solomon Snyder, to investigate the workings of opiates in the human nervous system. It had long been assumed that drugs interact with specific receptors in the brain, but Snyder and his colleague Candice Pert became the first scientists to identify a specific site when they discovered receptors perfectly designed for the receipt of opiates. The discovery of these receptors, which are now known to be distributed throughout the brain's pain systems, made another question unavoidable: "Why do opiate receptors exist? Humans were not born with morphine in them. Might the opiate receptor be a receptor for a new transmitter that regulates pain perception and emotional states?" The question was later raised again in relation to the cannabis receptor: "The receptor had to be there for a purpose," said Roger Pertwee, the pharmacologist researching its effects. "Presumably it didn't evolve so that people could smoke cannabis and get high."

In 1975, John Hughes and Hans Kosterlitz began to answer some of these questions when they isolated a chemical they called enkephalin. This is an endemic opiate, a substance similar to morphine, which the brain synthesizes for its own use. It was soon discovered that there were other opiate-like substances manufactured and used by the nervous system: beta-endorphin and the dynorphins, which are two hundred times stronger than morphine. All these substances are known as endorphins, a term derived from their status as endogenous morphines. These are the painkilling and pleasure-giving dragons that can be roused inside every human being.

"Though this discovery suggested a practical application in the relief of pain and of mood disorders, it also raised many questions," wrote the neurophilosopher Patricia Churchland. "What were the opiates doing in the brain in the first place? Will we find endogenous tranquilizers and endogenous antidepressants? Are certain diseases of the mind caused by imbalances in these chemicals? Can I be addicted to my own chemicals?" More to the point, can you be prosecuted for possessing them?

Many other receptors, and their native chemicals, have been discovered in the last few decades, and it is now widely accepted that psychoactive drugs interact with the brain at sites designed to receive them. A vast range of neurotransmitting chemicals are already present in a nervous system that does, in effect, have its own opiates, its own cocaine, its own version of every psychoactive compound that can affect the brain. Even the milk produced by nursing mothers and other lactating mammals is thought to contain some powerful opiates. And all of us are always on the drugs our bodies make. One of the most recent discoveries, in 1993, involves tetrahydrocannabinol, THC, the active ingredient in marijuana and hashish. It was Raphael Mechoulam, the Israeli chemist who had isolated THC from cannabis in 1964, who discovered the neurochemical to which the cannabinoids are related. He called it anandamide, from the Sanskrit word for bliss.

Of all these developments, it is the discovery of the similarity between serotonin and LSD and the other tryptamines that raises some of the most intriguing possibilities about the roles played by psychoactive compounds and neurotransmitting chemicals. The neurons containing serotonin are situated in a thin seam of cell bodies that runs along the brain stem, the raphe nuclei (*raphe* means seam), and serotonin is also widely distributed throughout the body, with a presence in some blood cells and certain muscular tissues.

> I could see a new world with my middle eye, a world
> I had missed before. I caught images behind images,
> the walls behind the sky, the sky behind the infinite.
> Anaïs Nin, *Diaries, 1947–1955*

By far the highest concentrations of serotonin are in the pineal gland, which until recently was assumed to be a leftover organ of no significance to the nervous system but is now known to play a crucial role in the body's regulatory systems. The pineal gland is situated in the middle of the forehead, the ancient site of the "third eye," which is still widely designated by the *bindi* painted by Hindu women on the forehead. René Descartes is one of many Western philosophers to have speculated about the role of the pineal gland as the site of communication between the body and the mind, and the gland has a stunning wealth of associations, which run all the way from the Vedas to the eye in the pyramid of the dollar bill. The pineal gland is located within the brain as a matter of anatomical fact but is actually on the outside of the blood-brain barrier and receives its nerve fibers not from the central nervous system but from the sympathetic part of the peripheral nervous system. Inside the pineal gland itself, serotonin is converted into melatonin, which is now known to influence a wide variety of superficially distinct effects: skin pigmentation, the body's ability to respond to light and darkness with its cycles of sleep, and the monthly cycle of the female reproductive system. Like serotonin, melatonin is present in many parts of the body, including the inner ear, a fact that has raised the intriguing possibility that far broader senses of balance, rhythm, and responsiveness are related to its activities.

The neurotransmitting chemical with which information travels on the fibers that extend between the peripheral nervous system and the pineal gland is noradrenaline, closely related to mescaline and the amphetamine cluster of psychoactive drugs. In addition to serotonin, the body's own LSD, the pineal gland contains endogenous equivalents of the short-acting tryptamines DMT and 5-methoxy-DMT, which have also been identified in spinal fluid, and both harmine and harmaline, the alkaloids present in harmal, one of the possible solutions to the mystery of *soma*.

The discovery of endemic psychoactive compounds and their receptors in the human brain has had an enormous impact on the neurosciences. It somehow failed to persuade

Nixon of the absurdity of any war on drugs, but it did begin to provide some understanding of how psychoactive drugs affect the human nervous system. Among the most significant implications of this research is the realization that many of the most powerful effects of drugs are caused by the nervous system's attempts to compensate for the disturbances they make. Just as the war on drugs displays more excitement, confusion, and paranoia than the drugs themselves, the brain's own search for equilibrium can become the most significant factor in drugs' ability to change states of mind.

This kind of compensation is thought to be a vital factor in the addictive effects of some drugs. When, for example, the heart rate is increased by the use of a substance such as nicotine, the nervous system adjusts the vagus nerve in order to slow the heart rate down. The system adjusts to its new supply, and equilibrium is restored—until, that is, the smoker quits. The vagus nerve, used to maintaining a slower beat, then has to speed the heart up again. This search for equilibrium is also played out in the molecular detail of the brain. Opiates, cocaine, and amphetamines all produce an increase in the levels and activities of dopamine, which is crucial to the brain's reward systems and its pleasure centers in the hypothalamus. If such drugs flood this part of the brain with dopamine, the brain may begin to compensate by, for example, cutting back on its own syntheses of the chemical. If the additional supply dries up, the brain continues to work with a diminished dopamine system until it can compensate again. Such adjustments can have large-scale effects, but they are all made at the molecular level, among the fine details of neurotransmission and chemical synthesis. In the case of opiates and their receptors, this kind of molecular addiction is thought to be compounded by second-messenger effects that inhibit the synthesis of certain proteins within cells. This encourages the neurons to produce more proteins, and, after a while, they get so used to it that they carry on the practice long after the supply of opiates has been withdrawn.

His body knew what vein could be hit. He let the body take over, as in automatic writing, when he was preparing to pick up.

William Burroughs, *Interzone*

Unlike other cells in the body and the brain, neurons do not replicate once the adult nervous system has developed to a certain point. But the mature brain is not a finalized machine, incapable of any further change. It may well have made its most rapid and formative developments before it was even born, but at the level of synaptic transmission the brain has amazing plasticity. New connections are continuously made as new data is learned and new skills are acquired. Dendrites and synapses can multiply and change in the brains of many animals that are exposed to stimulating environments. These processes do not involve the production of new neurons, but they do make significant changes to the finer details of the brain's systems of communication. New synapses and dendrites can be produced; modifications can be made to the molecular structure of existing synapses; and the patterns and intensities of the networks they make up can be changed. Some of these processes were first identified in the 1940s by Donald Hebb, who proposed that synaptic connections are strengthened every time they are made within a brain that is continuously modified as it thinks and learns.

Glutamate is thought to be the neurotransmitter primarily responsible for making these changes to synaptic transmission. There are other messengers involved as well: among the most recent suggestions is that gaseous transmitters, including even carbon monoxide and nitric oxide, help to make these modifications. Studies of people with Alzheimer's disease suggest that acetylcholine plays some role in these material processes of learning and memory as well. Drugs that block the re-uptake of acetylcholine have the effect of enhancing memory, and those that counter its effects result in an impairment of memory. Anandamide, the brain's version of the active chemical in cannabis, is thought to have the opposite effect, allowing the brain to forget in an effort to avoid being overloaded with incoming data and stored memories.

Other neurotransmitting chemicals, especially those that work in the central and autonomic nervous systems, are thought to work as memory enhancers, too. Released in moments of high excitement or great stress, epinephrine and norepinephrine may excite not only the body's sympathetic systems but also the circuits on which it learns and remembers. The endorphins play a similar role. Released by the pituitary gland in an effort to diminish pain and enhance the organism's ability to cope with stress, they interact with receptors in the brain to induce a wave of euphoria, the endorphin rush emulated by opiates. Is this why certain memories tend to "stick in the mind"? People tend to retain vivid memories of times when they were under stress or in a state of high excitement. Flashbacks to such intense events can easily be induced when the conditions are repeated. Perhaps Freud's "compulsion to repeat" has found something of its chemistry.

> Renew the state of affection or bodily Feeling, same or similar—sometimes dimly similar, and instantly the trains of forgotten thought rise up from their living Catacombs!
> Samuel Taylor Coleridge, *Notebooks*

When opiates revealed their presence in the brain, it was as if the poppy had provided its users with the means to detect something of its own modus operandi. Opiates had caused the problem that necessitated the research that revealed their presence in the human brain. Neurotransmitting chemicals had always been carrying information through the nervous system, and now their relations from the outside world were bringing the news that this was how it worked. The dragon had become a meta-messenger.

There seems to be a sense in which drugs have always

given their users some prescient knowledge of the brain. The simple fact that drugs work at all has always suggested that the brain is, in part at least, a chemical system with some more or less direct relation between states of mind and the state of brain chemistry. At the very least, they have understood that states of mind were to some extent responsive to chemical change: drugs make it very obvious that thinking and perception have some inextricable relation to the workings of a chemical system of some kind. And at a time when most writers were still discussing the processes of thought in far more idealistic terms of the mind, the soul, or even, with Immanuel Kant, the faculty of knowledge, De Quincey was making bold materialist claims about the brain and the machinery of dreaming.

De Quincey's interest in this "machinery" led him to a pertinent analogy. In "Suspiria de Profundis," he likened the brain to an extraordinarily sensitive recording device, a palimpsest, "a membrane or roll cleansed of its manuscript by reiterated successions." The old texts had been erased, but, when treated with the right chemicals, all the hidden layers could be made to reappear. "What else than a natural and mighty palimpsest is the human brain?" he asked. "Such a palimpsest is my brain; such a palimpsest, O reader! is yours. Everlasting layers of ideas, images, feelings, have fallen upon your brain as softly as light. Each succession has seemed to bury all that went before. And yet in reality not one has been extinguished." Nothing is ever completely erased: "Countless are the mysterious handwritings of grief or joy which have inscribed themselves successively upon the palimpsest of your brain; and, like the annual leaves of aboriginal forests, or the undissolving snows on the Himalaya, or light falling upon light, the endless strata have covered up each other in forgetfulness."

It was what De Quincey described as the "elaborate chemistry of our own days" that allowed such strata to be brought back to life. The layers of a piece of parchment or vellum, inscribed and imperfectly erased many times, could now be restored: "The traces of each successive handwriting, regularly effaced, as had been imagined, have, in the inverse order, been regularly called back." If the hidden layers of a palimpsest were susceptible to such chemical analysis, so were those of the human brain. In effect, opium was a way of parting the veils "between our present consciousness and the secret inscriptions on the mind."

As De Quincey suspected, there really is a sense in which memories are inscribed in the brain. The neuroscientist Richard Thompson suggests that if "we knew how to 'read' memories from the synaptic connections we might someday be able to reconstruct the lifetime of memories stored in a brain." And if De Quincey was convinced that opium had given him some insights into "the machinery of dreaming" as well, the neurochemistry of dreams suggests that they, too, have a crucial part to play in the development of long-term memory.

Dreams vivid enough to be recalled the next day tend to occur during intermittent periods of a certain kind of sleep. For about a quarter of an average night's sleep, the whole body falls into a state of amazing inactivity. Temperature drops, and even the heartbeat and breathing become irregular. The only activities that increase involve the penis or the clitoris, which become engorged with blood, and the muscles of the eye and the inner ear. These periods of rapid eye movement (REM) sleep are, however, characterized by extraordinary levels of brain activity. The brain consumes more oxygen and uses more energy during REM sleep than when it is, for example, being used to think about its own neurochemistry. As it happens, one of the chemicals thought to stimulate REM activity is acetylcholine, the substance of which Loewi dreamed in 1921. Other synaptic transmissions, including those of the serotonergic raphe neurons with which LSD interferes, are turned off in REM sleep, and there are suggestions that it is this shutdown that allows certain transmissions to occur randomly, triggering images and memories that the dreaming mind then tries to string together into some coherent whole. When the sleeper begins to awake, the serotonin circuits start to fire again. The dreams that come in this moment, "when the waking state of the brain is re-commencing and most often during a rapid alternation, a *twinkling,* as it were, of sleeping and waking," are, as Coleridge knew so well, the finest dreams of all.

> One must make an end to the myth of opium-visions. The episodes in dreams, instead of dissolving on some nocturnal screen and evaporating quickly, make deep veins like agate on the confused surfaces of our bodies.
>
> Jean Cocteau, *Opium*

Hallucinations can seem far more real and tangible than the events in more ordinary dreams and imaginings. Fitz Hugh Ludlow, writing on hashish, found his hallucinations far more impressive than figments of his sober imagination. "Truly, this was imagination," he wrote, "but to me, with eyes and ears wide open in the daylight, an imagination as real as the soberest fact." At their most intense, these hallucinations seem as real as or, indeed, far more real than events in the familiar world. At a certain "pitch of intensity," wrote Henri Michaux in *Infinite Turbulence,* mescaline produces images and events that, although they are "in the mind," are also "a hundred times more real than reality." Michaux called his mescaline hallucinations "admirably synergic, synthetic, 'global,'" and "infinitely more real than the sight of ordinary reality," which, with its "contradictory elements and impressions," is always "open to doubt, distracting, fragmentary." Ironically, he knew where he stood with these visions. "One is never more sure of reality than when it is illusion," he wrote.

But it is still easy for these visual effects to throw the tripper back into old questions and categories. "However agile your mind may have become at apprehending on several fronts," Michaux wrote, "you return often, too often, to the visions because, of all the elusive things crossing through you, they seem the least elusive." Were they to be trusted? Were they really real? Was he seeing visions of the infinite or just another version of Baudelaire's artificial paradise? Michaux was impatient with such lines of thought: "What did it matter what I believed, SINCE THEY WERE THERE!" But what did they mean? What was going on? Too many questions: "It happened, that's all."

> Whoever has taken mescaline took a bowl of vibrations, that is what he took, that is what is possessing him now.
>
> Henri Michaux, *Darkness Moves*

No matter how ephemeral their shifts may seem, drugs are material substances, and they have material effects. Cocteau's opiated visions are like neural tattoos: the images persist as recollections in the mind, but it is the body on which opium makes its mark. Michel Foucault's hallucinations in "Theatrum Philosophicum" shared this ability to "function at the limit of bodies; against bodies, because they stick to bodies and protrude from them, but also because they touch them, cut them, break them into sections, regionalize them, and multiply their surfaces." In his eloquent discussions of the auras perceived during migraine, Oliver Sacks made some similar remarks: "Lattice hallucinations," he wrote, "may not only be seen, and not only projected upon the body surface, but may cut it up, or replace it—so that the body itself is felt as a mosaic or lattice." Sacks quoted Heinrich Kluver's account of a man who said he "saw fretwork before his eyes . . . his arms, hands, and fingers turned into fretwork and . . . he became identical with the fretwork." When Elias Canetti described the symptoms of delirium tremens and cocaine poisoning, he observed that the visual phenomena—which tend to consist of tiny animals or insects crawling on or under the skin—are interpretations of some bodily effect. "The visual hallucinations often become 'microscopic'; innumerable tiny details are registered—animalcules, holes in the walls, dots"—but the "crowd-sensation on the skin is what comes first." It is as if the body becomes aware of its own microscopic processes: the "constant trend of delirium tremens towards the concrete and the small (in cocaine-delirium, often the microscopically small)," Canetti wrote, "has some resemblance to a dissociation of the body into its component cells." He finds it difficult to "dismiss the suspicion that the hallucinations of alcoholics express an obscure awareness of this fundamental condition of the body."

> After smoking, the body thinks. Catastrophe, riots, factories blowing up, armies in flight, flood—the ear can detect a whole apocalypse in the starry night of the human body.
>
> Jean Cocteau, *Opium*

Much of Deleuze and Guattari's work is underwritten by suggestions that visceral effect and sensation precede and produce perceptions that are later grasped, remembered, and expressed as images, ideas, representations. In *Anti-Oedipus*, they argue that particular hallucinations are merely indications of more abstract and less figurative changes: not what one becomes, or what manifests itself, but the process of becoming. "The basic phenomenon of hallucination (*I see, I hear*) and the basic phenomenon of delirium (*I think* . . .) presuppose an *I feel* at an even deeper level, which gives hallucinations their object and thought delirium its content . . . Delirium and hallucination are secondary in relation to the really primary emotion, which in the beginning only experiences intensities, becomings, transitions." The body loses its own categories, the boundaries that normally present it as an organized structure, each of whose organs has its proper function and place. It becomes the Body without Organs: "connection of desires, conjunction of flows, continuum of intensities."

> Need we wonder at Plato's opinions concerning the Body, at least, need that man wonder whom a *pernicious Drug* shall make capable of conceiving & bringing forth Thoughts, hidden from him before, which shall call forth the deepest feelings of his best, greatest, & sanest Contemporaries? and this proved to him by actual experience?
>
> Samuel Taylor Coleridge, *Notebooks*

When De Quincey found himself haunted by "dreams of lakes—and silvery expanses of water," he began to fear "that some dropsical state or tendency of the brain might thus be making itself (to use a metaphysical word) *objective*; and the sentient organ *projects* itself as its own object." De Quincey acknowledged that this suggestion would probably "appear ludicrous to a medical man." Such literal, figurative images are obviously very different for particular individuals, involving all their personal memories, cultural associations, and a host of activities presumed to occur in the highest levels of the cortex and completely beyond the reach of contemporary neuroscience. But De Quincey's basic intuition that certain brain states could become perceptible was not as ludicrous as he feared.

There are compelling suggestions that many of the world's intricate, abstract, repeating patterns—from the colors and designs of Persian carpets to the "paisley" patterns of the Indian subcontinent—have some more or less direct connection with the intense colors and designs that can accompany the use of mescaline, cannabis, LSD, psilocybin, DMT, and many other psychoactive substances, as well as a variety of trancelike states induced by sensory deprivation, sleep deprivation, and fasting and, most commonly, some involuntary states of mind such as epilepsy and migraine. To some extent, they can even be induced by the simple exertion of pressure on closed eyelids. Benoit Mandelbrot's famous series of self-similar fractal images, published in the late 1970s, seemed to reveal the same patterns once again when they displayed precisely the sense of vertiginous travel through speeds, dimensions, spaces that so many drugs had rendered accessible and perceptible. Mandelbrot seemed to have given such patterns a mathematical formula, which turned out to repeat itself in complex structures recurring throughout the natural world. "One may well wonder why it has taken so long for these material effects to be recognized," writes Manuel De Landa in "Non-organic Life." "Of the many possible explanations, one undoubtedly deserves special mention: our 'mathematical technology' was simply incapable of modeling self-organizing behavior." But it seems as if our chemical technologies have long been capable of rendering them perceptible.

The mathematical precision with which these patterns recur with such perfect regularity on so many drugs, in so many cultures, at so many very different times, and in such different brains has led many drug users to explore the possibility that psychoactive substances were allowing them to perceive something of the workings of the brain itself. "Innumerable scales. Infinite segmentation," wrote Michaux in *Infinite Turbulence*, a book alive with mescaline's "sparkling diamonds," and the "fulgurations for microbes," which come "rolling down upon me, towards me, loops, and infinite number of loops and twirls, and cables, plaits and braids, coiling and intertwining in twirls, twirls everywhere, intricately laced, lacework upon lacework, ceaselessly intertwined with yet more lacework, twisting and coiling, an infinity of ornaments for the sake of ornamentation."

"Is it absurd," asked Michaux on mescaline, "to think that brain waves, actually quite slow, become perceptible in some states of violent nervous hyperexcitation, especially that of the visual cortex? New experiments must be performed." Havelock Ellis was less tentative: "Such spontaneous evolution of imagery is evidently a fundamental aptitude of the visual apparatus which many very slightly abnormal conditions may bring into prominence." In *Mescal and Mechanisms of Hallucination*, published in 1928, Heinrich Kluver suggested that amid all the shocking variety of hallucinatory events, and for all the random chaos they were tacitly assumed to put on display, there were indeed recurring patterns of hallucination, universal geometric constants common to many drug-induced and other disturbed states of mind.

When Oliver Sacks pursued this research in the 1992 edition of *Migraine*, he also found that certain processes and patterns of hallucination recur with amazing regularity. Describing the spontaneous, involuntary, and abstract hallucinations associated with the migraine aura, he wrote of "spiderwebs, honeycombs, mosaics, networks, lattices" that creep across the visual field, forming a "mosaic vision" in which

> circles may spin, rotate into spirals, a spiral may deepen into a vortex, a large vortex may break up into little scrolls or eddies. The whole visual field—or sometimes half of it—may be taken over by a violent, complex turbulence, sweeping the perceived forms of objects into a sort of topological turmoil; straight edges of objects may be swept into curves, bits of a scene magnified or distorted as if stretched on a rubber sheet.

The entire "perceptual world, in such states, seems to run completely amok, everything moving and alive, in a state of gross distortion and perturbation. There may be a sense of winds and waves and eddies and swirls, of space itself—normally neutral, grainless, immobile and invisible—becoming a violent, intrusive, distortive field." Sacks described complex lattices, geometric forms, elaborate polygonal networks that "may grow visibly, sometimes with sudden jerks, 'like frost on a windowpane,' or 'primitive plants.' Sometimes there are radially symmetrical forms like flowers or pinecones, continually unfolding in a constant revelation of themselves. Or 'maps,' 'landscapes,' pseudogeographies of great complexity, which constantly create themselves before the inward eye, enlarging endlessly in self-similarity."

Both Sacks and Ronald Siegel emphasize the movements that recur in these patterns, as well as their formal designs. "There is incessant movement at this stage of hallucinosis," wrote Sacks, "not only concentric, rotational, and pulsating . . . but with sudden fluctuations as well, sudden replacements of one pattern or one image by another." This kaleidoscopic quality of abstract hallucinations recalls the "nervous illness" suffered by Flaubert as he worked on *The Temptation of Saint Anthony*. "Each attack was a sort of haemorrhage of the nervous system," he wrote. "It was like seminal losses of the pictorial faculty of the brain, a hundred thousand images at once, exploding into fireworks."

The new experiments Michaux hoped to see performed suggest that such hallucinations are manifestations of cortical rhythms that become perceptible when their oscillations are synchronized and extreme. Such oscillations are thought to be an inevitable corollary of the extreme complexity of the visual cortex. With so many neural networks, circuits, paths, and loops in play, it is hardly surprising that normally moderate rhythms can lose their equilibrium and begin to oscillate to extremes: just as a boat can start to roll at sea, the waves can begin to synchronize; all the neurons start to fire together, and the whole system can be overwhelmed as if by a literal brainstorm. Epileptic seizures involve such synchrony in the whole cerebral cortex, and migraines are among many kinds of partial seizure, brainstorms that affect some particular region of the cortex. Such escalating cycles can also be directly induced by psychoactive drugs, whose specific, local actions at the level of synaptic connections can induce far more global changes in the speeds, amplitudes, and frequencies of brain waves.

Sacks raised the possibility that the waves or rhythms of the visual cortex and, indeed, of the cortex as a whole, "if driven to critical, far-from-equilibrium conditions, actually generate spatial and temporal patterns similar to those of the aura" common to all these disturbed states of mind. It begins to seem as if these abstract matrices really are direct manifestations of the self-organizing processes at work in the visual cortex. Even though they "are normally local, microscopic, and, as such, invisible," these chaotic, self-organizing processes are the basis for all visual perception: "It is only in pathological conditions that they cohere, synchronize, become global, become visible, take over, and thrust themselves as patterned hallucinations into awareness."

If Fitz Hugh Ludlow was ascribing too much to hashish when he argued that the drug was more or less directly implanting the contents of his hallucinations into his mind, it seems that there is a level of basic hallucinatory experience that proceeds independent of the user's personal and cultural preconceptions. Sacks is one of many writers to suggest that these hallucinated patterns occur at a particular stage of hallucination that can then become more figurative and literal: "The geometric patterns might form a 'screen' or 'matrix' upon which, or within which, true images could arise—often tiny images of people and places *within* the interstices or links of the lattice." In the 1950s, Donald Hebb had suggested that the hallucinations that accompany sensory deprivation pass through several distinct stages on their way "from simple to complex." With the eyes closed, the visual field moves from dark to light, and then displays "dots, lines, or simple geometric patterns," which are followed by isolated objects and then more integrated, dreamlike scenes. As Sacks pointed out, this final stage of figurative hallucination is beyond the capacity of the visual cortex. "But the higher cannot occur without the lower," he wrote. "One knows that the primary visual cortex, though it cannot generate complex imagery by itself, is none the less a prerequisite for its generation."

Sacks's discussions of the mechanisms of hallucinations lend some fascinating support to drug users' intuition that something of the drug experience crosses all the boundaries between particular drugs and the cultures, individuals, and historical periods in which they are used. But one of the most extensive implications of Sacks's research is that the brain is a complex, self-organizing system whose chaotic activities become visible in certain extreme states but are by no means peculiar to such disturbances: "chaotic and self-organizing processes occur normally in the cortex" and are "a prerequisite for sensory processes and perception." The cortex is complicated in the most literal sense of the word: it is folded many times, and its "neuronal events and integrations are determined less by local considerations of microanatomy . . . than by global considerations of wave actions and interactions in an alive, spontaneously active, enormously complex neuronal medium."

> When you trip, you liquefy structures in your brain, linguistic structures, intentional structures . . . You think concepts you were not able to think before. Information rushes in your brain, which makes you feel like you're having a revelation. But of course no one is revealing anything to you. It's just self-organizing. It's happening by itself.
>
> Manuel De Landa, interview in *Mondo 2000*

Contemporary neuroscientific research draws much of its inspiration from work on machine intelligence. After devoting years to the development of computers capable of reproducing the abilities of the human brain—an artificial intelligence—this field has more recently advanced to the simulation of neural networks, which are not programmed with preexisting knowledge but given only the most basic capacity to learn and evolve for themselves. The emergence of such machine intelligence is by no means confined to individualized networks in computer labs: in the last decades of the twentieth century, a vast self-organizing network was growing and connecting itself all around the world. Connected to the Net, individual computers and their users find themselves transformed into elements of a vast communications network with its own emergent behavior.

> Imagine . . . the response of a computer to the sort of high-speed transmission of data that occurs when one system dumps its memory load on to another. That must be almost hallucinogenic, the mechanical equivalent of a chemical rush or "peak experience," something like the fleeting feeling we sometimes get of being part of something larger.
>
> Lyall Watson, *The Nature of Things*

If individuated computers have extended themselves into the Net, the late twentieth century's drug experiments have also given individuated people an unprecedented sense of the interconnectivities at work within and between individuals themselves. Gregory Bateson's "slight experience of LSD" allowed him to perceive a complex network of communications links where once he had perceived a discrete and centered self. "Prospero was wrong when he said, 'We are such stuff as dreams are made on,'" he wrote. "It seemed to me that the pure dream was, like pure purpose, rather trivial. It was not the stuff of which we are made, but only bits and pieces of that stuff. Our conscious purposes, similarly, are only bits and pieces. The systemic view is something else again." And from this systemic view, the same one cultivated by the later Freud as well as Foucault, Deleuze, and Guattari, "the system is not a transcendent entity as the 'self' is commonly supposed to be," but rather a "network of pathways" that is "not bounded with consciousness but extends to include the pathways of all unconscious mentation—both autonomic and repressed, neural and hormonal." It is "not bounded by the skin, but includes all external pathways along which information can travel."

These external pathways are traversed by pheromones, the chemical transmitters that are thought to underwrite the chemistry of sexual attraction and the syndrome that allows the menstrual cycles of women living in close contact to synchronize. If so many crucial neurotransmitting chemicals also function as hormones, it seems more than possible that a number of otherwise enigmatic phenomena associated with the use of psychoactive drugs might be related to such pheromonal routes. The "contact high," for example, which seems to allow people who have not taken drugs to pick up something of their effects from people who have taken them, suggests that the chemical messengers at work within individuals might also pass between them. Perhaps the ubiquity of reports that psychoactive plants "call" their hunters to them is also related to the simple fact that psychoactive drugs are communicating substances.

When *Naked Lunch* defined the "junk virus" as "public health problem number one of the world today," Burroughs made himself unpopular with many critics of the war on drugs, who felt that he was fueling drug hysteria. The notion that drugs are contagious diseases has indeed fed into a great deal of overexcited paranoia about drugs: Alfred McCoy reports that, in the 1970s, GIs returning from Vietnam came "home as carriers of the disease and are afflicting hundreds of communities with the heroin virus."

But there is something compelling about Burroughs's intuition that drugs are at least a little like viruses: they spread between people, through the body and the brain, and around the world in ways that do at least have a metaphoric resonance with viral contagions. Viruses are far too active to be defined as dead, inert matter but far too simple to be defined as living things: not unlike Burroughs himself, they are poised on the brink of life and death, defined as "fluid living contagions" when they were first observed in the late nineteenth century. Viruses are parasites that have no independent lives of their own but are obliged to latch on to far more complex hosts: bacteria, or organisms, plants, and animals. The vast majority of viral activity within, for example, a human body is benign and sometimes positively useful. Viruses persist in mutually beneficial relationships with their hosts, with whom they have more genetic common ground than with other viruses. These are semi-living entities that grow and duplicate themselves only in the context of their hosts.

Drugs are viruses only in the most loose and metaphoric terms. But psychoactive substances do seem to display something of this same liveliness, and perhaps it is this that singles them out for the very special treatment that they have always received. The detective starts to wonder if they might belong to another, as yet unidentified, strand of compounds somewhere between viruses and the even more inert stuff of the inorganic world. Neurotransmitters, hormones, pheromones: are these all communicating chemicals, compounds in a league of their own?

Psychoactive substances seem to fit the brain with uncanny precision. But most of them first evolved as weapons in ancient wars, those played out between plants and their predators. Unable to attack their enemies or run away from them, plants have developed surprisingly sophisticated systems of defense. Their resources include physical weapons, such as thorns, bristles, needles, and gums, and more subtle tactics, such as camouflage. But the most refined and effective plant defenses are their chemical weapons: tannins, flavonoids, terpenoids, proteinase inhibitors, saponins, lipids, photosensitizers, and alkaloids. These compounds rarely play important metabolic roles in the plants that contain them: their primary function is defensive. They are the chemical armaments of the vegetable world.

The chemical weapons deployed by plants can be vicious and elaborate. Ronald Siegel describes plants whose photosensitizers affect some insect predators by burning up their cells on exposure to light and kill others by inducing lethal chromosomal abnormalities. Some chemicals function by dissuading predators from eating too many of the plants; others have long-term effects on the growth of the offensive population rather than on individual predators. In what is often an escalating arms race, many predators take steps to counter plant defenses and are met in turn by new plant techniques.

Chemicals that have evolved to affect specific predators may prove fatal to other consumers too. They may not work on them at all. This is often a question of dosages: too much of anything can be fatal, just as small quantities of many lethal substances can be harmlessly absorbed. Many of these weapons are transferable: certain predators not only survive the ingestion of toxic alkaloids but effectively requisition them as their own means of self-defense. Among the repellents used by tiger moths are the toxic alkaloids they ingest with the flowers of a plant on which they feed. In other cases, these compounds can have very different effects on the biochemistries of their new predators. *Nepeta cataria*, or catnip, employs terpenoids called nepetalactones to repel its insect predators. It just so happens that these terpenoids mimic tomcat pheromones. Although other mammals are less impressed, the cats who chew and rub themselves on the plant become so highly excited that it seems as if the terpenoids were made for them. But this singular convergence of chemicals and receptors appears entirely coincidental. Neither the name nor the distribution of catnip seems to have anything to do with cats themselves, which are simply the accidental beneficiaries of a chemical war played out between the plant and its insect predators.

Other plants produce compounds that work on humans and on other species. Cocaine stimulates the llamas who graze on coca leaves; caffeine excites goats when they eat the berries of the coffee bush; fly agarics and peyote buttons send deer into catatonic trances. Since these are among the many alkaloids that also affect human beings, it is widely assumed that people learned about the properties of these plants by observing their effects on animals. Like cats on catnip, humans who drink coffee or chew coca leaves are the unintended beneficiaries of this ancient conflict between plants and predators. They, too, are enjoying the spoils of wars played out elsewhere.

Gregory Bateson's systemic view of human culture extends far beyond the lines connecting individuals: drugs bring out the intricate complexities of a vast chemical economy, a meshwork of reactions and syntheses connecting humans and animals with the most innocent molecular processes of plants.

After many thousands of years of synthesis in vegetable life, the manufacture of these compounds now extends to machines as well. Once morphine, the most powerful constituent of opium, had been extracted from its natural source in 1804, it was quickly joined by codeine, quinine, and caffeine. By the end of the century, many other alkaloids and other compounds had been detached from their native plants. The isolation of these compounds was a landmark in their history. Once inside the lab, they could be altered and combined, designed to treat particular conditions and induce specific effects. But for all the opportunities extraction opened up, this was still a kind of "bucket chemistry"—a haphazard trawl through combinations of chemicals on the off chance of therapeutic discovery. The scales at which it worked were relatively large, the speeds of its processes were slow, and its engineering was far from precise.

By the end of the twentieth century, the research and development of chemical compounds had moved to much smaller scales, higher specifications, and faster processes. New techniques allowed compounds to be engineered at the level not only of their molecular composition but also of molecules themselves. When they met computing in the 1990s, these fields of chemistry became even more sophisticated and advanced. The sheer speeds and capacities of the microprocessor have made it possible to search through vast swathes of molecular combinations with unprecedented efficiency. Mathematical modeling allows chemicals to be designed and assembled as virtual compounds, tried, tested, and manipulated atom by atom on the screen, meeting the wetware world only in the closing stages of their development.

The digitization of drug synthesis marked a dramatic point in its history. But there is a sense in which the continuities in the move from vegetable matter to animals, animals to humans, and humans to labs are more striking than the jumps between these sites. Some kind of preparation has always attended the use of these compounds, from the simple gathering or harvesting of plants to their preparation for consumption: tobacco leaves are dried and cured; coffee beans are roasted and ground. For all the sophistication of modern pharmaceutical techniques, many of today's most popular drugs remain surprisingly close to the plants in which they naturally occur. In the forms of coffee and tobacco, caffeine and nicotine are among the most widely used compounds in the world. Even cocaine, morphine, and heroin continue to be processed from their native plants. The most natural psychoactive substances have emerged from their plant synthesizers, and even the most artificial, inorganic drugs have close relatives in the vegetable world. And all of them can be processed in the vast complexity of a brain that is continuously manufacturing analogous chemicals for itself.

Psychoactive drugs defy all easy distinctions between organic and synthetic substances, natives and aliens at work in a nervous system that is always predisposed to receive them. Their introduction may disturb the equilibrium of the human brain, but they change the speeds and intensities at which it works rather than its chemicals and processes.

> Beyond plants, whose speed is different from our own, and the speed of metals, which shows an even greater relative immobility, lie other realms, whose speed is too slow or too fast for us even to see them or be seen by them.
>
> Jean Cocteau, *Opium*

Mescaline "installs a new tempo in you, but only one," wrote Michaux in *Infinite Turbulence*. "An extremely rapid tempo— too rapid (the tempo of unrest the tempo of hypomaniacs)." LSD implants "two tempos—the mescalinean and an extremely slow tempo—both of which are abnormal, psychotic." Hashish has its own sense of time as well: "impressions of descending at an insane speed and of ascending outrageously," wrote Michaux. Cocteau described the "slow speed" of opium, a drug for which everything "is a question of speed (Immobile speed. Speed in itself. OPIUM: speed in silk)." All the ups and downs, the highs and lows of drugs are ups and downs of tempo, highs and lows of speed. This is the quality that, in Deleuze and Guattari's terms, makes it possible to describe "an overall Drug assemblage in spite of the differences between drugs." All drugs share in this ability to change both the speeds of perception and the perceptions of speeds and speed itself: "All drugs fundamentally concern speeds, and modifications of speed."

All that can be said is this: "Nothing is moderate," whatever the speed, whatever the drug. Even the trade is infected. "Delay is a rule in the junk business," as Burroughs said in *Naked Lunch*. "The Man is never on time."

> "You'll get used to it in time," said the Caterpillar; and it put the hookah into its mouth and began smoking again.
>
> Lewis Carroll, *Alice in Wonderland*

Trade Wars

By the 1990s, more than a hundred psychoactive compounds had been listed in the United Nations Conventions on Narcotic Drugs and Psychotropic Substances, and the illegal trade in these scheduled drugs had grown to extraordinary proportions. This is not a business that keeps accounts: secrecy is one of the secrets of any black-market economy's success, and the drug trade makes no obvious appearance in the books or the figures on the screens of the world's stock markets. There are, however, estimates, and all of them suggest that the traffic in illegal drugs now constitutes one of the largest, most profitable, and most extensive markets in the world. In the mid-1990s, the United Nations Commission on Narcotic Drugs calculated that the volume of sales was somewhere between $400 billion and $500 billion a year. This gives the drug trade something like a 10 percent share of the world's international commodity trade, compared with oil, mineral fuels, and lubricants, which together account for 9.5 percent, the chemicals industry, which accounts for some 9 percent, and the combined market in food, live animals, beverages, and tobacco, which also constitutes some 9 percent of international trade. The legitimate pharmaceutical industry—which includes the licit cultivation and processing of opium poppies in Spain, Australia, India, and Turkey—is estimated to be about half the size of the illicit-drug industry.

This vibrant economy has developed in conjunction with some of the world's most extensive and oldest international laws, a vast legal edifice that authorizes high levels of surveillance and intervention in a wide range of social, economic, and political affairs. The 1988 convention includes opium poppies, opium, and more than eighty opiates and opium derivatives; coca leaves and cocaine; marijuana and hashish; some twenty hallucinogens, including MDMA and its relatives; and dozens of depressants and stimulants.

Nearly all the countries in the world have signed this convention, requiring them to enact legislation that extends far beyond the control of drugs themselves. As they appear in U.S. law, for example, drug laws prohibit imports, exports, and sales of a bewildering variety of "drug paraphernalia," defined as "any equipment, product, or material of any kind which is primarily intended or designed for use in manufacturing, compounding, converting, concealing, producing, processing, preparing, injecting, ingesting, inhaling, or otherwise introducing into the human body a controlled substance, possession of which is unlawful." The list makes specific reference to such items as metal, wooden, acrylic, glass, stone, plastic, or ceramic pipes, water pipes, chillums, bongs, wired cigarette papers, roach clips (which are endearingly defined as "objects used to hold burning material, such as a marihuana cigarette, that has become too small or too short to be held in the hand"), and "miniature spoons with level capacities of one-tenth cubic centimeter or less."

Signatory nations are required to monitor the movement of money in the banking sector, as well as the manufacture and distribution of precursor chemicals, the compounds used in the illicit manufacture of synthetic drugs and the illicit processing of cocaine and opiates. Most of these substances have legitimate medical or industrial uses; some of them are common household chemicals. Acetic anhydride, which is used to process heroin, is also crucial to the manufacture of plastics and a variety of pharmaceuticals. Acetone, a solvent widely used for cleaning paintbrushes and removing nail varnish, is also used in the refinement of cocaine, as is potassium permanganate, widely used as a disinfectant and water purifier. Surveillance extends even to *potential* precursors, chemicals that could be used in the future manufacture of future drugs.

The 1988 convention also deals with the distribution of information and opinion on drugs. In 1997, the International Narcotics Control Board reminded member states that the convention "requires them to establish as a criminal offense public incitement or inducement to use drugs illicitly. The Board urges Governments to ensure that their national legislation contains such provisions and that those provisions are enforced, making violators liable to sanctions that have an appropriate deterrent effect." The board expressed concern about "the constant messages that are in favour of drug use and abuse, particularly from pop culture and some media," and called on governments "to use new forms of communication, particularly the Internet, in order to disseminate objective information about drug abuse. Governments are also invited to seek the co-operation of the telecommunications industries and software providers in removing illegal subject matter from the Internet."

The laws have had an incalculable effect on attitudes, opinions, and perceptions of drugs, their users, their uses, their effects. They have also changed the realities: the risks and the dangers, the profits and the costs, the quality, the quantity, and even the variety of drugs themselves. Illegality has altered all the patterns of their use, proliferating cultures as it tried to drive drugs and their users underground. It is barely possible to speculate about what might have been the case in the unlikely absence of laws that are themselves vague, indiscriminate, and full of holes. The small print suggests that there is no war on the substances themselves: the problem is controlling their use. As the UN itself says, "drug control Conventions do not recognize a distinction between licit and illicit drugs and describe only *use* to be illicit." Drug enforcement is as much a matter of prescription as proscription: many of the scheduled drugs have legitimate uses as medicines, and the readiness with which drugs such as Prozac, Ritalin, Rohypnol, and a wide variety of addictive and debilitating tranquilizers are prescribed makes it clear that governments are more than happy to sanction the use of some psychoactive drugs. Heroin and cocaine, the primary targets in what has become an international drug war, are responsible for only a small number of deaths, injuries, and diseases compared with nicotine and alcohol, and although both opiates and coke can be highly addictive, this cannot be said of drugs such as cannabis, ecstasy, and LSD. Such enormous discrepancies make it difficult to see the logic of the current legal status of psychoactive drugs. The laws seem irrational or disingenuous. The Chinese dragon whispers of conspiracy.

> As the war against heresy was in reality a war for
> "true" faith, so the war against drug abuse is in re-
> ality a war for "faithful" drug use.
>
> Thomas Szasz, *Ceremonial Chemistry*

There is no end to the ironies, the absurdities, the crazy vicious circles at work in this war. But there is no secret here, no
single explanation, no overriding rationale, and certainly no
final solution to a problem that cannot even be defined. The
so-called drug problem has assembled itself as a patchwork of
short-term, piecemeal measures, private interests, tactical necessities. But it is the case that what the UN now describes as
"the drug phenomenon" has emerged from a long and tangled history in which even the most virulent opponents of the
trade are inextricably involved.

They may be excluded from the figures, but, like those of
any black-market economy, the fortunes of the drug trade are
closely entangled with the interests of legitimate trade. With
precious stones and metals, drugs move around the world on
their own distinctive routes, close to the basic currents and
currencies of trade. Cannabis hemp was used as legal tender
in seventeenth-century America; tobacco was once worth its
weight in silver; opium still trades as the black gold standard
of the world's black-market economies. And, as Vernon Coleman observed in the 1980s, cocaine and heroin "are so light
and so easily transportable that they are now preferred to diamonds as an international currency." The covert financial networks stimulated by the traffic in drugs open up new
opportunities for criminal activities and black markets of all
kinds—illicit arms, bootleg goods, and smuggled people—
and with extensive financial, commercial, and industrial links
to the official economy, the money generated by the trade is
widely distributed throughout the global economic system.
The laundering of drug money has become a vast enterprise
in its own right: cleansed in banks, casinos, and other cash-
intensive sectors of the economy, drug profits become indis-

tinguishable from their legitimate equivalent. And hardly any money is completely clean. In 1987, it was reported that one in three bills in U.S. circulation had been used in cocaine transactions. Ninety-four percent of American paper currency was said to be contaminated with traces of cocaine. As Ronald Siegel remarked, the sniffer dogs of the Drug Enforcement Administration are "no more likely to detect illicit activities than the new smell of American capitalism." Not to mention the old smell of European trade. Cocaine and American capitalism are only the most recent examples of a complex history of commercial activity and government control that says as much about the increasingly fraught relationship between markets and the state as about drugs themselves.

Black Markets

> Stupefacients, foods or medicines, these were great factors destined to transform and disturb men's daily lives.
>
> Fernand Braudel, *Capitalism and Material Life*

When Europe's early traders started doing business beyond their shores, they suffered from a peculiar disadvantage. Wherever they went, they encountered cultures that were not merely self-sufficient but also rich in resources: there was plenty to buy, but Europe had so little of its own to sell. As a consequence, the commodities traded by the Europeans were those they found on their travels. There were many important sources of revenue, including silks, dyes, and cotton, precious stones and metals, sugar, spices, perfumes, and, of course, people. As Jean-François Lyotard once remarked, capitalism was "not constituted by a slow process of birth and growth like a living being, but by intermittent acts of vampirization: it merely seizes hold of what was already there." Among the first and most lucrative of these new commodities were those that had some psychoactive effect.

Tea, as everybody knows, was first imported into Europe by Dutch, British, and Portuguese traders in the early seventeenth century, and by the mid-eighteenth century the British East India Company had become the world's leading tea merchant. The British planted tea in India, and the drink became extremely popular in England, Holland, Russia, and much of the Muslim world. In many other European countries, it was rivaled by coffee.

Both tea and coffee are now known to contain the stimulant caffeine, but in tea the alkaloid is mixed with a calming variety of other chemicals. Coffee has much higher concentrations of caffeine, and it is to this chemistry, so the story goes, that coffee owes its very discovery. Noticing that his goats seemed to get excited when they chewed on the berries of the coffee bush, an Ethiopian goatherd decided to take some of the berries to a nearby monastery. According to the legend, the monks brewed them up and discovered that the drink allowed them to pray long into the night without feeling tired. It was later discovered that the roasted beans were even more effective. Although it was sometimes argued that coffee was anti-Islamic, a taste for coffee spread through the Arab world, and the drink was widely used by the end of the sixteenth century. The cultivation of coffee began to spread to the European colonies, and the drink became extremely popular in Venice, Paris, and London in the seventeenth century. European governments imposed strict taxes on the importation of both coffee and tea, and colonial governments collected generous revenues from the trades.

Although some murmurs of disapproval greeted the spread of coffee, less so tea, the sale of tobacco aroused much higher passions across the world. Tobacco is said to have been one of the first gifts made to Columbus and his sailors on their arrival in Cuba. (Visit Havana, and the greeting's still the same:

"Hey, hey, Americano? You want *puro, sí*? Cigars? My father works in cigar factory, good cigars, best *puro*, you want to buy?") According to later reports, one of which appears in C. Cabrera Infante's eloquent history of the cigar, *Holy Smoke*, the sailors saw men who "sucked or blew or absorbed with each breath some sort of smoke, of which it is said that it drowses the flesh and almost makes you drunk in such a way that you never feel tired." At first, the dried leaves of tobacco and the strange practice of smoking them were as incomprehensible to the Europeans as the rituals, healings, and ceremonies that accompanied its use. But tobacco was easy to cultivate and highly profitable and seemed to have only mild, pleasant, and, at first, innocuous effects on its European users.

Although it was in Cuba that the first Europeans came across tobacco, the plant turned out to be widely used across North and South America and was commonly associated with a wealth of myths and shamanic rituals. Nothing of these cultures appeared to spread with its use and cultivation. Tobacco was effectively reinvented when it became an international commodity. But it certainly retained its charm. Whether it was used as snuff, or smoked, or chewed, tobacco was popular wherever it went, and it seems to have spread more quickly and widely than any other cultivated plant in the history of world trade. From here, it moved to Spain in the mid-sixteenth century, and then to England, Italy, Turkey, eastern Europe, and Russia. In the early seventeenth century, it was being grown in many regions of the world: India, Japan, China, Java, Scandinavia, and, of course, Europe's new American colonies.

It also aroused unprecedented hostility. Although its effects were relatively mild and apparently benign, tobacco provoked prohibitionist responses everywhere it went. In early-seventeenth-century Turkey, for example, where smoking was considered to contravene the principles of the Quran, the use of tobacco was prohibited and punishable by death. And in Britain, opposition was led by James I, who described tobacco as "the lively image and pattern of hell" and a "stinking and loathsome thing" in his famous *Counterblaste* against the drug, quoted at length in *The Forbidden Game* by Brian Inglis. He observed that "many in this kingdom have had such a continual use of taking this unsavoury smoke, they are not now able to resist the same, no more than an old drunkard can abide to be long sober." James was appalled by these compelling qualities. Smoking had a glamour and a charm he thought he had dispatched with the burning of the last witches, and he was horrified by the possibility that tobacco might be bringing shamanism home again: "He that taketh tobacco saith he cannot leave it, it doth bewitch him." Health and morality were being eroded by the seductive smoke, and "a great part of the treasure of our land is spent and exhausted by this drug alone." Even more pertinent were James's fears that a population hooked on nicotine threatened the security and efficiency of the nation: "Men who took time off to smoke could be expected to expend much of that time in talk; and the talk might turn to gunpowder, treason and plot."

There was, however, no escaping the extraordinary commercial viability of a substance with such high and repeatable demand. Tobacco seemed to have the knack of making itself indispensable, even to those who opposed it. Prohibition was attempted all over the world, and everywhere it proved ineffective. Governments that had first prohibited its use began to realize the legal and financial potential of its fiscal control. In Britain, the Crown was struggling, and new sources of revenue were desperately sought. In 1622, in spite of his disapproval of tobacco, James decided not to prohibit importation of the drug but to prohibit the domestic production of tobacco, grant monopolies to Bermuda and Virginia, and raise the taxes originally imposed by Elizabeth I by some 4,000 percent. Such high prices, it was hoped, would deny tobacco to the masses and make tobacco profitable to the Crown. The money rolled in, but the high prices did little to affect demand. Smuggling and corruption came to rival the depraving effects of tobacco itself, and soon the Crown was reducing the tariffs, regulating quality, and generally facilitating the availability of tobacco.

The first moves to regulate the tobacco industry were prompted by the recession that hit Virginia and the other tobacco-growing colonies in the seventeenth century. Tobacco was a victim of its own success: thriving production had become overproduction; the market was saturated, and prices dropped. The recession undermined the whole economy, not least because tobacco was used as currency in Virginia. Tobacco paid for goods and services; fines and taxes were levied in it. In the southern colonies, where tobacco farmers relied on slave labor, the tobacco industry fueled and was supported by the slave trade.

The most successful attempts to deal with the glut of tobacco involved the introduction of quality controls. By 1730, a warehouse and inspection system had been established in Virginia; by the 1750s, the system had been put in place in Maryland and Carolina too. Only tobacco of a certain quality now found its way onto the market, and prices began to rise again. Regulation rescued the industry and, with it, the fortunes of the colonies. The success of the tobacco plantations also underwrote the colonies' bid for independence from Great Britain. Hemp, which was only later used as a drug, was also an important source of revenue, but it was tobacco that provided the colonists with the resources for a war that, when they tried to eradicate the colonists' tobacco crops, the British fought as a war on drugs.

By the end of the eighteenth century, tobacco had demonstrated both the futility of prohibitionist policies and the economic advantages of regulation and taxation. There was some opposition to its use on grounds of health and morality: in 1884, the *New York Times* declared that the "decadence of Spain began when the Spaniards adopted cigarettes, and if this pernicious practice obtains among adult Americans the Ruin of the Republic is at hand." In 1921, at the height of enthusiasm for the prohibition of alcohol, tobacco was illegal in fourteen American states. But on the whole, America embraced the commodity that had been so important to its early success. The industry was powerful and continued to enjoy federal protection and subsidy. Tobacco became closely associated with the dream spirit of America.

Until 1911, when the U.S. Supreme Court broke up the monopoly, the world's tobacco market was carved up between the American Tobacco Company and Britain's Imperial Tobacco Company, which had been established to contest America's market lead. Philip Morris, whose Marlboro brand was later to take the market lead, was only a small company in those days. Established in London in 1847, it had opened an American subsidiary in 1902 but enjoyed only limited success until the 1950s, when it rode into the sunset with the Marlboro man. Launched in 1954, this cowboy made Marlboro the world's leading brand name. The corporate motto on the pack is appropriate: *Veni Vidi Vici*, "I came, I saw, I conquered." To smoke a Marlboro was to spend a moment in America, to ride through Marlboro country and gaze toward the frontier with the Marlboro man.

> If soma ever existed the Pusher was there to bottle it and monopolize it and sell it and it turned into plain old time JUNK.
>
> William Burroughs, *Naked Lunch*

In China, opium was a benign and sleeping dragon until it was roused by tobacco in the seventeenth century. When the Portuguese began to sell opium from the Middle East alongside pipes and tobacco from South America, the combination proved irresistible. What had been a long-standing and unproblematic relationship began to blossom into the world's first drug problem.

China had once been one of the world's most advanced and wealthy nations. The Chinese had the abacus, canals, the printing press, paper money, binary mathematics, and the drawloom long before Europe had dreamed of such things. Although they were far in advance of any Western achievements, China's technical and commercial developments were made in the context of a careful Confucian philosophy that allowed none of them to get out of hand. This was, for example, a state that "closed the mines as soon as the reserves of metal were judged sufficient, and which retained a monopoly or a narrow control over commerce (the merchant as functionary)." There was, in other words, no instability, no profit, no surplus, no accumulation. The "vast Chinese territory was crossed and enlivened by chains of regular markets, all linked to one another and all closely supervised," and all excess in the system was turned back into the system as a whole. Although China had all the infrastructure and technologies that might have enabled it to have an industrial revolution of its own, it continually refused to allow such dramatic changes to take hold: whenever "capitalism expanded as a result of favourable circumstances, it would eventually be brought back under control by a state that was virtually totalitarian," wrote Braudel in *Afterthoughts to Civilization and Capitalism*. If this ability to maintain equilibrium was the secret of China's success, it was also one of the underlying reasons why the country found itself overtaken by the European powers in the late eighteenth century. If China wanted for nothing, Europe was unstable, dissatisfied, hungry for change, driven to explore, always looking for more. As this sense of weakness was transformed into the strengths of industrial capitalism and global trade, China's strengths became liabilities.

The Chinese system might have had its own internal tensions, but from Europe's point of view, the empire was formidable and apparently impenetrable. Awed by its sheer size, longevity, and stability, De Quincey in his essays on the Opium Wars described a landmass "defensible, without effort of her men, by her own immeasurable extent, combined with

the fact of having no vulnerable organs—no local concentrations of the national power in which a mortal wound can be
planted." And yet, he wrote,

> the day may come when the empire boasting its thou-
> sands of years shall reach the term of its immortality—
> when, invulnerable on all points but one . . . on that point
> a formidable and outraged power shall press and inflict
> the first wound—a wound which, once open, will be-
> come the standing sore for future mark by one or other
> foe or rival, until a final break-up of the system be accom-
> plished.

De Quincey hated China and couldn't wait for this moment to
come. When he plotted the empire's decline, he thought he
was taking revenge on the Orient he feared in his dreams: the
wound was "the intemperance of opium-eaters or opium-
smokers," and Britain was determined to aggravate it. China
was neither occupied nor colonized but instead broken down
by the aggressive trading practices of the British opium dealers.

> The Celestial Empire possesses all things in prolific
> abundance and lacks no product within its borders.
> There is therefore no need to import manufactures
> of outside barbarians in exchange for our products.
> Emperor Ch'ien Lung, in Martin Booth, *Opium*

The Portuguese were the first European traders to establish
themselves in East Asia, settling Macau in 1557. Then came
the Spanish, to the Philippines, and the Dutch, to Java. But it
was the British merchants who really made their mark and
their fortunes when they started trading with the Chinese. By
1715, the British East India Company had become the main
European agency in Canton. Although the Chinese were wary

of foreign traders, the European merchants were generally welcomed in. Their activities had little impact on China as a whole and were often to the benefit of all parties.

For much of the eighteenth century, the British paid for the tea and silks they purchased from the Chinese with silver. But when the Mogul Empire fell in India, the British inherited a new source of wealth: the Mogul princes' vast fields of opium. As Marx pointed out in *Capital*, Indian opium presented the British with an opportunity to make

> gold out of nothing . . . Great fortunes sprang up like mushrooms in a day . . . Here is an instance. A contract for opium was given to a certain Sullivan at the moment of his departure on an official mission to a part of India far removed from the opium district. Sullivan sold his contract to one Binn for £40,000; Binn sold it the same day for £60,000, and the ultimate purchaser who carried out the contract declared that after all he realized an enormous gain.

As well as such extraordinary commercial opportunities—these were, after all, enormous sums of money in the eighteenth century—the expansion of Indian opium cultivation presented the British with a potential problem: that the use of opium would become widespread in India itself. The drug had to be for export only. And China was the perfect destination. For the first time, the British had something to sell to the Chinese in exchange for tea and silks. "China was now literally being paid in smoke (and what smoke!)," exclaimed Braudel.

The smoking of opium was already a matter of concern to the Chinese authorities. Opium had grown in popularity ever since the Portuguese had mixed it with tobacco, and, as early as 1729, an imperial edict had prohibited its domestic sale and use for nonmedical purposes. But all attempts at prohibition were disastrous. Opium continued to flourish, and when the

British began to import it from India in the 1770s, they found an enthusiasm for the drug that further legislation did nothing to quell. In the late eighteenth century, the British East India Company enjoyed monopolies on the cultivation of opium in India and a large share of its sale in China. It was not the only Western outfit to deal in drugs—Dutch, French, Spanish, Portuguese, and a few American merchants were all involved in the trade. But the British grip on opium was unique. Trading without regard for either Chinese or British law, the East India Company was the world's first drug cartel. Even when the Chinese introduced heavy penalties for trafficking the drug in 1799, the British continued to import it. In 1729, they had moved 13 tons of opium from India to China. In 1839, 2,558 tons were shipped.

The activities of European merchants in Canton were limited by strict Chinese trading restrictions. Trading and settlement were confined to the city, and overseas trade was designed to maximize the emperor's revenue. His representatives collected high, and unevenly levied, dues, and all overseas trade was conducted through the Hong merchants, who effectively monopolized exports on behalf of the emperor. Trade was an imperial monopoly, with the emperor taking both taxes and some of the profits of all overseas trade. The Chinese rejected early-nineteenth-century British appeals for the relaxation of these commercial laws, but in the 1830s the legislation could no longer contain the thriving markets of Canton. The emperor's officials became increasingly open to corruption, and Canton developed into an anarchic trading zone with its own alternative system of trade.

Opium was not directly imported by the British East India Company. The drug was sold in India to smaller companies that smuggled it into Lintin, where Chinese officials collected their own revenues from the illicit trade on which they all grew rich. The British East India Company disowned all involvement with the Lintin trade. "We have no responsibility whatever for what may be happening at Lintin. The vessels there are not owned by the Company, but are country firms whose business is quite separate and over whom we have no authority." But the British government was concerned about the affairs of the East India Company and, by implication, its own complicity in a trade that was sometimes compared with slavery. Reports that the East India Company was trafficking dangerous drugs were embarrassing for the Whigs. Public awareness of the undesirable effects of opiates had grown in the early nineteenth century, and the British government could hardly pretend ignorance and condone the Chinese trade. The company argued that it was up to the Chinese to enforce their own laws and insisted that its monopoly was functioning to restrict the production of opium and so ameliorate the Chinese opium problem. There may have been an element of truth in these arguments for a while. But as the cultivation of opium in India began to extend beyond the British fields, the company dropped all pretensions to restriction, and with them the price of opium. It bought or forced out the new Indian growers and increased its monopoly still further.

By 1830, the company had become the main player in a highly profitable network of organized crime, a business riddled with bribery, corruption, and violent coercion. A government investigation was launched that year, and the company lost its monopoly in 1833. But the government had no option but to allow the traffic to continue. Opium was a "necessary exchange for tea." The British were as hooked as the Chinese. At this time, the opium trade was worth in excess of two million pounds, an income that effectively paid for half the annual costs of the British Crown and the civil service. The investigating committee found against the practices of the East India Company on a number of counts but condoned the traffic in opium. It would not be desirable, it reported, "to abandon so important a source of revenue as the opium trade."

In the 1830s, the Chinese were also desperately looking for

solutions to the opium problem. Many imperial advisers were in favor of legalizing and taxing the trade and use of opium, pointing out that prohibition had meant only that "the smokers of the drug have increased in number, and the practice has spread almost through the whole empire." By the early nineteenth century, the use of opium had become prevalent as far north as the capital, where even the emperor's courtesans and officials were using the drug to what he considered unacceptable excess. Although, as De Quincey reported, "The punishments of the traffic and use of opium had been gradually increased, until made 'death by strangling,' yet the desire of gain and the desire of the drug was superior to the fear of death."

Others were more sympathetic to opium and acutely aware of the revenue a homegrown trade would bring: "To shut out the importation of it by foreigners, there is no better plan than to sanction the cultivation and preparation of it in the empire." Given that foreign intervention was one of China's greatest complaints about the opium trade, legalization was a tempting proposal that would have kept the trade in Chinese hands. Nevertheless, the emperor's conservative advisers finally persuaded him that only prohibition would preserve the highest laws and best interests of the empire. In an 1839 edict, the imperial commissioner, H. E. Lin, insisted that "ships afterward to arrive here shall never, to all eternity, dare to bring any opium."

The British companies regarded such statements as provocative in the extreme. William Jardine, of Jardine and Matheson, which became the leading British company in China when the East India Company lost its monopoly on Asian trade in 1833, made vehement representations to the foreign secretary, Lord Palmerston, in 1839, pointing out the benefits of a military intervention to force the Chinese to trade freely with the Western world. There was also an outstanding matter of compensation for opium cargoes seized by the Chinese authorities. Palmerston continued to press the Chinese to legalize the traffic and open up their ports. When they still refused, the warships were dispatched.

At the end of the events that became known as the First Opium War, prohibition was no longer tenable, and as a war-weary China gave in to the trade, British imports of opium doubled in the next ten years. In 1856, hostilities were reopened when a renewed campaign against opium led to the arrest of a British-registered smuggling ship. Palmerston waded in again, meeting his opposition in Parliament with a successful general election, which gave him a mandate for war. With the support of both France and America, the British ensured that this Second Opium War was the final blow for Chinese protectionism. Britain continued to reap the rewards of the opium trade until the early decades of the twentieth century. And at the time the Great War broke out, Britain was manufacturing vast quantities of morphine for the use of its troops and also for export to China and the Far East.

China suffered greatly when it lost its fight against the trade. The Treaty of Nanking opened Canton, Amoy, Foochow, Ning-po, and Shanghai to foreign trade and ceded Hong Kong to the British Crown. The Russians won the Maritime Province, where they built Vladivostok, and war with Japan led to the loss of Korea. What De Quincey had seen as a "vast country, pure, homogeneous, unmixed, and uncontaminated alone of all the earth in its people and lineage," was now wide open to all the corruptions of foreign influence and trade, and the old empire had been torn apart.

> For the first time, the European economy . . . aspired to control the economy of the entire world and to be its embodiment all over the globe, where every obstacle collapsed before the Englishman, first of all, and eventually before the European. This held true until 1914.
>
> Fernand Braudel, *A History of Civilizations*

But the Englishman laughed too loud and too soon. The industrial and economic changes from which De Quincey was so desperate to escape were being funded by the drug to which he had so optimistically turned for relief. And when he thought he was plotting China's decline, De Quincey was writing his own story and the script for the future of his own Western lands. If Coca-Cola's cocaine taught the mass consumer markets of the twentieth century its tricks, opium taught mercantile capitalism some even more basic lessons about trade. Its eighteenth-century merchants changed the speeds and scales at which it traveled around the world, opening trade routes, blazing trails for other markets and commodities, and triggering an opium diaspora that has continued to this day. The drug resisted, ignored, or overcame all attempts to bring it under control and became, in every sense, a dream commodity: supplies were easily arranged, demand was guaranteed to repeat itself. Its users were the perfect consumers, and opium the perfect commodity, "the ideal product," as Burroughs later said, "the ultimate merchandise. No sales talk necessary. The client will crawl through a sewer and beg to buy."

> The spectacle is a permanent opium war which unleashes a limitless artificiality in the face of which all living desire is disarmed.
>
> Guy Debord, *The Society of the Spectacle*

Raw opium was the very stuff of raw capitalism, and not only because of the size of the trade and the heights of the profits it made. All markets learned the secrets of its success. Opium was "the mold of monopoly and possession," a graphic demonstration of the ease with which desires could be turned into necessities and demand manipulated to satisfy supply. The opium trade was the first story of runaway success for markets that have chased the dragon ever since.

As Flaubert said to Baudelaire, it is always difficult to say "what will come of it all later." In the China of the twenty-first century, the very cities that were once forced open and destroyed by the East India Company are now emerging as the site of the world's first true megalopolis, a city that is growing beyond anyone's control and will soon turn Macau, Hong Kong, and Canton into thriving suburbs of its own. But things were very different in the nineteenth century. The extreme poverty and instability into which China was plunged in the wake of the Opium Wars triggered waves of emigration that took Chinese workers to Europe, Australia, and America and led to the first large-scale Chinese settlements in the countries of Southeast Asia. This was the heyday of European colonial power: Burma and Malaya were British colonies, and Vietnam, Cambodia, and Laos were French. The Philippines were Spanish, until 1898, and Indonesia was Dutch. Only Siam resisted European colonization: although the Siamese accepted some degree of British influence, they cherished their autonomy and remained so independent that they later named their nation Thailand, land of the free.

All the region's European colonial powers built railroads, mines, and cities where once there had been only sleepy villages. Many of the workers they employed to construct this new world were emigrants from the coastal regions of China's southern states. With these Chinese migrants traveled knowledge of the use and cultivation of opium. Most colonial governments saw this as a golden opportunity to supplement the income they received from home: they developed poppy plantations and licensed the use of opium, and at the end of the century, government-sponsored opium dens were "as common as the pith helmet." As Alfred McCoy pointed out, "Every nation and colony in South East Asia—from North Borneo to Burma—had a state-regulated opium monopoly." When a later wave of emigrants, many of them Chinese nationalists in flight from Maoist China, moved south as well, the region on the borders of Burma, Laos, and Thailand became established as the Golden Triangle, an area from which most of the world's heroin is exported to this day.

Chinese migrants moved far beyond Southeast Asia in the late nineteenth century. By the end of the century, Chinatowns had nestled in many European, Australian, and American cities. And in these enclaves, there were other enclaves, too.

Charles Dickens's unfinished *The Mystery of Edwin Drood*, written in 1869, begins with an Oriental dream: "Ten thousand scimitars flash in the sunlight, and thrice ten thousand dancing-girls strew flowers. Then, follow white elephants caparisoned in countless gorgeous colours, and infinite in number and attendants." But the dream is interspersed by visions of an English cathedral town and a spire the dreamer gradually realizes belongs to a collapsed bedstead. As the dreamer collects his "scattered consciousness," he finds himself in

the meanest and closest of small rooms. Through the ragged window-curtain, the light of early day steals in from a miserable court. He lies, dressed, across a large unseemly bed, upon a bedstead that has indeed given way under the weight upon it. Lying, also dressed and also across the bed, not long-wise, are a Chinaman, a Lascar, and a haggard woman. The two first are in a sleep or stupor; the last is blowing at a kind of pipe, to kindle it.

De Quincey, who couldn't cope with the visit of a single Malayan, would have been horrified by the prospect of finding opium dens in his precious English towns. But they were increasingly common in the late nineteenth century. England was hardly unused to opium, but, as the Chinese themselves knew all too well, opium smoking was a very different thing. And as Chinese migrants moved around the world, the smoking of opium, which had been encouraged with such careless enthusiasm by the British traders in China, had come home. The empire was returning fire.

> The patience of a poppy. He who has smoked will
> smoke. Opium knows how to wait.
>
> Jean Cocteau, *Opium*

In Britain, America, and many other countries, the Chinese were resented and rarely welcomed in. In America, where they built the railroads coast to coast, Chinese workers met with great hostility from the labor organizations to which their white counterparts belonged. In San Francisco, the smoking of opium was banned as early as 1875. In the early 1900s, American unions led attacks on the country's hundred thousand or so immigrants in what Thomas Szasz described as an attempt "to handicap them as competitors by depriving them of opium, whose habitual but moderate use helped them to cope with life and its vicissitudes." Chinese economic success was often jealously ascribed to their use of the drug, and rumors of debauchery in opium dens fueled popular—and hardly implausible—beliefs that opium gave Chinese men an unfair sexual advantage in their dealings with white women. These arguments were later repeated in Britain, where the Opium Wars and the work of writers such as De Quincey and Dickens had paved the way for vehement racist hostility. In 1907, the National Seamen's and Firemen's Union won a campaign to restrict opium smoking to private houses in London.

If the Chinese association with opium legitimized this kind of racist attack, later waves of drug hysteria served racist interests too: in the 1930s, "reefer madness" was said to be the Mexican weakness, and cocaine was supposed to make the black population of the southern states strong enough to resist even a .32 caliber bullet (this is often said to be the reason for the development of the .38). The pattern has repeated itself with every subsequent antidrug campaign that has swept the Western world. And the syndrome is by no means peculiar to European cultures: when nineteenth-century China struggled to contain the opium problem, a drug that had been used at home for centuries became "a poisonous substance from over-seas."

As the Western world introduced its first domestic opium controls, the Chinese authorities were still struggling with what had become a crippling problem. In 1906, China entered into the Ten Years Agreement with India, a treaty in which each nation gave the other a decade to eradicate the opium trade. The treaty recognized that it was impossible to control opium on a national basis. But it was already clear that even such bilateral moves were insufficient to the task of dealing with a trade in which so many nations were involved. Any effective treaty would have to be agreed on by them all. And China was by no means the only Asian nation to be swamped by opium. In the United States, there was great concern about the use of opium in the Philippines, won by America from Spain in 1898. Although the Spanish had instituted a system of supplying opium to registered addicts, a new American commission reported that its use on the islands was out of control. Prohibition, it concluded, was the only way. And, as the Chinese had discovered, prohibition demanded some kind of international control.

It was President Roosevelt who instigated the first multilateral discussions about drugs. In Shanghai in 1909, delegates from thirteen nations with some interest in the opium trade met to discuss the problems it posed. Although it had no legislative powers, the meeting paved the way for a later convention in The Hague, where three years later the articles of the Hague Opium Convention were drawn up.

The Shanghai conference was the first time so many nations had ever gathered to discuss trade of any kind. As the first of many U.S. interventions in the history of international drug control, this was also the event with which the United States began to emerge as leader of the drug-free world. Roosevelt's administration did have legitimate concerns about the Philippines. But there were other, deeper reasons for Roosevelt's campaign against the trade. Although some American companies were involved in the opium economy, the United States was one of the few leading nations to which opium brought virtually no economic advantage. Britain was raking in the profits, and France, Holland, Spain, Portugal, Japan, and even China itself were earning revenues from opium. But America was largely out of the loop. On top of this, it was also clear that many Asian nations were buying opium from Europe when they could have been buying other goods—tobacco, for example—from the United States. In this sense, the Shanghai conference was simply an American attempt to remove the competition by changing the rules.

If America's workers had once argued that opium gave their Chinese counterparts unfair economic advantages, its politicians now made the same point to the nations that met in Shanghai. The prospect of an end to the opium trade was politically and economically momentous for them all. Britain was especially vulnerable. In the United States, it was said that "the financial problem which the situation offered her was one of the most difficult which any nation ever has been called upon to solve." A 1911 article in the *New York Times* declared, 'She recognizes, though, that the opium traffic, while it is not exactly a parallel to the slave traffic, is, after all, analogous to it, and she is arranging to destroy the one as she destroyed the other."

The 1912 Hague convention recognized that control of the production, distribution, and consumption of drugs could never be achieved by nations working on their own. And there was more than opium at issue: the Hague convention also extended the remit of the Shanghai meeting to include cocaine. As a unique piece of international legislation, the Hague convention was later incorporated into the Treaty of Peace that settled the First World War and established the League of Nations. Drugs were high on the agenda of the league. It convened a committee on the subject at its inaugural meeting in 1920 and committed itself to encouraging member states to pass and enforce laws to limit the manufacture, import, sale, distribution, export, and use of all narcotic drugs to medical purposes.

These aims were reiterated and reinforced by the 1931 Geneva Convention, which Brian Inglis described as the first ruling "not merely to apply the principles of a controlled economy to a group of commodities by international agreement, but also to regulate all phases of the production of dangerous drugs from the time the raw material entered the factory to the final acceptance of the finished product." Subsequent international treaties have been composed under the auspices of the United Nations, which superseded the League of Nations after the Second World War. Current treaties include the 1961 Single Convention on Narcotic Drugs, the 1971 Convention on Psychotropic Drugs, and the 1988 Convention against Illicit Traffic in Narcotic Drugs and Psychotropic Substances.

> The drug phenomenon is unique in the number of aspects of people's lives which it affects—the health of the individual, political and economic development, the safety of the streets and the stability of governments.
>
> United Nations International Drug Control
> Programme, *World Drug Report*

It was also with the 1909 conference in Shanghai that America began to develop its own federal drug laws. Hamilton Wright, the American delegate to the conference, later said that although he went to the meeting expecting to learn about "the dreadful things the Chinese had been doing to themselves with opium," he soon discovered that they were not alone. When his comments were reported in the *New York Times*, the headline said it all: UNCLE SAM IS THE WORST DRUG FIEND IN THE WORLD. Wright realized that "we were importing into the United States, and legally importing, in our selfish greed to fill our own fat purses, undreamed of quantities of the same drug which we believed the Chinaman should cease to use."

He thinks in terms of losers and winners. He will be a
winner. He will take it all. So he sets out to do just
that. He will eliminate all unpredictable factors. He
will set up the American Non Dream.

William Burroughs, *Ah Pook Is Here*

The 1909 Smoking Opium Exclusion Act prohibited possession of opium, and five years later came America's first com-
prehensive drug legislation, the Harrison Narcotic Act. Like
the Hague Convention, the 1914 Harrison Narcotic Act was
backed by powerful moral arguments about the dangers,
temptations, and evils of drug use. But here, too, the moral issue was a smoke screen for the real imperatives of trade and
industry. America's domestic legislation was introduced as a
new tax, not an act of prohibition, and if its drug legislation
now amounts to a direct ban on the trade and use of certain
substances, it arrived at this point only after decades of piecemeal additions and amendments to what were first presented
as fiscal controls. The Harrison Narcotic Act provided for "the
registration of, with collectors of internal revenue, and to impose a special tax upon all persons who produce, import,
manufacture, compound, deal in, dispense, sell, distribute, or
give away opium or coca leaves, their salts, derivatives,
or preparations, and for other purposes." Licenses could
be bought by doctors, pharmacists, importers, and manufacturers, and patent-medicine manufacturers were not even
required to buy licenses as long as they used only small
quantities of opiates or cocaine. On paper, unlicensed users of
these substances were guilty of tax evasion rather than trafficking or possession.

The fiscal basis of this legislation won it widespread con-
gressional support. Politicians who might have been more
wary of overtly prohibitionist policies passed the 1914 act in
the belief that they were taxing commodities rather than re-
stricting constitutional rights. In practice, however, the act
was an act of prohibition. Licenses were difficult to get and

easily revoked if doctors or pharmacists were suspected of supplying addicts with the drugs. But by the mid-1920s, there were hundreds of thousands of heroin addicts in America. Many of them had picked up a taste for opiates from using morphine in the First World War. And as medical outlets for opiates and cocaine were gradually closed down, black markets grew to fill the gap.

> With adequate profit, capital is very bold. A certain 10 per cent will ensure its employment anywhere; 20 per cent will produce eagerness; 50 per cent positive audacity; 100 per cent will make it ready to trample on all human laws; 300 per cent and there is not a crime at which it will scruple, nor a risk it will not run, even to the chance of its owner being hanged. If turbulence and strife will bring a profit, it will freely encourage both. Smuggling and the slave trade have amply proved all that is stated.
>
> Karl Marx, *Capital*

Although opium was the first substance subjected to such extensive federal control, it was by no means America's most controversial intoxicant. Sobriety was a virtue in these puritanical times, and while the temperance movement expressed some concerns about the widespread availability of opium, its real targets were liquor and beer.

America's Protestant origins meant that alcohol had always been a matter of dispute and disrepute, and the first prohibition dates back to 1838, when its sale and manufacture were prohibited in the state of Tennessee. By 1917, there were twenty-three dry states in America. Two years later, with the ratification of the Eighteenth Amendment to the U.S. Constitution and the Volstead Act, which dealt with the enforcement of the amendment, the production, distribution, and consumption of alcohol were prohibited by federal law.

One of the immediate effects of this policy was that the

federal government lost more than $400 million in annual revenue from the taxation it had previously applied to the interstate alcohol trade. It also acquired an increase of more than $9 million in expenditures necessitated by the administration and enforcement of the act. Bootlegging became a boom industry and home-brewed alcohol a health hazard. Piracy, smuggling, hijacking, and illegal manufacture fed the organization of crime, and law-enforcement officers became involved in bribery, corruption, and protection rackets. Judges, lawyers, government officials, and politicians were charged with violations of the law.

In the early years of Prohibition, vast quantities of alcohol were brought into the United States from the Caribbean. Just as they had pushed opium on a reluctant China, the British were some of the most enthusiastic traders of rum and whiskey from the Bahamas. Ships were anchored off the East Coast in such numbers that they formed a line that was dubbed Rum Row, and there were many celebrated chases as the Coast Guard struggled to cope with liquor smugglers. By 1922, Nassau had acquired the ambience of a gold-rush town: gunmen, dealers, sailors, sex, and alcohol. One of its great rumrunners, Bill McCoy, is said to have smuggled some three million dollars' worth of liquor into the United States in just three years. Liquor also entered the United States from Mexico and Canada, especially Montreal, and Chicago and Detroit became important distribution centers for alcohol from the north. Smaller operators were gradually squeezed out by increasingly sophisticated syndicates, and McCoy turned out to be the first in a long line of large-scale players: Mannie Kessler, Big Bill Dwyer, Lucky Luciano, Johnny Torrio, Al Capone. Some of the syndicates and combines were highly organized, with hundreds of employees, corporate structures, and factories in which even "the real McCoy" was cut or watered down. They ran underground speakeasies and nightclubs and integrated alcohol with older trades: racketeering, prostitution, gambling. And the profits were enormous. Wealthy syndicates invested in fast ships, sophisticated communications equipment, and generous payments in pursuit of close ties to politicians, the police, customs officers, and coast guards. As Prohibition continued, organized crime carved up the trade between itself, often with the knowledge and consent of law-enforcement agencies. At the height of his power, Al Capone was said to make an annual profit of sixty million dollars, most of it from his dealings with alcohol. In 1931, he was sentenced to eleven years in prison and fined fifty thousand dollars. In spite of a long and violent criminal career, Capone was famously charged with offenses relating to income-tax evasion.

Responsibility for the interdiction of liquor shipments lay with the U.S. Customs Service and the Coast Guard, which was assigned new ships—destroyers, cruisers, and patrol boats—in 1924. In the same year, a treaty gave the U.S. Coast Guard rights of search and seizure over British ships within an hour's distance of the coast. Ex-Navy destroyers were reconditioned, and cruisers, patrol boats, and thousands of new officers were assigned to the enforcement of the dry laws. But all these efforts were futile. Nothing stopped liquor coming into the United States. Demands for reform became more vociferous, and in 1930 President Hoover set up the Wickersham Commission to review the Prohibition laws. The commission's report recommended the repeal of Prohibition, and, with the passage of the Twenty-first Amendment under Roosevelt, alcohol was legal once again.

> For those who dare to face the truth, we know, don't we, the results of the suppression of alcohol in the United States. A superproduction of madness: beer on a diet of ether; alcohol larded with cocaine, which is sold secretly; multiplied drunkenness, a sort of general drunkenness. *In short, the law of the forbidden fruit*. The same for opium.
>
> Antonin Artaud, "General Security:
> The Liquidation of Opium"

The first American agency committed to drug control was the Federal Bureau of Narcotics, established by President Hoover in 1930. At its head was Harry J. Anslinger, who was to hold the position of commissioner of narcotics for more than thirty years, until he was removed from the post by John F. Kennedy. Anslinger had come to prominence during the years of alcohol prohibition when, in 1926, as a consul in the Bahamas, he sealed an agreement with the British to deal with a case of rum smuggling between Nassau and the American coast. He was appointed to the Prohibition Bureau, whose work at that time included narcotics, and then, in the aftermath of a scandal involving collusion between narcotics agents and drug traffickers, he took the job of commissioner of the new Bureau of Narcotics.

One of Anslinger's archenemies was the young mafioso Lucky Luciano, one of the most successful black marketers to have emerged from the years of Prohibition. For years after the establishment of the drug laws, the Italian Mafia refused to compromise its values by dealing in drugs. The bulk of the traffic was conducted by large and powerful Jewish gangs, while the Mafia traded in alcohol. But in the late 1920s, a new generation of mafiosi began to move into the heroin trade. Lucky Luciano, often described as "one of the most brilliant criminal executives of the modern age," transformed the Mafia and is credited with establishing many of the structures, operational principles, and alliances that continue to characterize international organized crime. He had no moral qualms about drugs. Anticipating the end of alcohol prohibition, which had previously been the Mafia's most lucrative source of income, Luciano's new-look Mafia broke with tradition, teamed up with the Jewish gangs, and invested in heroin and prostitution. Heroin proved the perfect commodity: substantial profits and an ever-increasing market that was easy to monopolize. Linked with prostitution, it became even more viable: Luciano soon discovered, as Alfred McCoy wrote, that "addicting his workforce to heroin kept them quiescent, steady workers, with a habit to support and only one way to gain enough money to support it." Prostitution has been entangled with such systemic drug use ever since.

By the mid-1930s, Luciano controlled two hundred New York City brothels and more than a thousand prostitutes; he was earning somewhere in the region of ten million dollars a year. Then Lucky Luciano's luck seemed to run out. He was convicted on charges of enforced prostitution and given a thirty-year minimum sentence.

Anslinger needed a new enemy and turned his attention to cannabis. Quietly overlooking the extent to which hemp had contributed to the economic health of the early colonies—George Washington had even made its cultivation mandatory for farmers during the War of Independence—Anslinger orchestrated a hysterical campaign against the use of hemp and encouraged the use of its Hispanic name—marijuana—in an effort to associate it with what he portrayed as the pernicious influence of America's own backyard. By the mid-1930s, several states had passed legislation that effectively added marijuana to the drugs covered by the Harrison Narcotic Act. And this creeping legislation paved the way for the federal control of marijuana in 1937. Just as the Harrison Narcotic Act had licensed and taxed users of opiates and cocaine, the Marijuana Tax Act avoided an outright ban on marijuana by outlawing its untaxed use. It specified that physicians, dentists, veterinarians, and others could continue to prescribe cannabis if they paid a license fee of one dollar per year; pharmacists, importers, and producers could operate, for higher fees, as well. The medical profession opposed the act, as did a variety of other interested parties: even birdseed distributors argued that canaries would stop singing without marijuana seeds.

But the parties with an interest in the eradication of the hemp crop were far more powerful and vocal than its supporters. Several large industries and wealthy industrialists stood to gain from the prohibition of a plant that had not only recreational uses but also medicinal value and a wide range of

other commercial uses in the textile and papermaking industries. And it just so happened that Harry Anslinger had close
associations with several leading industrialists in these fields.
He was also a close friend of William Randolph Hearst, whose
newspapers were happy to publicize wild stories of reefer
madness, mad Mexicans, marijuana-induced violent crime,
and sexual depravity.

> "Don't listen to Hassan i Sabbah," they will tell you.
> "He wants to take your body and all pleasures of the
> body away from you. Listen to us. We are serving
> The Garden of Delights Immortality Cosmic Con-
> sciousness The Best Ever In Drug Kicks."
>
> William Burroughs, *Nova Express*

Cannabis was the first of many drugs to join opiates and cocaine on the wrong side of national and international law. By
the late 1960s, the Johnson administration had consolidated
the tangle of state and federal policies that had evolved from
the 1914 act, and in place of the Federal Bureau of Narcotics
and the Bureau of Drug Abuse Control, a division of the Food
and Drug Administration, Johnson established the Bureau of
Narcotics and Dangerous Drugs in 1968. Its mission was
"to enforce the laws and statutes relating to narcotic drugs,
marihuana, depressants, stimulants, and the hallucinogenic
drugs."

This was the point at which U.S. politicians started to talk
about a war on drugs. Words like *war, evil*, and *peril* had pep-
pered discussions of drugs since the early years of the twentieth century, but it was in the late 1960s that the language of
drug control became increasingly aggressive. Military metaphors were used to convey the magnitude of both the drug
problem and the measures needed to contain it. In New York,
Governor Rockefeller asked, "Are the sons and daughters of a
generation that survived a great depression and rebuilt a
prosperous nation, that defeated Nazism and Fascism and

preserved the free world to be vanquished by a powder, needles, and pills?" Describing drug addiction as "a threat akin to war in its capacity to kill, enslave, and imperil the nation's future," Rockefeller launched New York State's Narcotics Addiction Control Program as "the start of an unending war." Rockefeller's legacy lives on: New York State still has some of America's most draconian drug laws. And when Richard Nixon was elected president of the United States, New York's governor was not alone. Drug abuse was described as a national emergency, America's public enemy number one, a threat to social, economic, and political stability. In the midst of this outcry, Nixon declared "a total war on dangerous drugs."

The metaphors of war became increasingly real: the U.S. Customs Air Interdiction Program was launched, and Nixon declared that international narcotics control was both a domestic priority and a foreign-policy issue. "I consider keeping dangerous drugs out of the United States just as important as keeping armed enemy forces from landing in the United States," he declared. "We are going to fight this evil with every weapon at our command." It was, he said in 1971, "imperative that the illicit flow of narcotics and dangerous drugs into this country be stopped as soon as possible." As a measure of the real intent behind these words, Nixon established the Cabinet Committee on International Narcotics Control, which included representatives from the Central Intelligence Agency, the State Department, the Treasury, and the Department of Defense, as well as the ambassador to the UN. This new organization was crucial to the "formulation and coordination of all policies of the federal government relating to the goal of curtailing and eventually eliminating the flow of illegal narcotics and dangerous drugs into the United States."

Nixon did enjoy some success. U.S. drug-enforcement officers collaborated with their counterparts in Marseilles to seize vast quantities of heroin and several heroin factories, and in 1972 Turkey bowed to U.S. pressure to ban the production of the opium with which this famous French connection began. Exports of opium had been controlled by the Turkish state since its inception in the 1920s, but within Turkey cultivation was widespread. The United States threatened to suspend economic aid and military support if Turkey did not eradicate the crop. But the Turks were not so easy to manipulate. The problem, they argued, was America's demand for heroin, not Turkey's ability to supply it. There were demands for economic compensation, and the United States eventually paid some 10 percent of the figure proposed by the Turks.

Nixon claimed victory: he had broken the French connection and disrupted America's heroin supplies. But these maneuvers simply encouraged the large-scale production of opium and the manufacture of heroin to move farther east, and, within a few years, the Turkish government had lifted restrictions on opium again.

The short-term success of Nixon's policy nevertheless boosted American enthusiasm for the war on drugs. Now that it had become a matter of foreign policy, drug enforcement legitimized widespread U.S. intervention in the military, political, and economic affairs of a number of other countries. In 1973, Nixon consolidated all federal antidrug forces into the Drug Enforcement Administration (DEA), an "elite drug-fighting organization," which remains the central player in the U.S. war on drugs. The DEA's mission is to enforce U.S. laws on drugs "by bringing to the criminal and civil justice system of the United States, or any other competent jurisdiction, those involved in the growth, manufacture, or distribution of controlled substances in or destined for the illicit traffic in the United States." Since any particular crop or consignment might well be destined for the United States, this mission legitimates DEA involvement in the global drug trade.

This had implications for the folks back home as well. Surveillance of overseas operations inevitably unearthed information about the activity of U.S. citizens, and, further down this slippery slope, U.S. intelligence agencies ended up tapping domestic phones and drawing up lists of American organizations and individuals with histories of illicit drug activities. As Nixon discovered on several counts, there were limits to such covert activities. But if his covert integration of military and civilian power was discontinued shortly after it began, Nixon's war on drugs set many precedents for later drug-enforcement strategies. When Ronald Reagan declared war again in 1982, his administration amended the Posse Comitatus Acts, which were passed in the 1870s to protect the distinction between military and civilian power in the United States, and so sanctioned the use of military personnel and equipment in the domestic enforcement of drug laws. Even the military feared that such a move would present an unprecedented threat to civilian government, but the Reagan administration was undaunted and determined to "do what is necessary to end the drug menace." And so the troops were rallied, the war declared. The First Lady smiled at the youth of America and told them "Just Say No" to drugs. No one can deny that the message hit home: soon JUST SAY YES was scrawled on the walls of the Western world.

Double Agents

If Nixon's war had centered on the heroin trade in the Middle East, Reagan's declared enemy was cocaine. The commercial cultivation of cocaine dates back to the first Spanish plantations established in the Andes in the sixteenth century. But the market for the drug was relatively small in the wake of the First World War, and the rise of the modern cocaine trade has much more recent sources in the 1940s development of Colombia, Bolivia, and Peru, the three Andean nations in which coca thrives. Successive postwar governments encouraged settlement in the Andean foothills and the Amazon Basin, and migrants to these areas were encouraged by the promise of a thriving agricultural economy. Hopes were invested in maize, cocoa, tea, tobacco, rubber, coffee, and rice, but all these crops failed to live up to the dreams of high yields and profits. In the mid-1970s, both marijuana and coca presented themselves as tempting solutions for the region. Trafficking gangs moved in, spreading cultivation and taking advantage of both government apathy in South America and an increasingly high demand for cocaine in the north. Marijuana proved profitable, but coca was the real thing. "At the outset of the coca boom," one commentator wrote in *Why People Grow Drugs*, "the people went wild. They woke up one day knee-deep in money and realized that they had been living in stark poverty. It took longer to count the money than to spend it."

By the 1980s, South American traffickers had grown into well-armed and organized cartels; cocaine was flooding onto the U.S. market, and vast sums of money were circulating in an underground cocaine economy. The power wielded by the cocaine markets was on display throughout the 1980s. As Steven Wisotsky reports, in the Bahamas it was said that you could "buy an airstrip, or an island. You can buy citizenship. You can buy protection. You can buy justice. And should your drug cargo get seized by police, you can even buy it back." And when financial investigations get too close to your laundry, why not simply buy the bank? Better still, take over the whole country: the 1980 Bolivian coup has been described as "the first known instance in which an entire government became a trafficking organization."

Cocaine always had its enthusiasts, but it was only in the early 1980s that its users and producers became major players in the war on drugs. The atmosphere of economic deregulation fostered by both Reagan and Thatcher encouraged an aggressive business culture in both the United States and the United Kingdom, and cocaine, the champagne drug, was an attractive way to spend what for many people was unprecedented wealth. Like the profits, the kicks were fast and high. There was another end of the market, too: as cocaine prices dropped in the 1980s, freebase and crack cocaine became increasingly popular. Harmless coca had now become a very different drug. It need take only a little baking powder to make the difference, but the effects of crack are even more compelling and instantaneous than those induced by injecting cocaine. John Mann describes crack as an "an orgasm in every cell of one's body." People will pay for that, several times a day.

By the early 1980s, Pablo Escobar, whose Medellín cartel then dominated the Colombian cocaine trade, had amassed a vast personal fortune of some five billion dollars. There were several attempts to arrest him during the 1980s, and other cocaine organizations, specifically the rival Cali cartel, were after him, as well as the Colombian, U.S., and Panamanian authorities. In 1991, Escobar offered to call a halt to the extreme violence that had characterized the cocaine trade for more than a decade. In return, he would be protected from extradition to the United States, where he was wanted on charges of drug trafficking and murder, and housed in a prison built specially for him, to his own specifications and at the site of his choice. The Colombian authorities agreed. Escobar was their only hope for peace, and they built him La Catedral, a luxurious suite with a football field, panoramic views, and security so lax that its principal inhabitant was more than able to continue conducting his business empire. In 1992, infuriated by Escobar's ability to run rings around them, the authorities moved in to take him to a more serious prison. But the first officials to enter La Catedral were taken hostage, and Escobar slipped past sixteen hundred Colombian troops to safety in the mountains. This was not entirely unexpected. "I'm surprised he stayed in jail for even a year," said a jaded spokesman from the DEA.

A few days later, Escobar was broadcasting an offer to surrender, but this time his overtures were rejected. Interpol, the CIA, the FBI, and the DEA put a price of seven million dollars on his head, and the Cali cartel offered a slightly reduced reward of five million dollars. Escobar was killed by the Colombian police in December 1993, trapped by the simple mistake of a traced telephone call to his family. Pablo Escobar was one of the last great public figures in an industry that no longer tends to throw up such powerful personalities. According to his obituary in the *Independent*, Escobar fell because, "like Capone, he publicly challenged the state." If only the sides were so clear-cut. Escobar might well have been at war with the Colombian state and the United States, but he was neither a liberal nor a revolutionary: he had built his empire in partnership with Carlos Lehder, a fascist whose great hero was Adolf Hitler. In 1994, Ernesto Samper Pizano became president of Colombia after an election in which, it is alleged, his campaign was largely funded by the Cali cartel, which picked up the pieces of Escobar's empire.

Millions of workers in Central and South America are now involved in the drug industry. Many of them are farmers selling coca and unrefined cocaine, often working in dangerous circumstances made even worse by the activities of U.S.-sponsored seizures, crop-eradication programs, and, especially in the midst of Colombia's vicious civil war, the maneuvers of the paramilitaries. They sell their coca for a tiny fraction of its eventual retail price. In 1997, Colombian coca growers could sell one kilogram of unrefined cocaine base for $690. Its value on the streets of America might be $200,000. But coca cultivation can also bring many advantages to the farmers who depend on it. Coca earns several times the income yielded from other cash crops. It is easy to cultivate and transport and yields several crops a year. Sales are guaranteed, returns are high, and, in spite of the extremes of uneven development that the trade inevitably brings, it can be accompanied by more general wealth. When the cocaine trade moved into Medellín, which was, in 1987, a depressed town, it created twenty-eight thousand jobs in that one year.

In 1982, Ronald Reagan launched his war against the cocaine trade in defense of all "individuals, families, communities, and governments." The politicians were excited by his determination to involve the military in his antidrug campaigns, but the armed forces despaired. War on drugs made a snappy slogan, but it was fraught with problems as a military campaign. The military was well aware that interventions at home, abroad, and of any kind would compromise the separation of military and civilian power and bring enormous military challenges as well. In spite of government claims that fighting drugs was exactly the same as defending the nation against any other hostile force, the military considered itself ill equipped to deal with the problem. The prospect of committing U.S. troops and equipment to such a vague and open-ended war had uncomfortable echoes of Vietnam. The war had no center of gravity, no single goal, no end point. Or perhaps it had too many: "At one end of the spectrum," wrote Francis Belanger,

> is the individual who crosses a border to purchase drugs, whether for personal use or for resale in a local market. At the other end are organizations which own or lease fleets of airplanes and ships for transporting large quantities of drugs from one country to another. In between is a full continuum of individuals and organizations, including terrorists and insurgents.

The military could see that a war on drugs would be subject to the worst excesses of mission creep: an amorphous market would be even more difficult to fight than the most diffuse guerrilla armies it had faced in Vietnam.

All the fears about the implications of a military war on drugs turned out to be well founded. The enforcement of drug laws has legitimized the involvement of military forces in matters of civilian law, often in countries where such maneuvers pose a significant threat to economic and political stability. Since the early 1980s, for example, the United States has offered funding, training, equipment, and sometimes personnel to counter-narcotics divisions of the military in several Latin American countries, encouraging military involvement in the internal security of Mexico, Colombia, and Peru. In Colombia, where many coca-farming areas are controlled by Marxist guerrillas, crops are regularly eradicated by crop-dusting planes flown by U.S. pilots, and both guerrilla and coca operations are continually disrupted by a Colombian military trained and funded by the United States. Resources intended for the war on drugs are often diverted to other campaigns. In 1997, it emerged that the helicopters deployed by Mexican authorities to transport troops to deal with the uprising in Chiapas had been supplied by the U.S. military to be used for counter-narcotics purposes.

Military and intelligence services were aware of an even greater obstacle to a successful war on drugs: they were bound to find themselves fighting on both sides. It is, for example, widely believed that the cheap cocaine that flooded into the United States during the 1980s and 1990s was being trafficked by the very same agencies enlisted to fight the war on drugs: according to a *New York Times* article from November 1993, the CIA shipped a ton of nearly pure cocaine from Venezuela to the United States in 1990 in an incident that was regarded as "a serious accident rather than an intentional conspiracy." The Iran-contra scandal made it clear that Panama's president Manuel Noriega had been on the CIA payroll for many years before the U.S. invasion in 1989, and there are allegations that U.S. military and intelligence agencies funded the contra opposition to Nicaragua's Sandinista regime with revenues from the cocaine trade. Some of this involvement can be ascribed to bribery, corruption, and incompetence. Most of it, however, has been little more than an incidental side effect of U.S. foreign policy. This was especially true during the Cold War, when, as virulent free traders, drug traffickers presented themselves as natural allies in the struggle against communism. Convinced that "the entire world was locked in a Manichean struggle between 'godless communism' and 'the free world,' " America's cold warriors saw themselves engaged in what Alfred McCoy characterized as a "desperate struggle to save 'Western civilization' " in which "any ally was welcome and any means was justified." In its efforts to keep free trade free, the CIA went on to forge close alliances with heroin traders in Europe, Southeast Asia, and the Middle East.

As far back as the late 1930s, the illegality of drugs had produced a thriving international network of organized criminal activity on which the security of the Western world was increasingly dependent. Troubled by a number of wartime sabotage incidents on the New York waterfront, the Office of Naval Intelligence, one of the CIA's predecessors, discovered it was powerless to organize surveillance without the cooperation of the real bosses of the docks, the Mafia. Lucky Luciano, only a few years into his thirty-year sentence, was moved to a more open prison from which he could take command of the waterfront and calm down the situation. At the same time, a somewhat bigger operation was being planned: the Allied landing in Sicily. The Mafia was vital to the success of the invasion, and cooperation between the organized-crime network and American intelligence extended as the Allies moved toward the mainland. When resistance to the German occupation, already armed and supported by the Allies, began to show its communist colors, the cooperation of the Mafia became increasingly important to the Allied governments. Lucky Luciano was happy to oblige, and, in return for this invaluable assistance, he and more than a hundred other mafiosi were released in 1946. Luciano then established the French connection that Nixon tried so hard to undermine.

> Necessity knows no law. That is why we deal with opium. We have to continue to fight the evil of Communism, and to fight you must have an army, and an army must have guns, and to buy guns you

must have money. In these mountains the only
money is opium.

General Tuan of the Kuomintang, in Alfred McCoy,
The Politics of Heroin in Southeast Asia

This is a story that has since been repeated many times. The
cooperation of drug traffickers was crucial to American operations in support of the Chinese nationalist forces, the Kuomintang, or KMT, in the 1950s, when some of what are now
the largest Burmese drug barons were either working directly
for the United States or supported by the CIA. Khun Sa, who
dominated the heroin trade for almost thirty years and, until
1996, was an outspoken and determined fighter for the freedom of the Shan states, had an army that was at one time
larger than that loyal to the Burmese state and a chief of staff
who ran clandestine operations from Laos into China for the
United States in the early 1950s. Those who were not working
for the Americans came to power in their attempts to resist
the influence of the CIA and the KMT. Lo Hsing Han, one of
Khun Sa's long-standing rivals, once defended his people, the
Kokang, against the KMT as a platoon commander under the
leadership of Olive Yang, a "pistol-toting lesbian" known as
the Opium Queen.

The heroin trade was also crucial to French operations during the Indochina War in the late 1950s. As the French said of
one hill tribe community in Laos: "To have the Meo, one must
buy their opium." By the time the Vietnam War began in
earnest in the 1960s, everyone had learned the importance of
fighting not with God but with the dragon on their side. It is
well known that America and its allies in the region were
complicit with the heroin trade during the Vietnam War: in return for their military and intelligence cooperation, the CIA
began flying the Meo's opium to markets beyond the Laotian
hills in 1965. Advice from the CIA even extended to cultivation. Belanger quoted one U.S. adviser saying, "If you're gonna
grow it, grow it good." With the arrival of hundreds of thou-

sands of American troops in Vietnam, the region acquired a vast new heroin market. No. 3 heroin, so named because it is the product of the third stage of refinement, had been produced in the area for years, but in the late 1960s, and just in time for the American GIs, Chinese chemists helped Southeast Asian refiners to reach the high purity of No. 4 heroin.

In 1979, the Soviet invasion of Afghanistan provided the United States with another chance to fight a proxy war on heroin. Afghanistan's opium fields form part of a region known as the Golden Crescent, which, like the Golden Triangle in Southeast Asia, stretches through three countries: Iran, Pakistan, and Afghanistan. Opium poppies have been grown in this mountainous landscape for several centuries, but it was the British who first encouraged their commercial cultivation when, in the late nineteenth century, they established plantations in the Mahaban Mountains, which divide Afghanistan and Pakistan. In the early years of the twentieth century, Iran was earning 15 percent of its foreign revenues from exports of the drug, and opium was widely used at home, first as a medicine and later as an intoxicant. In the 1950s, Iran was consuming some two tons of opium every day. The country's ruling elite profited from the cultivation of the poppies and their trade, and Tehran was full of licensed opium dens. Although the shah banned the use and farming of opium in 1955, this merely encouraged it in Afghanistan and Pakistan, and Iranian black markets in both opium and heroin thrived. Convinced that prohibition had caused more problems than it had solved, Iran modified the ban in 1969, and poppy cultivation was resumed.

Ten years later, the Iranian revolution flooded the global market with cheap heroin. Many of the people who fled Iran brought their money out as heroin, and the revolution pushed the cultivation of opium into Afghanistan and Pakistan, where the income from heroin soon came to outweigh the revenues the country gained from all its legitimate exports. When the USSR moved into Afghanistan, American involvement in this Cold War front line included military and financial aid to Afghanistan's mujahedin guerrillas—some of whom matured into the Taliban—who, like the Italian Mafia in the Second World War, the KMT in the 1950s, and the South Vietnamese government in the 1960s, were all dependent on the cultivation of opium and the manufacture of heroin. The repercussions of the war on drugs are always extensive and enduring.

Subsequent U.S. administrations have confirmed the military nature of the war on drugs. In 1989, George Bush—who had been director of the CIA and Reagan's drug tsar—named the Department of Defense the "single lead agency" for the monitoring and detection of drug routes into the United States and announced his administration's intention to concentrate drug-enforcement resources on the countries in which coca is grown and cocaine is produced. Bush's Andean Initiative was intended to cut the supplies at the source, eradicating crops in Peru and Bolivia, destroying refineries in Colombia, and disrupting the "air bridge" that connects them. The policy had moments of success, but by the mid-1990s the region had seen the area under coca cultivation increase by some 15 percent. Bush later changed the focus of his antidrug campaigns from source countries to the interdiction of shipments of cocaine, but the Clinton administration resumed U.S. intervention in the Andes and Central America, and as the United States returns the canal to Panama, it is also stepping up its drug-surveillance operations there.

The war on drugs has produced a vast and complex alternative economy that positively thrives on the laws and attempts to enforce them. There have been some supposed successes: battles have been won, crops destroyed, shipments seized, and arrests made. But the market rarely has gaps for long, and all these victories are small and short-lived. The U.S. federal budget for drug control rose from an annual one billion dollars in 1980 to some thirty billion dollars at the end of the 1990s, and for all this, as Vernon Coleman pointed out: "Customs and police officers around the world admit that they seize approximately five per cent of the drugs that are being smuggled. Many experts argue that this is an optimistic estimate." And even the most genuine efforts to arrest drug traders tend to backfire: roads intended for surveillance provide the traffickers with a smoother ride; arms destined for the authorities end up being used in defense of the trade. The drug economy is often compared to the Hydra, which grows new heads as its old ones are removed, or to a balloon or an old mattress, which, squeezed in one place, will expand elsewhere. Steven Wisotsky quotes one Colombian police chief who might as well be talking for them all: "The worst thing is that even if we could get all the bosses, new ones would immediately take their place. They'd pop up like mushrooms." Sweep them under the carpet, and the carpet flies away.

If the war on drugs has serious implications for the sovereignty of many nations, in America the domestic implications of such extensive laws and intensive enforcement are also significant. The war on drugs has eroded what was once a sacrosanct distinction between military and civilian policing, resulting in at least one civilian death at the hands of U.S. Marines on U.S. soil, and America now has a higher proportion of its population in prison than any other nation in the world. In 1995, there were more than 1.5 million adults imprisoned in the United States and 25 percent of them were convicted for drug violations. This is three times the number incarcerated in 1980, when only 8 percent of inmates were convicted on drug charges. And these statistics deal with only the most serious drug crimes and punishments. Behind them lie huge numbers of minor drug convictions and arrests, an unprecedented culture of policing, surveillance, and social control and unprecedented opportunities to contain specific neighborhoods, communities, and racial groups. America's black and Hispanic populations are often subject to the summary justice of a harsh penal code, which allows vast swathes of the white population to take drugs with impunity. The illegality of drugs produces a syndrome defined by Foucault in

Discipline and Punish as a kind of "useful delinquency." "The existence of a legal prohibition creates around it a field of illegal practices, which one manages to supervise, while extracting from it an illicit profit through elements, themselves illegal but rendered manipulable by their organization in delinquency. This organization is an instrument for administering and exploiting illegalities." Criminals function as informers even before they give anything away: delinquency facilitates and authorizes a "generalized policing," constituting "a means of perpetual surveillance of the population: an apparatus that makes it possible to supervise, through the delinquents themselves, the whole social field."

In the late 1980s, there were admissions that all attempts to stop the production and trafficking of drugs, in America and abroad, were being "undermined by corruption of government officials and law enforcement officers, intimidation and violence," and by what Belanger described as "the stark fact that nations are outmanned, outgunned, and outspent by narcotics criminals." Other commentators saw the end of the Cold War bringing an unprecedented chance for the development of a global drug squad: Richard Clutterbuck optimistically suggested that NATO and Warsaw Pact countries "would be able to divert many army, naval and air patrol units to the drugs war," allowing "previously rival power blocks to help police the world" and finally enact the global security system that "was precisely the original concept of the UN."

The absence of the two rival superpowers and their proxy wars served only to increase political and economic instability in many drug-producing regions of the world. The drug traffic now funds and is protected by warring parties, insurgent groups, and terrorist organizations in many of the world's most intractable war zones, and the governments of several leading drug-producing countries are complicit with the trade. There are a number of countries in which the black market in drugs rivals the scale and vigor of the official economy, and nations that once exported the bulk of their crops and products have now become consumers, too. One of the most tragic examples of this syndrome is Burma, where Khun Sa could once claim that heroin addiction in the West was simply a matter of karma, a payback for the West's attempt to flood the East with opium a hundred years before. But things are no longer so clear-cut. Under military rule, Burma has become one of the world's largest opium-producing nations, and also one of its most repressive states. It now supplies more than half of the U.S. heroin market, and its drug exports have more than doubled since 1988, when Burma's military government, the State Law and Order Restoration Council, SLORC—renamed the State Peace and Development Council in November 1997—seized power. The dragon has run riot here, and the consequences are appalling. After several offers to end the trade in the 1970s and 1980s—all of which were refused by the United States—Khun Sa ignored an indictment from a U.S. court and continued to dominate the trade until 1996, when, faced with increasing splits and disputes among his followers, he "surrendered" to the Burmese government and effectively gave them his trafficking network and much of his accumulated wealth. Khun Sa's great rival, Lo Hsing Han, has followed him to become a leading Burmese industrialist. Rangoon and Mandalay are awash with heroin and cheap speed, and in some rural areas workers are paid in drugs: a third of the hundred thousand jade miners at the SLORC-owned Hpakant mine, in the Kachin region, take their wages in heroin. HIV infection and deaths from AIDS are rife in both Burma and the border regions of its neighbors: India, China, Thailand, and Laos.

Khun Sa and Pablo Escobar were among the last kingpins of the drug trade, which is now far more decentralized, anarchic, and violent than it was in the days of the Cold War. The collapse of the Soviet Union had dramatic effects on production and trafficking in the Near and Middle East, and volatility in both Russia and the central Asian states has encouraged a proliferation of mafias and cartels: in 1996, there were said to be some nine thousand Mafia-style gangs organizing Russia's illegal-drug trade, and organized-crime networks now seem to control more than half of the Russian economy. The cultivation of opium, the manufacture of heroin, and, to a lesser extent, the trade in hashish continue to complicate both political and military scenarios in Israel, Syria, Lebanon, Turkey, and Iran. The cocaine cartels continue to do battle with each other and the DEA across the Americas, and the whole continent of Africa is crisscrossed with drug trade routes, whose control has been crucial to the course of recent wars in Rwanda, Uganda, and the Congo. Struggles for control of the Balkan trade have been far from incidental to the course of the war in former Yugoslavia: Serb, Croat, and Albanian gangs had been involved in the drug trade through Yugoslavia for years before the war, and these links were intensified when war broke out. Iraq is widely assumed to be exporting heroin as a means of evading the UN embargo, and all the factions in Afghanistan are beneficiaries of the trade.

> We are at a crossroads, and if we do not design some more effectual means of combating this malady, our world, as we now know it, is doomed. We have had our last chance. Time is running out!
> Francis W. Belanger, *Drugs, the US, and Khun Sa*

In the face of this chaotic situation, the UN continues to insist that the illegal cultivation, manufacture, trade, and use of drugs can be brought to an end. In 1997, when he became director of the new United Nations Office for Drug Control and Crime Prevention, Pino Arlacchi declared his intention to eradicate the cultivation of coca bushes and opium poppies by 2008. His first moves were made in Afghanistan, where, by 1998, the Taliban controlled more than three-quarters of the country. Establishing an extreme form of *Shari'a*, Islamic law, the Taliban prohibited women's employment and education,

banned television and all intoxicants, and earned Afghanistan
a reputation as the most extreme fundamentalist Islamic state.
But Afghanistan is also one of the world's leading producers
of opium. UN estimates suggested that 200,000 farmers produced 2,800 tons of opium in 1997, 25 percent more than in
the previous year.

"You have two problems: women and drugs," Arlacchi told
the Taliban as he tried to persuade them to relax their control
of women and take control of drugs instead. Like those of
other drug-producing regions of the world, opium farmers in
Afghanistan earn a tiny fraction of the vast incomes their produce goes on to generate. But their revenues—and those they
bring the Taliban—are still far greater than what can be derived from alternative crops, and demands for the eradication
of opium inevitably meet with demands for compensation. So
Arlacchi struck a deal with the Taliban. They agreed to eradicate the cultivation of opium poppies within a decade, in line
with UN plans, and the UN agreed to finance this program to
the tune of twenty-five million dollars a year. The sum in
question is about eight million dollars more than the annual
revenue collected by the Taliban in taxes on the opium trade,
and although the Taliban issued decrees banning the production of opium and the manufacture of heroin in 1998, it also
continued to impose the tax. As the UN finds itself supporting
a trade and a regime to which it is supposedly opposed, the
war on drugs is once again chasing its own tail. Someone is
laughing all the way to a bank he probably already owns.

> Exhausted by the effort of concentrating on the
> traffic and holding the cars around us in their lanes,
> I took my hands off the wheel and let the car press
> on.
>
> J. G. Ballard, *Crash*

To write on drugs is to plunge into a world where nothing is
as simple or as stable as it seems. Everything about it shim-

mers and mutates as you try to hold its gaze. Facts and figures dance around each other; lines of inquiry scatter like expensive dust. The reasons for the laws and the motives for the wars, the nature of the pleasures and the trouble drugs can cause, the tangled webs of chemicals, the plants, the brains, machines: ambiguity surrounds them all. Drugs shape the laws and write the very rules they break, they scramble all the codes and raise the stakes of desire and necessity, euphoria and pain, normality, perversion, truth, and artifice again. Endlessly repeating their patterns and their themes, time after time to their opening scenes.

And so the year of the dragon comes around again. You keep running; it keeps running. Dragons never tire. It dances at the head of a long parade whose colors twist and turn in a dream that will not fade. It has written your stories, changed your mind, shaped your cultures and economies. And still it runs, imperious and wise, refusing your judgments, blurring all the lines. It scorns your efforts to leave the border town and scoffs at your attempts to write it down. It runs ahead; it laughs at you. It knows you'll always fail. You hear it all, and still you try to tell the dragon's tale.

Bibliography

Acker, Kathy. *Empire of the Senseless.* New York: Grove, 1988.

Anonymous. *Anaesthetic Inspiration.* Birmingham, U.K.: John Hannon, 1998.

Artaud, Antonin. "Coleridge the Traitor." In *Artaud Anthology.* San Francisco: City Lights, 1965.

———. "General Security: The Liquidation of Opium." In *Artaud Anthology.* San Francisco: City Lights, 1965.

———. *Les Tarahumaras.* Paris: Gallimard, 1971.

———. *The Theatre and Its Double.* London: John Calder, 1981.

Ballard, J. G. *Cocaine Nights.* London: Flamingo, 1996.

———. *Crash.* London: Flamingo, 1993.

Bamford, James. *The Puzzle Palace: A Report on America's Most Secret Agency.* London: Penguin, 1983.

Barthes, Roland. *Camera Lucida: Reflections on Photography.* London: Jonathan Cape, 1972.

Bateson, Gregory. *Steps to an Ecology of Mind.* London: Paladin, 1973.

Baudelaire, Charles. "My Heart Laid Bare." In *Intimate Journals.* San Francisco: City Lights, 1983.

———. *Les Paradis artificiels.* Paris: Flammarion, 1966.

———. *Selected Poems.* London: Penguin, 1986.

Belanger, Francis W. *Drugs, the US, and Khun Sa.* Bangkok: Duang Kamol, 1989.

Bell, Ian. *Robert Louis Stevenson: Dreams of Exile.* Edinburgh: Mainstream, 1992.

Benjamin, Walter. "Hashish in Marseilles." In *One Way Street.* London: New Left Books, 1979.

———. "Surrealism." In *One Way Street.* London: New Left Books, 1979.

———. "The Work of Art in the Age of Mechanical Reproduction." In *Illuminations.* London: Jonathan Cape, 1970.

Bernstein, Dennis, and Leslie Kean. "People of the Opiate." *Nation*, 16 December 1996.*

Berridge, Virginia, and Griffith Edwards. *Opium and the People: Opiate Use in Nineteenth Century England*. London: Allen Lane/St. Martin's Press, 1981.

Bibra, Baron Ernst von. *Plant Intoxicants*. Rochester, Vt.: Healing Arts Press, 1995.

Booth, Martin. *Opium: A History*. London: Simon and Schuster, 1996.

Braudel, Fernand. *Afterthoughts to Civilization and Capitalism*. Baltimore and London: Johns Hopkins University Press, 1977.

———. *Capitalism and Material Life, 1400–1800*. London: Weidenfeld & Nicolson, 1979.

———. *Civilization and Capitalism, 15th–18th Century*. Vol. 2: *The Wheels of Commerce*. New York: Harper & Row, 1982.

———. *A History of Civilizations*. London: Penguin, 1993.

Burroughs, William. *The Adding Machine: Collected Essays*. London: John Calder, 1985.

———. *Ah Pook Is Here and Other Texts*. London: John Calder, 1979.

———. *Interzone*. London: Picador, 1989.

———. *The Job*. New York: Grove, 1970.

———. "Literary Autobiography." In *A Descriptive Catalogue of the William S. Burroughs Archive*. London: Miles Associates, 1973.

———. *Naked Lunch*. London: Corgi, 1968.

———. *Nova Express*. London: Panther, 1978.

———. *The Soft Machine*. London: Calder and Boyars, 1968.

Burroughs, William, and Allen Ginsberg. *The Yage Letters*. San Francisco: City Lights, 1963.

Burroughs, William, and Brion Gysin. *The Third Mind*. London: John Calder, 1979.

---

*This and many other articles on the war on drugs, the drug trade, and especially Burma can be found at the invaluable Lindesmith Center Web site, hosted by the Soros Foundation.

Cadigan, Pat. *Synners*. London: HarperCollins, 1991.

Campbell, Joseph. *The Hero with a Thousand Faces*. London: Fontana, 1993.

Canetti, Elias. *Crowds and Power*. London: Penguin, 1984.

Carmichael, Michael. "Wonderland Revisited." In *Psychedelia Britannica: Hallucinogenic Drugs in Britain*. Edited by Antonio Melechi. London: Turnaround, 1988.

Carroll, Lewis. *Alice in Wonderland*. London: W. H. Cornelius, 1946.

Castaneda, Carlos. *The Teachings of Don Juan: A Yaqui Way of Knowledge*. Berkeley: University of California Press, 1968.

Charters, Ann. *Kerouac: A Biography*. London: André Deutsch, 1984.

Chesterton, G. K. "The Dagger with Wings." In *Father Brown Stories*. London: Penguin, 1994.

Churchland, Patricia. *Neurophilosophy: Toward a Unified Science of the Mind-Brain*. Cambridge, Mass.: MIT Press, 1989.

Clarke, William M. *The Secret Life of Wilkie Collins*. London: W. H. Allen, 1989.

Clutterbuck, Richard. *Terrorism, Drugs, and Crime in Europe: After 1992*. London: Routledge, 1990.

Cocteau, Jean. *Opium: The Illustrated Diary of His Cure*. London: Peter Owen, 1990.

Coleman, Vernon. *The Drugs Myth: Why the Drugs War Must Stop*. London: Green Print, 1982.

Coleridge, Samuel Taylor. *Biographia Literaria*. London: Everyman, 1997.

———. *The Notebooks of Samuel Taylor Coleridge*. Edited by Kathleen Coburn. London: Routledge and Kegan Paul, 1957.

———. *Poetical Works*. Oxford: Oxford University Press, 1992.

Collins, Wilkie. *The Moonstone*. London: Penguin, 1994.

Collis, Maurice. *Foreign Mud: Anglo-Chinese Opium War*. Singapore: Graham Brash, 1946.

Crowley, Aleister. *The Diary of a Drug Fiend*. York Beach, Maine: Samuel Weiser, 1970.

Daftary, Farhad. *The Assassin Legends: Myths of the Isma'ilis.* London: I. B. Tauris, 1995.

Daumal, René. "A Fundamental Experiment." In *The Drug User: Documents, 1840–1960.* Edited by John Strausbaugh and Donald Blaise. New York: Blast Books, 1991.

———. *Mount Analogue.* London: Penguin, 1986.

Davis, Mike. *City of Quartz: Excavating the Future in Los Angeles.* London and New York: Verso, 1990.

Debord, Guy. *The Society of the Spectacle.* Detroit, Mich.: Black & Red, 1977.

De Landa, Manuel. Interview in *Mondo 2000,* issue 8, 1993.

———. "Non-organic Life." In *Incorporations, Zone 6.* Edited by Jonathan Crary and Sanford Kwinter. New York: Zone Books, 1992.

Deleuze, Gilles. *Cinema 2: The Time-Image.* London: Athlone, 1992.

———. *Foucault.* Minneapolis and London: University of Minnesota Press, 1988.

———. *The Logic of Sense.* New York: Columbia University Press, 1990.

Deleuze, Gilles, and Félix Guattari. *Anti-Oedipus: Capitalism and Schizophrenia.* London: Athlone, 1984.

———. *A Thousand Plateaus: Capitalism and Schizophrenia.* London: Athlone, 1988.

De Quincey, Thomas. *Confessions of an English Opium-Eater and Other Writings.* Oxford: Oxford University Press, 1990.

———. Two articles on the Opium Wars, *Blackwood's Edinburgh Magazine,* 47 (January–June 1840).

Dick, Philip K. *Do Androids Dream of Electric Sheep?* London: Panther, 1977.

———. *A Scanner Darkly.* London: HarperCollins, 1996.

———. "We Can Remember It for You Wholesale." In *Collected Stories 5.* London: Grafton, 1991.

Dickens, Charles. *The Mystery of Edwin Drood.* London: Penguin, 1980.

Doyle, Arthur Conan. "The Final Problem." In *The Memoirs of Sherlock Holmes*. London: Penguin, 1950.

———. *The Return of Sherlock Holmes*. London: Penguin, 1981.

———. *The Sign of Four*. London: Cape, 1974.

———. "Silver Blaze." In *The Memoirs of Sherlock Holmes*. London: Penguin, 1950.

———. *The Uncollected Sherlock Holmes*. Compiled by Richard Lancelyn Green. London: Penguin, 1983.

Ebin, David, ed. *The Drug Experience*. New York: Grove, 1965.

Eisner, Bruce. *Ecstasy: The MDMA Story*. Berkeley, Calif.: Ronin, 1994.

Eliade, Mircea. *Shamanism: Archaic Techniques of Ecstasy*. London: Penguin, 1989.

Ellis, Havelock. *The World of Dreams*. London: Constable, 1931.

Escobar obituary. *Independent*, 4 December 1993.

"Escobar's Escapade." *Newsweek*, 3 August 1992.

Flaubert, Gustave. *Lettres à Charles Baudelaire*. Edited by Claude Pichois. Paris: Neuchatel, 1973.

———. *Madame Bovary*. London: Penguin, 1995.

———. *The Temptation of Saint Anthony*. London: Penguin, 1980.

Followers of the Tipi Way. "Straight with the Medicine." In *The Drug User: Documents, 1840–1960*. Edited by John Strausbaugh and Donald Blaise. New York: Blast Books, 1991.

Foucault, Michel. *Discipline and Punish: The Birth of the Prison*. New York: Random House, 1995.

———. "Fantasia of the Library." In *Language, Counter-memory, Practice*. Ithaca, N.Y.: Cornell University Press, 1977.

———. *History of Sexuality: Volume 1: An Introduction*. New York: Random House, 1978.

———. *Madness and Civilization*. London: Tavistock, 1971.

———. "Theatrum Philosophicum." In *Language, Counter-memory, Practice*. Ithaca, N.Y.: Cornell University Press, 1977.

Freud, Sigmund. "Beyond the Pleasure Principle." In *On Metapsychology: The Theory of Psychoanalysis*. Penguin Freud Library. Vol. 11. London: Penguin, 1984.

———. *Cocaine Papers*. Edited by Robert Byck. New York: Stonehill, 1974.

———. "The Economic Problem of Masochism." In *On Metapsychology: The Theory of Psychoanalysis*. Penguin Freud Library. Vol. 11. London: Penguin, 1984.

———. *The Interpretation of Dreams*. Penguin Freud Library. Vol. 4. London: Penguin, 1985.

———. *Introductory Lectures on Psychoanalysis*. Penguin Freud Library. Vol. 1. London: Penguin, 1991.

———. "The Moses of Michelangelo." In *Art and Literature*. Penguin Freud Library. Vol. 14. London: Penguin, 1984.

Gibson, William. *Neuromancer*. New York: Ace, 1984.

Ginsberg, Allen. *Howl and Other Poems*. San Francisco: City Lights, 1956.

Ginzburg, Carlo. *Ecstasies: Deciphering the Witches' Sabbath*. London: Hutchinson Radius, 1990.

———. "Morelli, Freud, and Sherlock Holmes: Clues and Scientific Method." In *The Sign of Three: Dupin, Holmes, Peirce*. Edited by Umberto Eco and Thomas A. Sebeok. Bloomington and Indianapolis: Indiana University Press, 1988.

Graves, Robert. *The White Goddess: A Historical Grammar of Poetic Myth*. London: Faber and Faber, 1952.

Grinspoon, Lester. *The Speed Culture: Amphetamine Use and Abuse in America*. Cambridge, Mass.: Harvard University Press, 1975.

Halifax, Joan. *Shamanic Voices*. London: Arkana, 1991.

Hayter, Alethea. *Opium and the Romantic Imagination*. London: Faber and Faber, 1968.

Hebb, Donald. *The Organization of Behavior: A Neuropsychological Theory*. New York: John Wiley & Sons, 1949.

Hofmann, Albert. *LSD, My Problem Child*. Los Angeles: Jeremy P. Tarcher, 1983.

Holmes, Richard. *Coleridge: Darker Reflections.* London: HarperCollins, 1998.

Homer. *The Odyssey.* London: Penguin, 1948.

Huxley, Aldous. *The Doors of Perception.* New York: Perennial Library, 1970.

Infante, C. Cabrera. *Holy Smoke.* London: Faber and Faber, 1985.

Inglis, Brian. *The Forbidden Game: A Social History of Drugs.* London: Hodder & Stoughton, 1975.

James, William. *The Varieties of Religious Experience: A Study in Human Nature.* London: Longmans, Green & Co., 1952.

Jeffrey, Ian. *Photography: A Concise History.* London: Thames & Hudson, 1981.

Jones, Ernest. *The Life and Work of Sigmund Freud.* London: Penguin, 1962.

Jones, Jill. *Hep-Cats, Narcs, and Pipe Dreams: A History of America's Romance with Illegal Drugs.* New York: Scribner, 1996.

Jung, Carl. *Letters.* Vol. 2. London: Routledge, 1976.

Jünger, Ernst. *Approches: Drogues et ivresse.* Paris: Vermillon, 1974.

―――. *Heliopolis: Rückblick auf eine Stadt.* Tübingen: Heliopolis-Verlag, 1949.

Kadrey, Richard. *Metrophage.* London: Victor Gollancz, 1988.

Kerouac, Jack. *On the Road.* London: Penguin, 1991.

Kluver, Heinrich. *Mescal and Mechanisms of Hallucination.* Chicago: University of Chicago Press, 1966.

Kohn, Marek. *Narcomania: On Heroin.* London: Faber and Faber, 1987.

Kramer, Heinrich, and James Sprenger. *Malleus Maleficarum.* London: Arrow, 1971.

Laing, R. D. *The Politics of Experience; and, the Bird of Paradise.* London: Penguin, 1990.

Land, Nick. *The Thirst for Annihilation: Georges Bataille and Virulent Nihilism.* London: Routledge, 1992.

Lautréamont, Comte de. *Maldoror.* London: Penguin, 1978.

Leary, Timothy. *Flashbacks: A Personal and Cultural History of an Era: An Autobiography.* Los Angeles: Jeremy P. Tarcher, 1990.

Leary, Timothy, Ralph Metzner, and Richard Alpert. *The Psychedelic Experience: A Manual Based on* The Tibetan Book of the Dead. New York: Citadel Press, 1990.

Lee, Martin A., and Bruce Shlain. *Acid Dreams: The Complete Social History of LSD: The CIA, the Sixties, and Beyond.* New York: Grove Weidenfeld, 1992.

Lewin, Louis. *Phantastica: Narcotic and Stimulating Drugs, Their Use and Abuse.* London: Routledge and Kegan Paul, 1964.

Lilly, John C. *The Centre of the Cyclone.* London: Boyars, 1990.

————. *Programming and Metaprogramming the Human Biocomputer.* New York: Julian Press, 1968.

Loewi, Otto. *An Autobiographic Sketch.* Chicago: University of Chicago Press, 1960.

Lovell, Richard. Letter on Churchill's use of amphetamines and barbiturates. *British Medical Journal,* June 1995.

Ludlow, Fitz Hugh. *The Hasheesh Eater: Being Passages from the Life of a Pythagorean.* Hypertext version compiled by Dave Gross at http://www.lycaeum.org/~sputnik/Ludlow/THE/index.html.

Lyotard, Jean-François. *Libidinal Economy.* London: Athlone, 1993.

Mabry, Donald, ed. *The Latin American Narcotics Trade and US National Security.* London and New York: Greenwood, 1987.

Macey, David. *The Lives of Michel Foucault.* London: Vintage, 1994.

Mandelbrot, Benoit. *The Fractal Geometry of Nature.* San Francisco: Freeman, 1982.

Mann, John. *Murder, Magic, and Medicine.* Oxford: Oxford University Press, 1994.

Mantegazza, Paolo. "On the Hygienic and Medicinal Virtues of Coca." In *The Coca Leaf and Cocaine Papers.* Edited by George Andrews and David Solomon. New York: Harcourt Brace Jovanovich, 1976.

Marcuse, Herbert. *An Essay on Liberation*. London: Penguin, 1969.

Marx, Karl. *Capital: A Critique of Political Economy*. Vol. 1. London: Lawrence & Wishart, 1970.

McCoy, Alfred W. *The Politics of Heroin in Southeast Asia*. New York: Harper & Row, 1989.

McKenna, Terence. *Food of the Gods: The Search for the Original Tree of Knowledge*. New York: Bantam Books, 1992.

McLuhan, Marshall, and Quentin Fiore. *War and Peace in the Global Village*. New York: Bantam Books, 1967.

Mestel, Rosie. "Cannabis: The Brain's Other Supplier." *New Scientist*, no. 1884 (31 July 1993).

Michaux, Henri. *Au pays de la magie*. London: Athlone, 1977.

———. *By Surprise*. Madras and New York: Hanuman Books, 1987.

———. *Darkness Moves: An Henri Michaux Anthology, 1927–1984*. Berkeley: University of California Press, 1994.

———. *Infinite Turbulence*. London: Calder & Boyars, 1975.

———. *Miserable Miracle*. San Francisco: City Lights, 1963.

Miller, James. *The Passion of Michel Foucault*. London: Harper Collins, 1993.

Nietzsche, Friedrich. *The Birth of Tragedy*. New York: Vintage, 1967.

———. *The Gay Science*. New York: Vintage, 1974.

Nin, Anaïs. *Diaries, 1947–1955*. Vol. 5. London: Quartet, 1974.

Nuttall, Jeff. *Bomb Culture*. London: Paladin, 1972.

Paz, Octavio. *Alternating Current*. London: Wildwood House, 1974.

Pendergrast, Mark. *For God, Country, and Coca-Cola: The Unauthorized History of the Great American Soft Drink and the Company That Makes It*. London: Weidenfeld & Nicolson, 1993.

Plant, Sadie. *The Most Radical Gesture*. London: Routledge, 1992.

———. *Zeros + Ones*. London: Fourth Estate, 1997.

Plato. *The Last Days of Socrates*. London: Penguin, 1975.

Poe, Edgar Allan. *The Portable Poe.* Edited and introduced by Philip van Doren Stern. London: Penguin, 1977.

———. "The Thousand-and-Second Tale of Scheherazade." In *The Science Fiction of Edgar Allan Poe.* Edited by Harold Beaver. London: Penguin, 1976.

Raus, Charles. "Postscript: An Interview with Michel Foucault." In *Death and the Labyrinth: The World of Raymond Roussel,* by Michel Foucault. London: Athlone, 1987.

Reynolds, Simon. *Energy Flash: A Journey through Rave Music and Dance Culture.* London: Picador, 1998.

Rimbaud, Arthur. *Collected Poems.* London: Penguin, 1986.

Robinson, Victor. *Victory over Pain: A History of Anaesthesia.* London: Sigma, 1947.

Ronell, Avital. *Crack Wars: Literature, Addiction, Mania.* Lincoln: University of Nebraska Press, 1992.

Rudgley, Richard. *The Alchemy of Culture: Intoxicants in Society.* London: British Museum Press, 1993.

———. *The Encyclopaedia of Psychoactive Substances.* London: Little, Brown, 1998.

Sacks, Oliver. *Migraine.* London: Picador, 1995.

Schneider, Elisabeth. *Coleridge, Opium, and "Kubla Khan."* Chicago: University of Chicago Press, 1953.

Scholem, Gershom. *Walter Benjamin: Story of a Friendship.* New York: Schocken Books, 1981.

Schultes, Richard Evans. *Plants of the Gods: Origins of Hallucinogenic Use.* London: Hutchinson, 1980.

Shelley, Mary. *Frankenstein, or the Modern Prometheus.* London: Penguin, 1985.

Siegel, Ronald K. *Intoxication.* New York: Simon and Schuster, 1989.

Smith, Michael L., et al. *Why People Grow Drugs: Narcotics and Development in the Third World.* London: Panos, 1992.

Snyder, Solomon H. "Finding Opiate Receptors." In Mark F. Bear, Barry W. Connors, and Michael A. Paradiso. *Neuroscience: Exploring the Brain.* Baltimore: Williams & Wilkins, 1996.

Sontag, Susan. *On Photography*. London: Penguin, 1979.

Sophocles. *The Theban Plays*. London: Penguin, 1985.

Stafford, Peter. *Psychedelics Encyclopedia*. Berkeley, Calif.: Ronin, 1992.

Stephenson, Neal. *Snow Crash*. London: Bantam Books, 1992.

Sterling, Bruce, ed. *Mirrorshades: The Cyberpunk Anthology*. London: Paladin, 1988.

Stevens, Jay. *Storming Heaven: LSD and the American Dream*. London: Paladin, 1989.

Stevenson, Robert Louis. "A Chapter on Dreams." In *Essays and Poems*. London: J. M. Dent, 1992.

———. *The Strange Case of Dr. Jekyll and Mr. Hyde*. London: Bantam Books, 1981.

Szasz, Thomas. *Ceremonial Chemistry: The Ritual Persecution of Drugs, Addicts, and Pushers*. London: Routledge and Kegan Paul, 1975.

Tales from the Thousand and One Nights. London: Penguin, 1973.

Teresa of Ávila. *The Life of Saint Teresa of Ávila by Herself*. With an introduction by J. M. Cohen. London: Penguin, 1957.

Thamm, Berndt Georg. *Andenschnee: Die Lange Line des Kokain*. Basle: Sphinx Verlag, 1986.

Thompson, Hunter S. *Fear and Loathing in Las Vegas*. London: Paladin, 1972.

Thompson, Richard F. *The Brain: A Neuroscience Primer*. New York: W. H. Freeman, 1993.

Trocchi, Alexander. *Cain's Book*. London: Calder Publications, 1992.

———. "Trocchi on Drugs." In *Psychedelia Britannica: Hallucinogenic Drugs in Britain*. Edited by Antonio Melechi. London: Turnaround, 1988.

Twain, Mark. "The Turning Point of My Life." In *Tales, Speeches, Essays, and Sketches*. London: Penguin, 1994.

United Nations International Drug Control Programme. *World Drug Report*. Oxford: Oxford University Press, 1997.

Virilio, Paul. *War and Cinema: The Logistics of Perception*. London: Verso, 1989.

Wasson, Gordon, and Valentina Wasson. *Mushrooms, Russia, and History.* New York: Pantheon, 1957.

Watson, Lyall. *The Nature of Things: The Secret Life of Inanimate Objects.* London: Hodder & Stoughton, 1990.

Wilson, Andrew. Introduction to "Trocchi on Drugs," by Alexander Trocchi. In *Psychedelia Britannica: Hallucinogenic Drugs in Britain.* Edited by Antonio Melechi. London: Turnaround, 1988.

Wisotsky, Steven. *Breaking the Impasse in the War on Drugs.* London and New York: Greenwood, 1986.

Wolfe, Tom. *The Electric Kool-Aid Acid Test.* New York: Farrar, Straus and Giroux, 1968.

Index

279

INDEX